LET'S TALK LISP

LAURENT SIKLÓSSY

Department of Computer Sciences
The University of Texas at Austin

LET'S TALK LISP

Prentice-Hall, Inc., Englewood Cliffs, New Jersey

Library of Congress Cataloging in Publication Data

SIKLÓSSY, LAURENT
    Let's talk LISP.

    Bibliography.
    Includes index.
    1. LISP (Computer program language) I. Title.
QA76.73.L23S55   001.6'424   75–19297
ISBN 0–13–532762–8

10 9 8 7 6 5 4 3 2

Printed in the United States of America

PRENTICE-HALL INTERNATIONAL, INC., *London*
PRENTICE-HALL OF AUSTRALIA, PTY. LTD., *Sydney*
PRENTICE-HALL OF CANADA, LTD., *Toronto*
PRENTICE-HALL OF INDIA PRIVATE LIMITED, *New Delhi*
PRENTICE-HALL OF JAPAN, INC., *Tokyo*
PRENTICE-HALL OF SOUTHEAST ASIA (PTE.) LTD., *Singapore*

CONTENTS

v

3   **Elementary DEFINE**   *24*

4   **Elementary Recursive DEFINE**   *31*

5   **Additional Recursive Definitions**   *51*

6   Introduction to MAP Functions and LAMBDA Expressions   *82*

7   PROG, CONSTANTS AND GENERATORS   *96*

11   Miscellaneous Functions and Features   *160*

12   Some Larger Examples   *169*

Appendices

C　A LISP Bibliography

D　Some Errors in LISP Programs

PREFACE

LISP is a *LISt Processing* programming language based on John McCarthy's work on nonnumeric computation published in 1960. The first LISP system was implemented at M.I.T. and was described in the *LISP 1.5 Programmer's Manual*. Since then, LISP has been implemented on a variety of computers. It is the language of choice for research requiring nonnumeric computation. To a large extent, it remains unique among programming languages, possessing a flavor and "feel" all of its own. In 1973, in an invited talk at the University of Texas at Austin, Jean Sammett said, "Programming languages can be divided into two categories. In one category, there is LISP; in the second category, all the other programming languages!" The pedagogic value of LISP has indeed been recognized in computer science curricula.

This text gives a reasonably complete exposition of LISP, but avoids the details of the implementations of the language. The first seven chapters give a slow-paced introduction to the more elementary features of the language: elementary functions, recursive functions, the PROG feature, MAP functions, and generators. The experienced programmer will find a condensation of these seven chapters in Appendix B.

Chapters 8 to 11 encourage the use of property lists, explain a particular interpreter for EVAL, describe the storage structures in LISP and their manipulations, and finally pull together various features that had not found a niche in the previous chapters. The notion of *cell-value*, i.e. the address of the beginning of a structure, is introduced to overcome the difficulties created by nonstandard storage structures.

Chapter 12 describes a variety of larger LISP programs, sometimes omitting details of implementation. The chapter ends with a number of more substantial exercises for the reader.

Seldom is LISP taught as a first programming language, and so we have assumed that the reader of this text knows the mechanics of accessing computers, running his programs and debugging them. We did, however, emphasize some programming approaches.

- How do you write recursive functions? Start with the simplest cases, and try to bootstrap yourself.
- How do you write "good" code? Use mnemonics,† auxiliary functions (especially MAP functions and generators); think of property lists.

We also emphasized the more advanced features of LISP: the use of functional arguments, the generation and manipulation of functions within programs, the efficiency of property lists, and benefits of direct modifications of storage structures. Often, the same function was defined in different ways with the aid of different features of the language.

The success of LISP has lead to a variety of implementations with the unfortunate result that the LISP of machine A is usually different from the LISP of machine B (or another LISP of machine A!). The user should consult the manual of his own LISP system to check whether his LISP agrees with the one described here. In some important cases, we were familiar with differences among implementations, and instead of giving constant warnings in the text, adopted warning signals in the margin. The code used is the following:

Code	Meaning
§	Usually a system function. Functions not so marked may not exist in a LISP system.
✓	Check this function in your system to determine whether it agrees fully with the definition that we have given.
✓n	Check the name of this function in your system. It may be somewhat different from the one used here.
✓O	Check the order of the arguments of this function. It may not be the same as the one used here.

†We should have gone even farther with mnemonics, preferring LISONE and LISTWO to LIS1 and LIS2.

Parts of this book were used in classes that I taught at the University of Texas at Austin. The book has benefited greatly from the many comments that my students have made. While visiting Austin, Dr. Richard Duda, of the Stanford Research Institute, read a partial draft and made many excellent suggestions.

Learning a language should be fun. To the rather dry list (A B C D E) we have preferred silly sayings, aphorisms or even bilingual puns such as (AMENOPHIS HAD HIS SONS BROUGHT). Whether such examples amuse, irritate, or disgust the reader, we hope that they will keep him awake.

Oscar Wilde said that no one is perfect.† This author will gratefully receive suggestions for improving this text.

And now, it is time to talk LISP!

L. Siklóssy

Austin, Texas

---

†For example, he did not like to sit in a draught.

LET'S TALK LISP

1

A LANGUAGE FOR
THE COMPUTER

If you want to communicate with a computer, you must have a way to communicate. A man mainly uses a language, such as English, to talk to another man. He can also use grunts, sighs, and a variety of more or less obscene gestures. To communicate with the computer, we use programming languages. These languages serve the same purpose as English does for communication between two men,† although they certainly do not look exactly like English, and in some cases do not look like it at all. We shall try to teach a particular programming language, called LISP, which is an acronym for LISt Processing Language. If you follow us faithfully, you will find LISP an easy language to learn, and you will find that many of the things that you want to tell the computer can be said very easily in LISP.

When you learn a language, you cannot grasp everything at once. You will learn some rules but will often find out that these rules are not totally general, that there are exceptions, or that we did not really tell you the whole story right away. You should not be worried. Our goal is to teach you to talk as soon as possible with the computer. At first, you will not talk as efficiently as you could. That is, you will learn subsequently that you could have told the computer the same thing in a different way

---

†Our subject being a language of communication between a human being and a machine, we do not feel obliged to include considerations about the communication possibilities among more than two men, or between a man and a woman, or among two or more women.

1

which would have been more elegant, shorter, or more efficient in the sense that the computer understands you better and can carry out your requests in a more efficient manner.

If you travel in a foreign country, you are certainly better off with a partial knowledge of the local language than with no knowledge at all. If you do not know the language, you may, of course, communicate by gestures or drawings†; but communication will be much more effective if you can express yourself verbally, even though a native speaker may say "razor blade" when you say "a piece of metal to cut the hair on the side of my head." You may have plenty of time and can wait to learn the foreign language perfectly before saying anything in it, or you may be in a hurry to shave or, for that matter, cut your mother-in-law's throat. It's a question of priorities. We shall assume here that you would rather start talking to the computer as quickly as possible.

1.1 Words in LISP

English consists of words, and so does LISP, except that there are two kinds of words in LISP: atoms and lists. When we do not care about which kind of word we are referring to, we shall use the term S-expression. We shall first consider the words of LISP, and then we shall discuss how to make sentences out of them.

1.1.1 Atoms

Atoms can be English words, such as HOUSE, HARRY, ATOM, and HERE,‡ or nonsense words, such as EDSEL, BXR, SSRR, and CDR. Furthermore, we can intersperse numbers inside the letters and still have atoms. For example, the following are atoms: Q5, B5C3Q4, B556, AB225, ABCD3AB. Basically, any combination of any of the 26 letters of the alphabet A, B, C, . . . , X, Y, Z with any of the ten digits 0, 1, 2, . . . , 8, 9, is an atom as long as we start with a letter. So, for example, 9ABC99 is not an atom since it starts with a 9, which is not a letter. But J9ABC99 is an atom, and so is ABC99, since they are both made up of letters and digits and start with a letter. In most computer systems, there is a limit to the number of letters and digits that you may use. We shall not be concerned with such limitations here, and, in any case, there is seldom any

---

†There is a story about a man who received an umbrella for having drawn a mushroom.

‡Many computers can print only capital letters, so we shall not use lowercase letters.

reason for using atoms of more than ten letters and digits.† Remember that it takes twice longer to write down ten letters than to write down five of them. Let us look at some more examples. The following are not atoms:

			Reason
✓	a.	5ABCDEF	Starts with a digit, not a letter.
	b.	AB CD	Includes a space, which is neither a letter nor a digit.
✓	c.	%BC	Does not start with a letter.
	d.	A5.)	Includes characters which are neither letters nor digits.

EXERCISE

Which of the following are atoms? Give your reasons.

a. HAPPY

b. HAPPY SAM

c. HAPPYSAM

d. (HAPPY)

e. HAPPY.

f. NINE

g. 9NINE

h. NINE9

1.1.2 Lists

The second type of word used in the LISP language is a list. We build up lists from atoms and other lists. A list starts with a left parenthesis, which is followed by any number of atoms and lists, and terminates with a right parenthesis. About the simplest list is (HARRY). It consists of a left parenthesis, the atom HARRY, and, finally, a right parenthesis. Another simple example is the list (POOR HARRY). It begins with (, followed by the two atoms POOR and HARRY, and terminates with). Notice that we separate the atoms by one or more spaces, since we want to distinguish between the lists (POOR HARRY) and (POORHARRY). The list (POORHARRY) is made up of the parentheses and the atom POORHARRY. The two lists are most definitely different.

The simplest list is (), which consists of a left parenthesis, followed by zero S-expressions (i.e., atoms or lists), and terminating with a right paren-

†Occasionally, we shall use long names for their mnemonic value.

thesis. This special list is called the *null list* or empty list and is extremely important in LISP.

Now that we have the lists (HARRY) and (POOR HARRY), we can build a more complicated list. We start with the (, then take the list (HARRY), then the list (POOR HARRY), and finally the). The result is the list ((HARRY) (POOR HARRY)). This new list can be used to build yet another list such as, for example, (((HARRY) (POOR HARRY)) HARRY (HARRY)).† The most general list is therefore of the form

$$\boxed{\text{(SEX1 SEX2 SEX3 . . . SEXk)}}$$

where SEX1, SEX2, . . . , SEXk (namely all the SEXes‡) are S-expressions, i.e., either atoms or lists. The integer k represents the length of the list. We have already seen the null list (), for which k = 0. Let us consider some additional examples and justify why they are lists.

a. (HARRY) is a list: We let k = 1, and SEX1 = HARRY, which is an atom—hence an S-expression.

b. (HARRY LOVES JANE) is a list; we let k = 3, SEX1 = HARRY, SEX2 = LOVES, and SEX3 = JANE.

At this point we should ask whether the O in the atom LOVES is the letter O or the digit 0 (zero). Our convention will be that 0 will be the digit and Ø the letter. However, in most contexts, it is obvious which character is used, and we shall usually dispense with Ø's.

Now to some more complicated examples. ((AB T56) HAT ()) is a list. Let k = 3, SEX1 = (AB T56), SEX2 = HAT, and SEX3 = (). SEX2 is fine, since it is an atom—hence an S-expression. We have only SEX1 to worry about. SEX1 is clearly not an atom, so it must be a list *if* ((AB T56) HAT ()) is to be a list. [You should verify that (AB T56) is indeed a list.]

Parentheses are very important in LISP, and a little care will avoid silly bugs in your program and much unnecessary wasted time. Thus it is highly advisable to use some check on the well-formedness of your LISP expressions.

GOLDEN RULE 1:

$$\boxed{\text{ALWAYS CHECK YOUR PARENTHESES.}}$$

†Is your name Harry?

‡The reader will have guessed the reason for calling LISP words S-expressions. It is a clever way to introduce the real problem with which this book should be dealing.

In Appendix A we shall describe three algorithms to help count parentheses.

1.1.3 Some Examples of Lists

Many kinds of information are easily represented as lists. For example, a sentence in English can be represented as the list of the words (MY NAME IS HARRY). A hand in some card game can easily be described as a list of lists. For example, the list ((KING HEARTS) (KING SPADES) (KING DIAMONDS) (ACE HEARTS) (ACE CLUBS)) describes a pretty good poker hand.†

Let us describe something more complicated. BOB has two sons, BILL and JACK, and two daughters, SALLY and SUZY,‡ born in the order given. SUZY is sterile, so she has no children. Although SALLY's husband is impotent, she still has a son FRED. BILL has two sons, BILLJR and JOE, while JACK has found no girl stupid enough to marry him. How does the family look?

```
(BOB (BILL (BILLJR JOE)
     JACK
     SALLY (FRED)
     SUZY
     ) )
```

Each parent is followed by a list of all his offspring. If any of these also has offspring, they are put in a list following the parent.

EXERCISES

1. What is the representation of the descendants of BOB if (a) JOE has a son TOM and a daughter SARAH and a grandson TOMJR, son of TOM, and (b) FRED has a daughter CLARA and a granddaughter HELEN?

2. Give husbands and wives (as seems appropriate) to BOB and his descendants, and design a list structure to represent the new family relationships.

3. Represent your own family tree as a list, going back as many generations as you can. How did you (or would you) take care of divorces, remarriages, etc. Give specific examples.

†That was my opponent's hand. Since I also had (ACE CLUBS), she was obviously cheating.

‡Notice the originality of the names.

2

ELEMENTARY SENTENCES

Now that we know how to write words in LISP, we shall learn to build sentences. What is beautiful about LISP is that its sentences look just like its words (namely lists) but the sentences carry a meaning. The sentences of LISP are elementary programs. A LISP program consists of functions applied to arguments. LISP functions have a single value. Complicated functions can be built from more elementary ones. Every LISP system has many built-in elementary functions. We shall consider some of these now.

2.1 CAR

Given a list, we may want to obtain its first element. Now a list is of the form (SEX1 SEX2. . . SEXk), and its first element is SEX1. The *function* CAR gives us the first element of a list. That is, given a list as *argument*, CAR returns as *value* the first element of the list.

Now we must present an unpleasant situation to you: There are two main dialects of LISP, i.e., two similar but still different ways of speaking. One we shall call EVALQUOTE-LISP, or EVQ-LISP for short; the other will be called EVAL-LISP, or EV-LISP for short. You should read all that follows independently of the LISP dialect that you have available on a computer.

6

2.1.1 CAR in EVQ-LISP

In EVQ-LISP, using CAR is easy. You write CAR, and then follow it by *a list* of the list of which you want the first argument. For example, to obtain the first element of the list (YOU ARE HARRY), write

```
CAR ( (YOU ARE HARRY) )
```

The computer will return YOU, the first element of the list, as the value of CAR.

Here are further examples:

```
CAR ( (YOU ARE HARRY) )
VALUE IS . . .
YOU

CAR ( ( (YOU ARE) HARRY) )
VALUE IS . . .
(YOU ARE)

CAR ( ( (YOU ARE HARRY) ) )
VALUE IS . . .
(YOU ARE HARRY)

CAR ( ( ( ) (YOU ARE HARRY) ) )
VALUE IS . . .
( )†

CAR ( ( ( ) ) )
VALUE IS . . .
( )
```

EXERCISE

If your computer talks EVQ-LISP, have it tell you the CAR of ten different lists of your invention.

2.1.1.1 Special Cases of CAR

Now let us consider some special cases. How about

```
  * CAR ( ( ) )‡
```

†Most systems would print the value ( ) as NIL; see Section 4.4.3.

‡Here and later on, a * in front of a LISP sentence indicates that it is bad and poorly formed.

( ) is a list of no arguments, and thus it has no first argument. We shall say that CAR of ( ) is undefined. Your actual LISP system may give you an error, or what computer programmers affectionately call *garbage*. How about

* CAR ((HI THERE) (YOU))?

Here we have another problem: CAR expects *one* list as argument; i.e., in the list that follows CAR there should be only *one* sublist. Depending on your LISP system you may or may not get garbage, but you certainly made an error. You must watch carefully for this type of error.

GOLDEN RULE 2:

> ALWAYS CHECK THAT YOUR FUNCTIONS ARE GIVEN THE RIGHT NUMBER OF CORRECT ARGUMENTS.

What does "correct argument" mean? Consider * CAR (HARRY). We have given CAR one argument, the atom HARRY. But CAR expects a (nonempty) list as its unique argument. Your EVQ-LISP should give you an error message. Let us recapitulate what we know about CAR:

> Function: CAR
> Number of arguments: 1
> Argument: nonempty list
> Value: first element of the list

2.1.2 CAR in EV-LISP

If you are talking with an EV-LISP computer, things are somewhat different. To calculate the CAR of (YOU ARE HARRY), write a list of two elements. SEX1 is CAR, while SEX2 is the list of the atom QUOTE followed by the list (YOU ARE HARRY).

(CAR (QUOTE (YOU ARE HARRY)))

which has value YOU.

Here are, in EV-LISP, the examples we considered in EVQ-LISP:

```
(CAR (QUOTE ((YOU ARE) HARRY)))
        VALUE IS...
        (YOU ARE)
```

```
    (CAR (QUOTE ((YOU ARE HARRY))))
     VALUE IS...
     (YOU ARE HARRY)
    (CAR (QUOTE (() (YOU ARE HARRY))))
     VALUE IS...
     ()
 * (CAR (QUOTE (YOU ARE HARRY))
```

The last example will not work since there is a) missing.

The special cases of CAR in EV-LISP are the same as in EVQ-LISP:
* (CAR (QUOTE ( ))) is undefined;

> * (CAR (QUOTE (HI THERE) (YOU)))

Here the diagnosis is somewhat different: QUOTE is a function of *one* argument, a SEX, i.e., an atom or a list. In the above bad example, QUOTE is given two arguments: (HI THERE) and (YOU). An error should result, since QUOTE was not given the correct number of arguments.

> * (CAR (QUOTE HARRY))

The value of QUOTE is the atom HARRY. An atom is an incorrect argument for CAR, so an error should result.

EXERCISE

If your computer talks EV-LISP, have it tell you the CAR of ten different lists of your invention.

2.2 QUOTE

While talking about CAR we have introduced the very important, yet most simple function QUOTE. We have only to write down its definition.

S

Function: QUOTE
Number of arguments: 1
Argument: any SEX
Value: the argument

An example in EV-LISP is

```
(QUOTE (ADD VICE TO ADVICE) )
VALUE IS...
(ADD VICE TO ADVICE)
```

Let us try to understand the use of QUOTE. In EV-LISP, the value of

```
(CAR (QUOTE (HARRY) ) )
```

is obtained as follows: EV-LISP recognizes the program (CAR (QUOTE (HARRY))) and sees that it will obtain the value of this program by applying the function CAR to *the value of the argument* of CAR, namely (QUOTE (HARRY)). The value of (QUOTE (HARRY)) is (HARRY), and the CAR of (HARRY) is HARRY. Hence when QUOTE is used, the argument of QUOTE is taken literally; i.e., it is not evaluated.

By contrast, let us consider the value of the (bad) EV-LISP program

```
* (CAR (HARRY) )
```

EV-LISP wants to take the CAR of the *value* of (HARRY), which is *not* (HARRY). [In fact, the value of (HARRY) is the function called HARRY applied to zero arguments. Since HARRY is not—supposedly—a function, an error was made. See also Section 2.8.]

So remember:
The simplest EV-LISP program which has value the SEX blooh is (QUOTE blooh).

2.3 CDR

Another very simple function is CDR (pronounced cooder). Like CAR, CDR is a function of a single argument that must be a nonempty list. The value of CDR of a list is what remains of the list when its CAR has been removed. For example, in EVQ-LISP, the value of CDR ((YOU ARE HARRY)) is the list (ARE HARRY) since CAR ((YOU ARE HARRY)) has value YOU and we take that off the list. Another way of looking at what CDR does is as follows: Grab the leftmost parenthesis of the list, lift it, and move it just to the right of the first SEX of the list. This way you obtain a new list, starting at the heavy leftmost parenthesis that you have happily put down, which is the value of the function CDR applied to the old list.

Let's come back to the example

(YOU ARE HARRY)

Grab the leftmost parenthesis of the list:

(YOU ARE HARRY)

Move it past the first SEX:

(YOU (ARE HARRY)

old   new

Here are some additional examples in EVQ-LISP:

```
CDR  ( (YOU ARE HARRY) )
 VALUE IS...
 (ARE HARRY)

CDR  ( ( (YOU ARE) HARRY) )
 VALUE IS...
 (HARRY)

CDR  ( ( (YOU ARE HARRY) ) )
 VALUE IS...
 ( )

CDR  ( ( ( ) (YOU ARE HARRY) ) )
 VALUE IS...
 ( (YOU ARE HARRY) )
```

Here are the same examples in EV-LISP:

```
(CDR (QUOTE (YOU ARE HARRY) ) )
 VALUE IS...
 (ARE HARRY)

(CDR (QUOTE ( (YOU ARE) HARRY) ) )
 VALUE IS...
 (HARRY)

(CDR (QUOTE ( (YOU ARE HARRY) ) ) )
 VALUE IS...
 ( )

(CDR (QUOTE ( ( ) (YOU ARE HARRY) ) ) )
 VALUE IS...
 ( (YOU ARE HARRY) )
```

2.3.1 Restriction on CDR

The restriction on CDR is the same as the restriction on CAR. Thus, the argument must be a nonempty list. What happens, for instance, if you try to take the CDR of the null list ()? You pick up the (and try to move it right one SEX. But then, WHAM!, you bump into the). Clearly CDR (()) should be undefined.

EXERCISE

Calculate the value of CDR in ten examples of your choice.

§

Function: CDR
Number of arguments: 1
Argument: nonempty list
Value: remaining part of list after deletion of the first element

2.4   CONS

2.4.1   Examples

CAR and CDR took apart lists, in the sense that their values were "smaller" than the list that was their argument. CONS is a function that builds bigger lists from its two arguments. The first argument of CONS can be any SEX, while the second argument must be a list. Let's look at some examples. Suppose that the two arguments of CONS are LIFE and the list (IS CONTAGIOUS). We write down the two arguments side by side:

LIFE   (IS CONTAGIOUS)

Since the second argument is always a list, it must start with a left parenthesis (:

LIFE   (IS CONTAGIOUS)
            ↑

We grab that left parenthesis and move it left past the first argument of CONS,

(LIFE   IS CONTAGIOUS)
↑...

to obtain the list (LIFE IS CONTAGIOUS). This list is the *value* of the function CONS applied to the two arguments LIFE and (IS CONTAGIOUS). Elementary, my dear Watson. Even an IBM computer could do it.

Consider another example. The arguments of CONS are

(LIFE)   (IS CONTAGIOUS)

We have already marked the left parenthesis of the second argument. We move it left, past (LIFE), to obtain

((LIFE) IS CONTAGIOUS)

A few more examples should suffice. Let the two arguments of CONS be

(LIFE)   ((IS (CONTAGIOUS)))

The value of CONS applied to these two arguments is

((LIFE) (IS (CONTAGIOUS)))

The second argument can be the empty list (). If the arguments are

GLOOBA   ( )

we move the left parenthesis of () left past GLOOBA, to obtain

(GLOOBA   )

or, equivalently, (GLOOBA).

If the arguments are

((LIFE IS) CONTAGIOUS)   ( )

then the value of CONS applied to these arguments is

(((LIFE IS) CONTAGIOUS))

2.4.2 *Relations Among CAR, CDR, and CONS*

Let us return to our first example. The CONS of LIFE and (IS CONTAGIOUS) is (LIFE IS CONTAGIOUS). Notice that the CAR of (LIFE IS CONTAGIOUS) is LIFE, which was the first argument of CONS, and that the CDR of (LIFE IS CONTAGIOUS) is (IS CONTAGIOUS), which was the second argument of CONS. These relationships always hold: The CAR of the CONS of two arguments is the first argument, while the CDR of the CONS of two arguments is the second argument. Remember that the second argument is restricted to being a list.†

§

```
Function:  CONS
Number of arguments:  2
Arguments:  first, any SEX; second, any list
Value:  a list, such that its CAR is the first argument
        and its CDR the second argument of CONS
```

2.4.3 CONS in EVQ-LISP

Remember that in EVQ-LISP we write the name of the function followed by *a list* of its arguments. Since CONS has two arguments, the list of arguments of CONS will contain two SEXes, the second one being a list. The program for calculating the CONS of the two arguments LIFE and (IS CONTAGIOUS) would be, in EVQ-LISP,

```
CONS (    LIFE    (IS CONTAGIOUS)    )
```

and the value would be (LIFE IS CONTAGIOUS). Without wasting too many blanks, here is the program as run on a computer with EVQ-LISP:

```
CONS (LIFE (IS CONTAGIOUS) )
 VALUE IS...
 (LIFE IS CONTAGIOUS)
```

Here is a program for all the examples discussed in Section 2.4.1:

```
CONS (LIFE (IS CONTAGIOUS) )
CONS ( (LIFE) (IS CONTAGIOUS) )
CONS ( (LIFE) ( (IS (CONTAGIOUS) ) ) )
CONS (GLOOBA ( ) )
CONS ( ( (LIFE IS) CONTAGIOUS) ( ) )
```

A run of the above programs would produce an output similar to

```
CONS (LIFE (IS CONTAGIOUS) )
 VALUE IS...
 (LIFE IS CONTAGIOUS)

CONS ( (LIFE) (IS CONTAGIOUS) )
 VALUE IS...
 ( (LIFE) IS CONTAGIOUS)
```

†This restriction will be lifted in Section 10.7.1.

```
CONS ( (LIFE) ( (IS (CONTAGIOUS) ) ) )
  VALUE IS . . .
  ( (LIFE) (IS (CONTAGIOUS) ) )

CONS (GLOOBA ( ) )
  VALUE IS . . .
  (GLOOBA)

CONS ( ( (LIFE IS) CONTAGIOUS) ( ) )
  VALUE IS . . .
  ( ( (LIFE IS) CONTAGIOUS) )
```

2.4.4   CONS in EV-LISP

In EV-LISP, the programs look somewhat different. The program to evaluate CONS of LIFE and (IS CONTAGIOUS) would be a list. The first SEX of the list would be the name of the function, namely CONS. The second and third SEXes of the list would be the first and second arguments of CONS, *but* these second and third SEXes are *evaluated*; that is, we must make sure that the *value* of the second SEX of the list is LIFE and that the value of the third SEX of the list is (IS CONTAGIOUS). The easiest way to do this is by using the function QUOTE. The program would be

```
(CONS (QUOTE LIFE) (QUOTE (IS CONTAGIOUS) ) )
```

The value of (QUOTE LIFE) is the argument LIFE of QUOTE. Similarly, the value of (QUOTE (IS CONTAGIOUS)) is the argument (IS CONTAGIOUS) of the function QUOTE. Note that (QUOTE LIFE) and (QUOTE (IS CONTAGIOUS)) are lists; their first SEX is the function QUOTE, while their second SEX is the argument of QUOTE.

A run of the above program would produce an output similar to

```
(CONS (QUOTE LIFE) (QUOTE (IS CONTAGIOUS) ) )
  VALUE IS . . .
  (LIFE IS CONTAGIOUS)
```

A complete program for the examples discussed in Section 2.4.1 is

```
(CONS (QUOTE LIFE) (QUOTE (IS CONTAGIOUS) ) )
(CONS (QUOTE (LIFE) ) (QUOTE (IS CONTAGIOUS) ) )
(CONS (QUOTE (LIFE) ) (QUOTE ( (IS (CONTAGIOUS) ) ) ) )
(CONS (QUOTE GLOOBA) (QUOTE ( ) ) )
(CONS (QUOTE ( (LIFE IS) CONTAGIOUS) ) (QUOTE ( ) ) )
```

A run of the above programs would produce an output similar to

```
(CONS (QUOTE LIFE) (QUOTE (IS CONTAGIOUS) ) )
VALUE IS...
(LIFE IS CONTAGIOUS)

(CONS (QUOTE (LIFE) ) (QUOTE (IS CONTAGIOUS) ) )
VALUE IS...
( (LIFE) IS CONTAGIOUS)

(CONS (QUOTE (LIFE) ) (QUOTE ( (IS CONTAGIOUS) ) ) )
VALUE IS...
( (LIFE) (IS CONTAGIOUS) )

(CONS (QUOTE GLOOBA) (QUOTE ( ) ) )
VALUE IS...
(GLOOBA)

(CONS (QUOTE ( (LIFE IS) CONTAGIOUS) ) (QUOTE ( ) ) )
VALUE IS...
( ( (LIFE IS) CONTAGIOUS) )
```

EXERCISE

Calculate the value of CONS on ten different pairs of arguments for CO NS. The second argument must be a list.

2.5 ATOM

There are three more elementary functions that we shall discuss in this chapter: EQ, NULL, and ATOM. Each of these functions is called a *predicate* or a test function: They test whether something is true or not. Their value can be either T (for true) if the outcome of the test is positive, or NIL (for false) if the outcome of the test is negative.

Remember that the universe of LISP consists of SEXes. The predicate ATOM tells us what kind of SEX its argument is. If it is an atom, the value of ATOM is T; if it is a list, then the value of ATOM is NIL. If we have two atoms, the predicate EQ tells us whether they are the same atom (value is T) or different atoms (value is NIL). If the SEX under consideration is not an atom (as we could have surmised from the predicate ATOM), then it must be a list, and NULL tells us whether the list is the empty list, in which case the value of NULL is T. We often test a list by the predicate NULL, since we can apply CAR and CDR only to non-NULL lists.

2.5.1 Examples of ATOM

The single argument of ATOM can be any SEX. The value of ATOM is T if the SEX is an atom; otherwise the value of ATOM is NIL. Here are three EV-LISP programs illustrating the behavior of the function ATOM:

```
(ATOM (QUOTE ABC54) )
 VALUE IS . . .
 T

(ATOM (QUOTE (CREATE THEN CREMATE) ) )
 VALUE IS . . .
 NIL

(ATOM (QUOTE (ABC54) ) )
 VALUE IS . . .
 NIL
```

The same examples in EVQ-LISP would be

```
ATOM (ABC54)
 VALUE IS . . .
 T

ATOM ( (CREATE THEN CREMATE) )
 VALUE IS . . .
 NIL

ATOM ( (ABC54) )
 VALUE IS . . .
 NIL
```

§

Function:	ATOM
Number of arguments:	1
Argument:	any SEX
Value:	T if the argument is an atom; NIL otherwise

EXERCISE

Test ATOM on three atomic and three nonatomic arguments.

2.6 EQ

EQ has two arguments. If both arguments are the same atoms, then the value of EQ is T. Otherwise the value of EQ is NIL.

2.6.1 Examples of EQ

In EV-LISP, a program to test for the equality of the two atoms LIFE and LIF is

```
(EQ (QUOTE LIFE) (QUOTE LIF))
```

and the computer would say

```
VALUE IS...
NIL
```

Similarly,

```
(EQ (QUOTE LIFE) (QUOTE LIFE))
VALUE IS...
T
```

In EVQ-LISP, the above two programs would be run as

```
EQ (LIFE LIF)
VALUE IS...
NIL
```

```
EQ (LIFE LIFE)
VALUE IS...
T
```

§

Function: EQ
Number of arguments: 2
Arguments: two SEXes
Value: T if both atoms are the same; otherwise NIL

EXERCISE

Test EQ on five pairs of atomic arguments.

2.7 NULL

The predicate NULL has one argument. The value of NULL is T if its argument is the empty list (). Otherwise, the value of NULL is NIL.

2.7.1 Examples of NULL

In EVQ-LISP, we write the function NULL, followed by the list of its unique argument:

```
NULL ( ( ) )
  VALUE IS...
  T

NULL ( ( ( ) ) )
  VALUE IS...
  NIL

NULL ( (SECRET LOVES SECRETE LOW VOWS) )
  VALUE IS...
  NIL
```

* NULL () is illegal since no argument is given to NULL.

The same examples in EV-LISP would be

```
(NULL (QUOTE ( ) ) )
  VALUE IS...
  T

(NULL (QUOTE ( ( ) ) ) )
  VALUE IS...
  NIL

(NULL (QUOTE (SECRET LOVES SECRETE LOW VOWS) ) )
  VALUE IS...
  NIL
```

EXERCISE

Test your NULL on five different lists.

2.8 Multiple Evaluations in EV–LISP

The following scenario is typical of LISP programming. Some function is given some arguments. The function has a value which is given, as argument, to some other function. The value of that function, together with perhaps the value of some other function, is given to a function of two arguments. The value of *that* function is given to some final function, and your friendly LISP system will give you only the value of this final function on its argument, printing VALUE IS... and the very last value.

Some of the functions may be the same; hence we had best turn now to clearing up some of the confusion that may arise.

Consider some examples:

```
(CAR (QUOTE (JOURNALISM IS UNREADABLE) ) )
```

LISP wants to evaluate the list (CAR (QUOTE (JOURNALISM IS UNREADABLE))). The first SEX of the list is an atom, CAR, and LISP expects this atom to be the name of a function. It verifies that CAR is, indeed, the name of a function and decides to apply CAR to the *value* of the second SEX of the list, (QUOTE (JOURNALISM IS UNREADABLE)). Once again LISP finds a list, the first SEX of which is a known function, QUOTE. The value of QUOTE is its argument, (JOURNALISM IS UNREADABLE). Therefore the value of (QUOTE (JOURNALISM IS UNREADABLE)) is (JOURNALISM IS UNREADABLE), and this value is given as argument to CAR, which returns as value JOURNAL-ISM. The run of the program would be

```
(CAR (QUOTE (JOURNALISM IS UNREADABLE) ) )
VALUE IS ...
JOURNALISM
```

Here is another example:

```
(CONS(CAR(QUOTE(LITERATURE)))(CONS(QUOTE IS)(CDR(QUOTE(RED NOT READ)))))
```

which is not particularly legible. A more legible version of the same program is

```
(CONS
    (CAR  (QUOTE (LITERATURE) ) )
    (CONS (QUOTE IS)
          (CDR (QUOTE (RED NOT READ) ) )
    )
)
```

where we tried to align the arguments of the CONSes. LISP finds a list and checks that the first SEX of the list is a known function, CONS. CONS will have two arguments, which must be evaluated. The value of the first argument is the value of (CAR (QUOTE (LITERATURE))). You should verify that the value of (CAR (QUOTE (LITERATURE))) is LITERA-TURE. The second argument of CONS is *the value of*

```
(CONS (QUOTE IS)
      (CDR (QUOTE (RED NOT READ) ) ) )
```

LISP finds another list, of which the first SEX is a function, another CONS. It evaluates the first argument of this second CONS by evaluating (QUOTE IS), the value of which is IS. It then evaluates the second argument of the second CONS; i.e., it evaluates (CDR (QUOTE (RED NOT READ))). The value of *that* is the function CDR applied to the value of (QUOTE (RED NOT READ)). Since the value of (QUOTE (RED NOT READ)) is (RED NOT READ), (CDR (QUOTE (RED NOT READ))) is CDR applied to (RED NOT READ) and has value (NOT READ).

The plot is beginning to clarify. The two arguments of the second CONS have been evaluated to IS and (NOT READ). The CONS of these two SEXes is (IS NOT READ), and this is precisely the second argument of the first CONS. Since LISP already knows that the first argument is LITERATURE, it can calculate CONS of LITERATURE and (IS NOT READ), and the value is the list (LITERATURE IS NOT READ). Since this list is the value of the original program, LISP will print it. The entire program will be

```
(CONS (CAR (QUOTE (LITERATURE) ) ) (CONS (QUOTE IS)
                    (CDR (QUOTE (RED NOT READ) ) ) ) )
VALUE IS...
(LITERATURE IS NOT READ)
```

Notice the (usual) structure of a program: a list, starting with the name of a function, followed by as many SEXes as the function takes arguments. Each of these arguments is in turn evaluated (unless the function is QUOTE), and, in fact, each of the arguments may itself be a program having the same structure as the original program. Since parentheses determine lists, they *cannot* be used for esthetics as in arithmetic and algebra. Let us look at some typical *bad* LISP programs that contain typical errors,† written by student Phf, who, as his name indicates, often gets F's for his homework.‡

To calculate the CAR of the list (A B), Phf wrote the program

```
* (CAR (A B) )
```

No, the answer is not A. The argument of CAR, (A B), *must be evaluated.* Defining a function of one argument called A and giving B a value might make some sense out of (A B), which would then be inter-

---

†In suitable contexts, the programs may have a meaning. However, at this stage, it is highly probably that they have bugs.

‡Having started from NIL, Phf has become president and chairman of the board of one of the most prosperous American corporations. Phf says that he enjoys the rat race and that he has three children, two sons and two daughters.

preted as the value of the function named A applied to the value of B. Phf should have written (CAR (QUOTE (A B))).

To show his understanding of multiple evaluations, Phf wanted to calculate the CAR of (A B), obtaining A, and the CDR of (C D), obtaining (D). Taking the CONS of A and (D) would give him (A D). His program was

```
*(CONS ((CAR (QUOTE (A B))) (CDR (QUOTE (C D))))) )
```

The first thing that is wrong is that CONS is given only one argument, the value of ((CAR (QUOTE (A B))) (CDR (QUOTE (C D)))), while we know that CONS requires two arguments. It is doubtful that a LISP system would spot that error first. It would take the first argument of CONS and would try to evaluate it, without noting whether there is a second argument. (It would find that out eventually, anyway.) So LISP wants to evaluate

```
((CAR (QUOTE (A B))) (CDR (QUOTE (C D))))
```

✓ The first SEX of the list is not the name of a function, as is usually the case, so LISP will evaluate (CAR (QUOTE (A B))), hoping that the value of this list will be the name of a function. The value of (CAR (QUOTE (A B))) is A, so that LISP wants to evaluate the function A on the value of the argument of A, i.e., the value of (CDR (QUOTE (C D))). Since it is likely that Phf did not define a function called A, an error will result. The correct program should have been

```
(CONS (CAR (QUOTE (A B))) (CDR (QUOTE (C D))))
```

and EV-LISP would have said

```
VALUE IS...
(A D)
```

Another common error is exemplified by the program

```
*(CONS A(B))
```

with which Phf wanted to calculate the CONS of the atom A and the list (B). Several things may be wrong here. First of all, LISP would want to evaluate A, i.e., find the value of A, which may not exist. Second, it would want to evaluate (B). The list (B) could be interpreted as the function called
✓ B applied to no arguments.† The correct program should have been

†There are other interpretations in some LISP systems.

```
(CONS (QUOTE A) (QUOTE (B) ) )
VALUE IS . . .
(A  B)
```

The above discussion has relevance beyond EV-LISP. We shall see in the following chapters that, in both versions of LISP, values of functions are passed to other functions as arguments. It is important to remember that, in general, what is evaluated is a list. *The first element of the list is the name of the function; the other elements of the list are the arguments of the function, and these arguments will also, in general, be evaluated.*

3

ELEMENTARY DEFINE

In the previous chapter, we introduced the six basic LISP functions CAR, CDR, CONS, ATOM, NULL, and EQ. With these functions, and a few auxiliary functions that we shall soon exemplify, you can construct any function that *can* be constructed. We make the restriction in italics because some functions cannot be constructed in LISP, nor, for that matter, in any programming language.

3.1 FIRST, SECOND, and THIRD

Suppose that you wish to define three functions FIRST, SECOND, and THIRD which will give you the first, second, and third SEX, respectively, of a list. For example, in the list (KEEP UP WITH YESTERDAY), the first SEX is KEEP, the second is UP, and the third is WITH. First, let us assume that the problem is solved and that we have defined the three functions. Then we could use these functions exactly as we have used CAR, NULL, or any other of the six basic LISP functions.

In EV-LISP, we would say

(SECOND (QUOTE (KEEP UP WITH YESTERDAY)))

24

and the system would respond

```
            VALUE IS ...
            UP
```

In EVQ-LISP, we would say

```
        THIRD ( (KEEP UP WITH YESTERDAY) )
```

and the system would respond

```
            VALUE IS ...
            WITH
```

Similarly,

```
        FIRST ( (KEEP UP WITH YESTERDAY) )
        VALUE IS ...
        KEEP
```

Thus our only problem is to tell the system what these functions FIRST, SECOND, and THIRD mean. So let's see how we can define them in terms of the six basic functions.

FIRST is clearly the same as CAR, so that's easy. Now to obtain the second SEX, we should first eliminate the first SEX, KEEP, obtaining the list (UP WITH YESTERDAY) and then take the CAR, or the FIRST, of this list. You will have noticed that (UP WITH YESTERDAY), besides being the motto of some conservatives, is the CDR of the original list (KEEP UP WITH YESTERDAY). To obtain the SECOND of a list, we first take its CDR, and then its CAR.

Now how do we get the THIRD of a list? You should verify that it can be done by first taking the CDR, obtaining (UP WITH YESTER-DAY); then taking the CDR again, obtaining (WITH YESTERDAY); and finally taking the CAR of that, leaving us the desired WITH, the THIRD of (KEEP UP WITH YESTERDAY).

Great! There is another way to define THIRD that may seem even prettier. Once we have taken the CDR, we have (UP WITH YESTER-DAY). And what is WITH in that list? It is the SECOND of the list. Hence we obtain the THIRD of a list by first taking the CDR, and then the SECOND. Let's do it this last way. We are now ready to DEFINE the three functions together. Each of them there functions (sic!) is a function of one argument, a list. Let us write down the definitions in EVQ-LISP and then discuss them.

3.2 DEFINE and LAMBDA in EVQ-LISP

```
DEFINE ( (

(SECOND (LAMBDA (LIS)  (FIRST (CDR LIS) ) ) )
(THIRD (LAMBDA (LIS)  (SECOND (CDR LIS) ) ) )
(FIRST (LAMBDA (LIS)  (CAR LIS) ) )

    ) )†
```

Let's try to understand the above LISP sentence. Look at the definition of FIRST:

(FIRST (LAMBDA (LIS) (CAR LIS)))

The definition is a list. The first SEX of the list is the name of the function. We have chosen a name that will make it easy for us to remember the meaning of the function. Any atom (that starts with a letter) will do, so long as it is not the name of a function that already has some meaning in LISP, such as, for example, CAR or EQ.

The second SEX of the definition is also a list. It starts with LAMBDA because the programmer who coded the first LISP system could never remember whether the first Greek letter α was spelled ALPHA or ALFA.‡ LAMBDA is followed by a list, the list of arguments of the function. The function FIRST has one argument, so the list of arguments will have only one SEX. Since the argument of FIRST is a list, the name of the argument of FIRST was chosen as LIS. We could have chosen any other atom but preferred one that was mnemonic. Since LIST is a function in most LISP systems, we have chosen LIS in order to avoid a possible confusion.

The third SEX of the second SEX of the definition, i.e., (FIRST (CDR LIS)), defines the function. Its form is the same as that used in EV-LISP. The value of FIRST is the value of (CAR LIS), which is the value of the function CAR applied to the *value* of LIS.

In general, the format for defining a function of n arguments is

(FUNCTION-NAME (LAMBDA (ARG1 ARG2 ... ARGN)
definition-of-the-function-as-an-EV-LISP-program))§

---

†The order in which the functions are listed within a DEFINE is immaterial. We emphasize this point by choosing some order different from FIRST, SECOND, THIRD.

‡Well, actually the name originates from a logical formalism due to A. Church and called the λ-calculus. See Alonzo Church, *Introduction to Mathematical Logic*, Vol. 1, Princeton University Press, Princeton, N.J., 1956.

§ARG1 ARG2 ... ARGN are also called the LAMBDA variables of the function FUNCTION-NAME.

Now let us look at the evaluation of FIRST. Suppose that FIRST has been defined and that we give the following sentence in EVQ-LISP:

FIRST ((TRY ANOTHER SIN))

The argument of FIRST is the list (TRY ANOTHER SIN). In the definition of FIRST, the argument is LIS. The value of LIS is made to be this list (TRY ANOTHER SIN). Now when we evaluate (CAR LIS), its value is therefore TRY, which is the value of FIRST ((TRY ANOTHER SIN)). Simple enough.

Okay, now let us turn to the definition of SECOND:

(SECOND (LAMBDA (LIS) (FIRST (CDR LIS))))

Again, we have used a mnemonic name, SECOND, for the name of the function. The function has a single argument, a list, so we have chosen LIS again as the name of the argument, and the argument list is (LIS). The value of the function is (FIRST (CDR LIS)). That is, we take the value of the FIRST of something, namely the value of (CDR LIS). The value of that is the CDR of whatever the value of LIS may happen to be. Here is an example. Let's evaluate

(SECOND (QUOTE (POP GOES THE WEASEL)))

in EV-LISP.

The *value* of the argument LIS of SECOND is the list (POP GOES THE WEASEL). The CDR of it is (GOES THE WEASEL), and we must calculate the FIRST of that. All right, the value of the argument LIS of FIRST is made to be (GOES THE WEASEL); its CAR is taken, giving GOES. So GOES is the value of (FIRST (CDR LIS)) in the definition of SECOND, and that is also the value of (SECOND (QUOTE (POP GOES THE WEASEL))). Remember, if you don't understand right away, don't worry. *You never learn anything, you only get used to it.*

Now we are coming to the third function, THIRD. It should be easy. Its definition is

(THIRD (LAMBDA (LIS) (SECOND (CDR LIS))))

Let's glance over the peculiarities of the function. Its name is THIRD; it has one argument, called LIS; and we can guess just by looking at the argument that it is probably a list. Its value is SECOND of the value of (CDR LIS), which in turn is the CDR of the value of LIS. Consider an example in EVQ-LISP:

THIRD ((GRUB FIRST THEN ETHICS))

The value of the argument LIS in THIRD is the list (GRUB FIRST THEN ETHICS). The value of (CDR LIS) is (FIRST THEN ETHICS), and you should verify that the SECOND of that is indeed THEN.

Now we can return to our friend the function DEFINE. As you would guess from its name, DEFINE is used to define new functions. It is a function of one argument, a list. This list has as its SEXes the definitions of any number of functions. This accounts for the two parentheses following DEFINE. The first parenthesis is always there, for the list of arguments of the function. The second parenthesis is *the* list of arguments of DEFINE. In this example, the argument of DEFINE is a list of three function definitions,

```
( (SECOND(LAMBDA(LIS)(FIRST(CDR LIS) ) ) )(THIRD(LAMBDA(LIS)(SECOND
(CDR LIS) ) ) )(FIRST(LAMBDA(LIS)(CAR LIS) ) ) )
```

but we preferred to write it more legibly.

What does DEFINE do? Like all functions, it returns a value. The value of DEFINE is the list of the new function names in the order in which they are encountered. Here the value of DEFINE would be the list (SECOND THIRD FIRST). But, more importantly, the execution of DEFINE causes the new functions to be remembered by the LISP system, so that they can be used as any of the other LISP functions, such as CAR, CDR, or CONS.

Putting everything together, here is how the LISP program will look:

```
DEFINE  ( ( (SECOND (LAMBDA (LIS) (FIRST (CDR LIS) ) ) )
            (THIRD (LAMBDA (LIS) (SECOND (CDR LIS) ) ) )
            (FIRST (LAMBDA (LIS) (CAR LIS) ) )   ) )
    VALUE IS . . .
    (SECOND THIRD FIRST)

SECOND  ( (KEEP UP WITH YESTERDAY) )
    VALUE IS . . .
    UP

THIRD  ( (KEEP UP WITH YESTERDAY) )
    VALUE IS . . .
    WITH

FIRST  ( (TRY ANOTHER SIN) )
    VALUE IS . . .
    TRY

SECOND  ( (POP GOES THE WEASEL) )
    VALUE IS . . .
    GOES
```

```
THIRD  ( (GRUB FIRST THEN ETHICS) )
    VALUE IS...
    THEN
```

Let us make some additional comments on the above program. Notice that the order in which the functions are defined by DEFINE is immaterial. For instance, SECOND is defined "before" FIRST, and that is fine even though the definition of SECOND includes the use of FIRST. And let us emphasize again that the names of the arguments in the definitions of functions need not differ from one function to another. However, care should be taken not to use atoms that are *reserved words* in your LISP system: These are atoms such as CAR, CDR, EQ or NIL which have a special meaning in LISP.†

EXERCISES

1. Define FOURTH and FIFTH to be functions that will have as values the fourth and fifth SEX of a list, respectively. Use THIRD and run a program testing your definitions.

2. Write a function REPONETHREE which will make the first SEX of a list into the third SEX, deleting the original first SEX (see example). In EVQ-LISP, the result of a run of REPONETHREE would be

REPONETHREE ((PRETTY PHOTOGRAPHS OF WOMEN))

has value

(PHOTOGRAPHS OF PRETTY WOMEN)

Hints: You need only CAR, CDR, and CONS in your definition. You can assume that the list has at least three SEXes.
    Run your program on several examples.

3.3 DEFINE and LAMBDA in EV-LISP

In EV-LISP, DEFINE looks very much like DEFINE in EVQ-LISP. The definition of FIRST and SECOND and its utilization would be

```
(DEFINE (QUOTE (
  (SECOND (LAMBDA (LIS) (FIRST (CDR LIS)) ))
  (FIRST (LAMBDA (LIS) (CAR LIS)))
)) )
```

and has value (SECOND FIRST).

†After you have become an expert, you will know that this rule can be bypassed. See Section D.4.10.

$$(\text{SECOND} \ (\text{QUOTE} \ (\text{PIGS RAISE PIGS})))$$

has value RAISE.

$$(\text{FIRST} \ (\text{QUOTE} \ ((\text{BALDNESS}) \ \text{IS NEAT})))$$

has value (BALDNESS).

3.4 Summary

§

Function: DEFINE
Number of arguments: one
Type of arguments: a list of function definitions
Value: the list of the names of the (newly) defined functions; these functions are added to the LISP system

1. Inside a DEFINE, the order in which functions are defined is arbitrary.

2. The names of arguments in the definitions of functions may be any ✓   alpha atoms† that are not reserved words in LISP. In particular, the same atoms may be used in different functions.

Note: There is no significant difference between DEFINE in EV-LISP and EVQ-LISP, so we shall drop the distinction between the two dialects of LISP. The user should only remember the slight difference between the forms in which functions are applied to their arguments.

✓   †An alpha atom starts with a letter and is distinguished from numeric atoms, such as 347, which will be considered later.

4

ELEMENTARY RECURSIVE
DEFINE

4.1 HASAND

In this chapter we shall consider ways of defining more complicated functions than those considered in the previous chapter. Let us start with a very simple example. We want to write a function that will have value T if the atom AND is found in a list—for example, the list

(EAT DRINK AND BE MERRY FOR TOMORROW YE DIET)

—and will have value NIL if the atom AND is not found in the list—for example, the list (FRIEND OR ENEMA). We shall assume that all SEXes of the list are atoms. If we call the function HASAND, then in EVQ-LISP the value of

HASAND ((EAT DRINK AND BE MERRY FOR TOMORROW YE DIET))

will be T, while in EV-LISP the value of

(HASAND (QUOTE (FRIEND OR ENEMA)))

will be NIL. In the terminology of Chapter 2, HASAND is a predicate since it can have only two values, T and NIL. Remember that EQ, NULL, and ATOM are also predicates.

Let us build up the function HASAND bit by bit. Since it will be a function of one argument, a list, the definition should start as

```
(HASAND (LAMBDA (LIS)   ...   ))
```

A good deal is missing, of course.

How does one design functions? There are no rules that will work in all cases, but here are some good *rules of thumb*.

RULE OF THUMB 1:

> *Start with the easiest cases.*

The atom AND is of course fixed; hence only the argument of the function HASAND, that is, LIS, can vary. What is the simplest case of a list? *The null list* (). If LIS is the null list, clearly the value of HASAND must be NIL. That was easy. Now let's look at a slightly more complicated case: LIS has a single SEX. There are essentially two subcases. Either LIS has value (AND), or the unique atom of the list is some atom other than AND. An example of such a list would be (DIET). How do we find out the value of HASAND? Clearly, we take the CAR of the list, and ask whether it is AND. How? By Using EQ. If LIS has exactly one SEX, the value of HASAND will be (EQ (CAR LIS) (QUOTE AND)). Let's look at that expression more closely. EQ has two arguments, which should be atoms. First, we should check that the arguments are atoms. Since we assumed that LIS has only atoms as SEXes, the *value* of (CAR LIS) is an atom. The value of (QUOTE AND) is AND, which is an atom also. Thus in the case of a list with either zero or one SEX, we know how to write HASAND. Finally, let us characterize these two simple cases. If LIS is the empty list, then the value of (NULL LIS) is T. That was easy. How are lists with one element characterized? If LIS has value (AND) or (DIET), then the CDR of the list is the empty list; i.e., the value of (NULL (CDR LIS)) is T.

4.1.1 COND

We can continue now with the definition of HASAND by using a new function: COND. COND will allow us to say that if (NULL LIS) is T, then the value of HASAND is NIL, and that if (NULL (CDR LIS)) is T, then the value of HASAND is the value of (EQ (CAR LIS) (QUOTE AND)). COND is a function of any number of arguments, each one a list.

Thus the way in which COND is used looks as follows:

```
(COND      (argument1)
           (argument2)
           (argument3)
                .
                .
                .
           (argumentn)  )
```

Each argument consists of a *pair* of SEXes, which we shall refer to as *left* and *right*. So, in greater detail, COND looks like this:

```
(COND      (left1 right1)
           (left2 right2)
           (left3 right3)
                .
                .
                .
           (leftn rightn)  )
```

COND is evaluated as follows: First, the value of left1 is computed. If it is not NIL, the value of COND is the value of right1. If the value of left1 is NIL, then right1 is *not* considered, but the value of the next left is calculated, namely left2. If the value of left2 is not NIL, the value of COND is the value of right2; otherwise (that is, if left2 has value NIL) the next left, namely left3, is calculated. To avoid running out of left's, it is good practice to make the last left, leftn, have value T. A SEX that always has value T is T, so that in most of our definitions the last left of a COND will be T.

How does our still incomplete definition of HASAND look now?

```
(HASAND (LAMBDA (LIS)
          (COND      ( (NULL LIS) NIL)
                     ( (NULL (CDR LIS)) (EQ (CAR LIS) (QUOTE AND)) )
                        · · ·
          )
       ))
```

where dots indicate that additional information must be added. But let's analyze what we have. The first argument of COND is the list ((NULL LIS) NIL). Its left is (NULL LIS), and its right is NIL. So, if the value of (NULL LIS) is T (i.e., if LIS is the empty list), then the value of COND will be the value of NIL, which is NIL.† If LIS is not the empty list, then (NULL LIS) has value NIL, and we skip down to the next argument of

---

†T and NIL are special atoms which have T and NIL as values, respectively.

COND, which is

```
( (NULL (CDR LIS) ) (EQ (CAR LIS)(QUOTE AND) ) )
```

Left2 is (NULL (CDR LIS)). Notice how important it is to know that, when we reach the second argument of COND, LIS is not the empty list; otherwise it would not make sense to evaluate (CDR LIS). If LIS has only one SEX, then (NULL (CDR LIS)) has value T; in addition the value of COND is the value of the corresponding (second) right, (EQ (CAR LIS) (QUOTE AND)), exactly W.W.W. (what we wanted.)

4.1.2   Use of Recursion

After this interlude concerning COND, let us return to the function HASAND and consider the next more difficult case—a list with two elements such as (AND PIGS), (PIGS AND), or (PIGGY PIGS). *We shall try to reduce this more complicated case to the previous cases*, according to

RULE OF THUMB 2:

> *Reduce difficult cases to simple cases.*

How could this rule work here? We can check the CAR of the list LIS to see whether it is AND. If it is AND, then the value of HASAND is T, and we have finished. If it is not AND, we wish to consider the remaining part of LIS, namely its CDR. Now the CDR of (PIGS AND) is (AND), while the CDR of (PIGGY PIGS) is (PIGS). Do you notice anything about the lists (AND) and (PIGS)? They are exactly of the form of the previously considered simple case. In other words, in the most general case, we test to see whether the CAR of the list LIS is AND, and if it is not AND, then we apply HASAND to the CDR of LIS. Simple enough.

So how does the definition of HASAND look?

```
(HASAND (LAMBDA (LIS)
           (COND    ( (NULL LIS) NIL)
                    ( (NULL(CDR LIS) ) (EQ (CAR LIS) (QUOTE AND) ) )
                    ( (EQ (CAR LIS) (QUOTE AND) ) T)
                    (T (HASAND (CDR LIS) ) )
         )
       ) )
```

The third argument of COND is ((EQ (CAR LIS) (QUOTE AND)) T). Its left is (EQ (CAR LIS) (QUOTE AND)). Notice again that it makes sense to evaluate (CAR LIS) since we know that left1, namely (NULL

LIS), is NIL, for otherwise we would never have reached left3. If (EQ (CAR LIS) (QUOTE AND)) has value T, it means that the first SEX of LIS, the argument of HASAND, is the atom AND, and therefore the value of COND (and therefore the value of HASAND) must be T, which is the value of right3, namely T.

If the value of left3 is NIL (that is, if the first SEX of LIS is not AND), then we shall calculate the value of the same function HASAND applied to the CDR of LIS. This is seen in the fourth argument of COND, (T (HASAND (CDR LIS))).

The definition of HASAND will work as given, but it is worth examining it a bit further. The second argument of COND was written to handle special cases such as (AND) or (PIGGY). Notice that the general case (arguments 3 and 4 of COND) will also take care of this special case. In other words, a list with only one atom is not a special case to be treated separately. The only special case is the null list. Therefore a shorter version of a definition of HASAND can be given:

```
(HASAND (LAMBDA (LIS)
          (COND ( (NULL LIS) NIL)
                ( (EQ (CAR LIS) (QUOTE AND) ) T)
                (T (HASAND (CDR LIS) ) ) ) ) )
```

We say that the definition of HASAND is *recursive* because HASAND is defined in terms of HASAND itself. Let us see how this definition works on several examples.

In EVQ-LISP, let us calculate

$$HASAND \ (\ () \ )$$

The value of LIS is the empty list (). The value of left1, (NULL LIS), is T; therefore, the value of COND is the value of NIL, which is NIL, and that is the value of HASAND, as it should be since the null list clearly does not contain AND.

The next example is in EV-LISP:

$$(HASAND \ (QUOTE \ (AND)))$$

The value of LIS is the list (AND). LIS is not empty; hence left1 has value NIL, and left2 is evaluated. The value of (CAR LIS) is AND, and the value of (QUOTE AND) is AND. The value of the predicate EQ applied to the two arguments AND and AND is T, so the value of COND, and hence of HASAND, is the value of T, which is T.

Now we try a much harder example:

$$(HASAND \ (QUOTE \ (BEG \ BORROW \ AND \ STEAL)))$$

The value of LIS is the list (BEG BORROW AND STEAL). LIS is not the empty list, nor is its CAR EQual to AND, so we arrive at left3, which is T. Since the value of T is T, we calculate (HASAND (CDR LIS)), with LIS having value (BEG BORROW AND STEAL). (CDR LIS) has value (BORROW AND STEAL), so we now calculate the function HASAND with a *new* value of the argument LIS, namely (BORROW AND STEAL). Neither left1 nor left2 is satisfied, since (CAR LIS) is BORROW; therefore we calculate (HASAND (CDR LIS)), where LIS has value (BORROW AND STEAL). Since (CDR LIS) has value (AND STEAL), we calculate the function HASAND with another new value for LIS, namely (AND STEAL). LIS is not the empty list; its CAR is AND, and thus left2 (EQ (CAR LIS) (QUOTE AND)), in the evaluation of HASAND, has value T. Therefore the value of (HASAND (QUOTE (AND STEAL))) is the value of right2, which is T.

Okay. From where did this last HASAND come? From the evaluation of (HASAND (QUOTE (BORROW AND STEAL))). The value of this LISP sentence is therefore the same as the value of (HASAND (QUOTE (AND STEAL))), which we have just seen to be T. Similarly, the value of (HASAND (QUOTE (BEG BORROW AND STEAL))) is the value of (HASAND (QUOTE (BORROW AND STEAL))), which we have just seen to be T. So the value of our original LISP sentence is T, as it should be.

```
DEFINE    ( (
(HASAND (LAMBDA (LIS)
          (COND ( (NULL LIS) NIL)
                ( (EQ (CAR LIS) (QUOTE AND) ) T)
                (T (HASAND (CDR LIS) ) )
          )))
 ) )
VALUE IS ...
(HASAND)

HASAND ( ( ) )
  VALUE IS ...
  NIL
```

In EV-LISP we have:

```
(HASAND (QUOTE (AND) ) )
  VALUE IS ...
  T

(HASAND (QUOTE (BEG BORROW AND STEAL) ) )
  VALUE IS ...
  T
```

4.1.3 TRACE and UNTRACE

A nice feature of LISP is that it is possible to obtain information of the arguments that a function assumes and of the values of the function for each of the arguments. In the above example, the arguments of HASAND were, respectively,

```
(BEG BORROW AND STEAL)
(BORROW AND STEAL)
(AND STEAL)
```

The value of HASAND was first found for the argument (AND STEAL), and it was T. Next, this result was used to find the value of HASAND for the argument (BORROW AND STEAL), and this was T. Then *this* result was used to find the value of HASAND for the original argument, (BEG BORROW AND STEAL), and this final value, T, is printed.

It is sometimes useful to follow the different arguments that a function takes, as well as the corresponding values that result. LISP makes it easy to do just that with the help of the function TRACE. TRACE is a function of one argument which is a list of functions to be traced. (You don't know what that means, but it is coming.) So if we wish to TRACE only the function HASAND, a call to TRACE would have as argument a list containing all the functions to be traced, namely (HASAND). We would write in EV-LISP

```
(TRACE (QUOTE (HASAND) ) )
```

The value of TRACE is unimportant, although it exists (it is NIL). After TRACE has been executed, each of the functions in the list of arguments of TRACE is marked to. . . trace. This means that every time one of these functions is entered, LISP will tell you what the list of arguments for it is, and each time a value is found for the function, this value is also printed. If you are tired of tracing a function, the function UNTRACE can be used. As with TRACE, the argument of UNTRACE is a list of functions. UNTRACE will unmark every function in its list of arguments so that each of these functions will no longer be traced. Let us make (EV-)LISP do some of our chores then by using TRACE and UNTRACE on HASAND.

```
(DEFINE (QUOTE  (
 (HASAND (LAMBDA (LIS)
         (COND  ((NULL LIS) NIL)
                ((EQ (CAR LIS) (QUOTE AND)) T)
                (T (HASAND (CDR LIS) ) )  ) ) )  ) ) )
```

```
VALUE IS ...
(HASAND)

(HASAND (QUOTE (PRAY MORE AND PREY LESS) ) )
VALUE IS ...
T

(TRACE (QUOTE (HASAND) ) )
VALUE IS ...
NIL

(HASAND (QUOTE (PRAY MORE AND PREY LESS) ) )
VALUE IS ... ←

[ A] ARGUMENTS OF†  ←
(PRAY MORE AND PREY LESS)

[ B] ARGUMENTS OF HASAND ←
(MORE AND PREY LESS)

[ C] ARGUMENTS OF HASAND ←
(AND PREY LESS)

[ C] VALUE OF HASAND ←
T

[ B] VALUE OF HASAND ←
T

[ A] VALUE OF HASAND ←
T
T ←

(HASAND (QUOTE (DONT DOUBLECROSS BRIDGES) ) )
VALUE IS ...

[ A] ARGUMENTS OF†
(DONT DOUBLECROSS BRIDGES)

[ B] ARGUMENTS OF HASAND
(DOUBLECROSS BRIDGES)

[ C] ARGUMENTS OF HASAND
(BRIDGES)

[ D] ARGUMENTS OF HASAND
NIL
```

†Note that the version of LISP used in this example has a bug. It failed to print
HASAND in the line starting with

[A] ARGUMENTS OF

```
[ D] VALUE OF HASAND
NIL

[ C] VALUE OF HASAND
NIL

[ B] VALUE OF HASAND
NIL

[ A] VALUE OF HASAND
NIL
NIL

(UNTRACE (QUOTE (HASAND) ) )
VALUE IS . . .
NIL

(HASAND (QUOTE (MY NOSE BLEEDS FOR YOU) ) )
VALUE IS . . .
NIL

(HASAND (QUOTE (AND NEVER DISCUSS DISCUSSIONS) ) )
VALUE IS . . .
T

(TRACE (QUOTE (HASAND) ) )
VALUE IS
NIL

(HASAND (QUOTE (SIMPLY AFFECTING) ) )
VALUE IS

[ A] ARGUMENTS OF
(SIMPLY AFFECTING)

[ B] ARGUMENTS OF HASAND
(AFFECTING)

[ C] ARGUMENTS OF HASAND
NIL

[ C] VALUE OF HASAND
NIL

[ B] VALUE OF HASAND
NIL

[ A] VALUE OF HASAND
NIL
NIL
```

Let us draw boxes around the two functions TRACE and UNTRACE.

§

```
Function:  TRACE
Number of arguments:  1
Argument:  a list of names of functions to be traced
Value:  NIL (but basically irrelevant)
Effect:  the functions will be traced
```

§

```
Function:  UNTRACE
Number of arguments:  1
Argument:  a list of names of functions that should
           no longer be traced
Value:  NIL (but basically irrelevant)
Effect:  the functions will no longer be traced
```

4.2 HAS

Now that we understand HASAND, TRACE, and UNTRACE, let us slightly generalize HASAND. Suppose that in some cases we wish to check whether a list contains the atom AND, sometimes NOT, sometimes GARTER, etc. We could write functions HASNOT, HASGARTER similar to HASAND, but it is really simpler to write a function of *two* arguments: The first argument ATM will be an atom that could be any of the values AND, NOT, or GARTER, while the second argument LIS will be a list of atomic SEXes. This function will be called HAS.

The results of some calls to HAS would be

```
HAS  (GRAVITY (LAW OF GRAVITY) )
 VALUE IS...
 T

HAS  (LAW (GRAVITY OF LAW) )
 VALUE IS...
 T

HAS  (LOVES (INFANTS LOVE INFANCY) )
 VALUE IS...
 NIL

HAS  (LOVE (ADULTS LOVE ADULTERY) )
 VALUE IS...
 T
```

So now let us DEFINE the function HAS. We can almost copy the definition of HASAND with some slight changes, replacing (QUOTE AND) where it occurs by ATM and making sure to remember that HAS possesses two arguments.

```
(HAS (LAMBDA (ATM LIS)
        (COND ((NULL LIS) NIL)
              ((EQ ATM (CAR LIS)) T)
              (T (HAS ATM (CDR LIS))) )))
```

That was pretty simple. Notice that we go down LIS by taking successive CDR's, and then for each successive LIS we test its CAR.

Note: In most LISP systems, there is a function MEMQ, which is very close to HAS:

```
(MEMQ (LAMBDA (ATM LIS)
        (COND ((NULL LIS) NIL)
              ((EQ ATM (CAR LIS)) LIS)
              (T (MEMQ ATM (CDR LIS)))  )))
```

EXERCISE

Write a program that defines both HAS and HASAND. Then TRACE both functions, then UNTRACE one, then the other, and then TRACE the other again. Show the results on examples.

4.3 HASTWO

We are now ready to consider a slightly more complicated function HASTWO, which will test whether two atoms ATM1 and ATM2 are in a list of atomic SEXes called LIS. We shall describe two ways in which HASTWO can be written. First we write down the beginning of the definition:

```
(HASTWO (LAMBDA (ATM1 ATM2 LIS)
         ...                    ))
```

Some results of HASTWO would be (in EVQ-LISP)

```
HASTWO  (WITH HURTS (TAXATION WITH REPRESENTATION HURTS))
    VALUE IS...
    T

HASTWO  (TAX HURTS (TAXATION WITH REPRESENTATION HURTS))
    VALUE IS...
    NIL
```

The definition of HASTWO is very simple if we use HAS. Clearly (HASTWO ATM1 ATM2 LIS) will be T if and only if (HAS ATM1 LIS) and (HAS ATM2 LIS) are both T. So a definition of HASTWO could be

```
(HASTWO (LAMBDA (ATM1 ATM2 LIS)
          (COND ( (HAS ATM1 LIS) (HAS ATM2 LIS) )
                (T NIL) )          ))
```

Let's look at the definition. If left1—that is, (HAS ATM1 LIS)—is T, then ATM1 is in the list LIS, and the value of HASTWO is the same as the value of (HAS ATM2 LIS), i.e., we check whether ATM2 is also in the list. If ATM1 is not in LIS, then we certainly do not need to check anything about ATM2, and since left1 is NIL and left2 is T, the value of HASTWO is right2, which is NIL.

We can define HASTWO in another way. We can go down LIS taking successive CDR's (as in the definitions of HASAND and HAS) and check whether the CAR of the successive lists is EQual to either ATM1 or ATM2. If either of the tests is T, we can concentrate on the other test using HAS. Here we go:

```
(HASTWOO (LAMBDA (ATM1 ATM2 LIS)
          (COND ( (NULL LIS) NIL)
                ( (EQ ATM1 (CAR LIS) )(HAS ATM2 LIS) )
                ( (EQ ATM2 (CAR LIS) )(HAS ATM1 LIS) )
                (T (HASTWOO ATM1 ATM2 (CDR LIS) ) )  )))
```

EXERCISE

Try to estimate the relative efficiencies of HASTWO and HASTWOO. You may assume that each operation—such as NULL, EQ, a test, or a call to another function (when HAS or HASTWOO is called again)—has the same cost.

4.4 EQAL

Until now we have considered mostly lists of atomic SEXes. In many cases we wish to manipulate more complicated lists, and we shall now introduce some operations on these. The most important thing to remember is that any list is still a simple list of SEXes which can be traversed by taking successive CDR's. However, each separate SEX may need to be processed further, since it is not necessarily an atom.

The fundamental question to ask about lists is whether two lists are equal. We shall develop in stages the definition of a function EQAL of two lists LIS1 and LIS2. (EQAL LIS1 LIS2) will be T if the two lists LIS1 and LIS2 are equal, i.e., if their SEXes are respectively equal. Otherwise the value of EQAL will be NIL.

§   *Note:* In all LISP systems there is a function EQUAL which checks whether two SEXes are the same. Our EQAL is restricted presently to lists.

We shall build up EQAL in stages. First, we shall define EQSIMPLE, which will test the equality of two simple lists having only atomic SEXes. Next, we shall define a function EQSTRUC, which will test whether two lists have the same structure. (We shall see what that means.) Finally, with all the practice we shall have acquired, we shall be ready to write down EQAL. So here we go.

4.4.1 EQSIMPLE

Just so that we shall not need to repeat ourselves, let's agree to a *definition:* A *simple list* is a list having only atomic SEXes.

Note that the empty list is a simple list according to this definition. Since the empty list is a list, how could it fail to be a simple list? By having a SEX that is not atomic. But () has no SEX; therefore, it must be a simple list. Tricky!

Our definition should look like this:

```
(EQSIMPLE (LAMBDA (LIS1 LIS2)
          (COND ( (NULL LIS1) (NULL LIS2) )
                ( (NULL LIS2) NIL)
                ((EQ (CAR LIS1) (CAR LIS2)) (EQSIMPLE (CDR LIS1)
                                                      (CDR LIS2)))
                (T NIL) )  ))
```

Let us look over this definition. If LIS1 is empty, then LIS2 must be empty also. If LIS1 is not empty, we fall down to left2, and if LIS2 is empty (LIS1 being nonempty), then the two lists are clearly not equal. If both LIS1 and LIS2 are not empty, then we are at left3, where we know that we can take CAR's and CDR's of both LIS1 and LIS2. This is an important consideration, and deserves a golden rule:

GOLDEN RULE 3:

> Make sure that you are not taking
> the CAR or CDR of an empty list.

At left3, we know that neither LIS1 nor LIS2 is empty, because left1 checked for an empty LIS1 and left2 checked for an empty LIS2. Back to left3. If the first SEX of the two lists, namely their CAR's, are EQual, then we calculate whether the CDR's of the two lists are equal. If the CAR's are not EQual, left3 is NIL and the lists are not equal. Since left3 is NIL, we fall down to left4, which is T, so that the value of EQSIMPLE would be NIL, as it should be. You must admit that EQSIMPLE was rather simple.

```
EQSIMPLE  ( (THE TIME TO GO IS NOW) (THE TIME TO START IS NOW) )
 VALUE IS . . .
 NIL

EQSIMPLE  ( (TOOO BAD) (TOOO BAD) )
 VALUE IS . . .
 T
```

4.4.2 EQSTRUC

We shall say that two SEXes have the same structure if they are both atomic or, if not both atomic, are both lists having the same number of SEXes, and if the 1st, 2nd, . . . , nth SEXes of these lists have, respectively, the same structures. For example, the SEXes RICH and BITCH have the same structures since they are both atoms. The lists (RICH PRESENTS ENDEAR ABSENTS) and (CHANGE WOMEN INTO RIBS) are structurally similar since they both have four SEXes, and the pairs of SEXes RICH and CHANGE, PRESENTS and WOMEN, ENDEAR and INTO, and ABSENTS and RIBS have, respectively, the same structure. The lists

and
```
( (RICH) (PRESENTS (ENDEAR) ) ( (ABSENTS) ) )
( (CHANGE) (WOMEN (INTO) ) ( (RIBS) ) )
```

taken as pairs are structurally the same, having three SEXes which, pairwise, have the same structure. On the other hand, the lists

and
```
( (THE) (WHOLE ( (BIG) ) ) (GAMUT) )
( (FROM) (A (TO) ) (B) )
```

do not have the same structure, because their second SEXes, (WHOLE ((BIG))) and (A (TO)) do not have the same structure, and *that* is due to the fact that the second SEXes of these lists, respectively, ((BIG)) and (TO), do not have the same structure, and *that* is caused by their first (and unique) SEXes, (BIG) and TO, not having the same structure, one being a list and the other an atom. Phoot!

The function EQSTRUC will test whether two lists LIS1 and LIS2 have the same structure. By now, the basic idea should be clear. The simple case is the empty list. Otherwise, we go down the CDR's of the lists and verify that the successive CAR's have the same structure.

```
(EQSTRUC (LAMBDA (LIS1 LIS2)
         (COND ( (NULL LIS1) (NULL LIS2) )
               ( (NULL LIS2) NIL)
     ...                )   ))
```

If neither list is empty, we look at their CAR's. They must either both be atoms or be lists with the same structure. Having checked the CAR's, we call EQSTRUC again on the CDR's of the lists. However, we need a function to test whether two things are atoms. Here we need some *help*. Since we do not have such a function, we assume that we have one. We shall call the help function BOTH and generalize it slightly: BOTH will have two arguments and will have value T if and only if both of its arguments are T. Of course, we shall need to define BOTH, but for the time being, we just scribble somewhere on the side:

BOTH: Two args;   T when both args are T, and NIL otherwise

Now life becomes easy (or so we think):

```
* (EQSTRUC (LAMBDA (LIS1 LIS2)
           (COND ( (NULL LIS1) (NULL LIS2) )
                 ( (NULL LIS2) NIL)
                 ( (BOTH (ATOM (CAR LIS1) ) (ATOM (CAR LIS2) ) )
                       (EQSTRUC (CDR LIS1) (CDR LIS2) ) )
                 ( (EQSTRUC (CAR LIS1) (CAR LIS2) )
                       (EQSTRUC (CDR LIS1) (CDR LIS2) ) )
                 (T NIL)
                     )   ))
```

Unfortunately, this definition is incorrect. The reason is that Golden Rule 3 is not satisfied. Let's see what happened. The first two pairs of the COND are clear. If left3 is T, then the CAR's of both LIS1 and LIS2 are atomic, so we need only check that the CDR's of the two LISts are EQSTRUC (sic.). If BOTH CAR's are not atomic, we fall down to left4, where we take the CAR's of LIS1 and LIS2. But is it certain that both of these CAR's are lists and are therefore legitimate arguments to EQSTRUC? From the failure of left3, we know that at least *one* is not an atom, but we are not sure about *both*. Let us look at an example. Suppose that we evaluate

EQSTRUC ((HELL) ((HO)))

Since the CAR of ((HO)) is the list (HO), we fall through to left4, where we wish to evaluate

(EQSTRUC (QUOTE HELL) (QUOTE (HO)))

But the first argument of EQSTRUC is HELL, which is not a list. There is an easy way out. At left3, if (CAR LIS1) is an atom, then we want want (CAR LIS2) to be an atom and the CDR's of LIS1 and LIS2 to have the same structures. If (CAR LIS1) is not an atom and (CAR LIS2) is an atom, the two lists cannot have the same structure. Now we have it!

```
(EQSTRUC (LAMBDA (LIS1 LIS2)
          (COND ( (NULL LIS1) (NULL LIS2) )
                ( (NULL LIS2) NIL)
                ( (ATOM (CAR LIS1) ) (COND ( (ATOM (CAR LIS2) ) (EQSTRUC
                                            (CDR LIS1) (CDR LIS2) ) ) (T NIL) ) )
                ( (ATOM (CAR LIS2) ) NIL)
                ( (EQSTRUC (CAR LIS1) (CAR LIS2) )
                          (EQSTRUC (CDR LIS1) (CDR LIS2) ) )
                (T NIL)
        )    ) )
```

We no longer need BOTH, but here is a definition anyway:

```
(BOTH (LAMBDA (ARG1 ARG2)
      (COND (ARG1 ARG2)
            (T NIL)    )    ) )
```

EQSTRUC ((RICH PRESENTS ENDEAR ABSENTS) (CHANGE WOMEN INTO RIBS))
VALUE IS . . .
T

EQSTRUC (((RICH) (PRESENTS (ENDEAR)) ((ABSENTS))) ((CHANGE) (WOMEN
        (INTO)) ((RIBS))))
VALUE IS . . .
T

EQSTRUC (((THE) (WHOLE ((BIG))) (GAMUT)) ((FROM) (A (TO)) (B)))
VALUE IS . . .
NIL

§   *Note:* In most LISP systems there is a function AND which does what BOTH does (and some more and some less; see Section 11.1).

4.4.3 BIGEQSTRUC

Let's return to EQSTRUC. The third and fourth pairs of COND were needed to take care of the particular case of atomic SEXes. If EQSTRUC worked on any type of SEXes, instead of working only on lists, then these two lines would be unnecessary: The fifth pair would take care of all contingencies. Let's, in fact, write another function which will test whether any two SEXes have the same structure. This function, BIGEQSTRUC, will have two SEXes, SEX1 and SEX2, as arguments. The particular cases are atoms and the empty list. When we know that both arguments are lists, then we call BIGEQSTRUC on the CAR's and then on the CDR's of the lists. The preliminary work consists in arriving at this case.

```
(BIGEQSTRUC (LAMBDA SEX1 SEX2)
            (COND ((ATOM SEX1) (ATOM SEX2))
                  ((ATOM SEX2) NIL)
                  ((NULL SEX1) (NULL SEX2))
                  ((NULL SEX2) NIL)
                  ((BIGEQSTRUC (CAR SEX1) (CAR SEX2))
                      (BIGEQSTRUC (CDR SEX1) (CDR SEX2)))
                  (T NIL)
            )))
BIGEQSTRUC  (((STERILITY (IS)) (NOT) ((HEREDITARY))) ((GRUB (FIRST))
             (THEN) ((ETHICS))))
 VALUE IS...
 T
BIGEQSTRUC  (((DOGS) ((CHASE (THEIR))) TAILS) (CATS (CHASE) THEIR ((BALLS))))
 VALUE IS...
 NIL
```

Let's go over this definition. If SEX1 is an atom, then SEX2 must also be an atom. If SEX1 is not an atom, we check left2, and if SEX2 *is* an atom, then the two structures are not equal. If neither SEX1 nor SEX2 is an atom, they must both be lists, and we check, as in EQSTRUC, for both or just one of the arguments to be the empty list. If both SEX1 and SEX2 are nonempty lists, then we can happily take CAR's and CDR's. Finally, as is often the case, it was easier to write the most general function BIGEQSTRUC than the restricted function EQSTRUC.

Notice the great similarity between pairs 1 and 2 and pairs 3 and 4 in the COND. If the empty list () were an atom, then pairs 3 and 4 would not be needed. In fact, all LISP systems make the convention that the empty list is an atom, namely the atom NIL. Therefore the atom NIL and the list () can be used interchangeably. Insofar as LISP is concerned, there is no difference whatsoever between NIL and (). NIL is biSEXual, both atom and list, and is the only biSEXual SEX. So remember: () ≡ NIL ≢ (NIL).

ESSENTIAL CONVENTION: The atom NIL and the empty list () are one and the same animal. The empty list is the only list that is also an atom, and NIL is the only atom that is also a list, the empty list.

With the knowledge of this convention, we can write a shorter definition for BIGEQSTRUC:

```
(BIGEQSTRUC (LAMBDA (SEX1 SEX2)
              (COND ((ATOM SEX1) (ATOM SEX2))
                    ((ATOM SEX2) NIL)
                    ((BIGEQSTRUC (CAR SEX1) (CAR SEX2))
                     (BIGEQSTRUC (CDR SEX1) (CDR SEX2)))
                    (T NIL))))
BIGEQSTRUC (((SOMETIMES (I ((THINK))))) ((SOMETIMES ((I) ((AM))))))
  VALUE IS
  NIL
BIGEQSTRUC ( (((FAMILIARITY) BREEDS) (CONTEMPT))
              (((FAMILIARITY) BREEDS) (CHILDREN)))
  VALUE IS ...
  T
```

4.4.4 EQAL

We are now ready to attack our major goal: the writing of a function that will test for the equality of two lists. In fact, as was the case for BIGEQST-RUC, it is just as easy to write an EQAL that will test for the equality of two SEXes. EQAL will be somewhat like BIGEQSTRUC since equal SEXes have the same structure, but in EQAL we must also check that corresponding atomic SEXes are the same. Thus we only need to change slightly the first pair in the COND of BIGEQSTRUC: If SEX1 is an atom, then SEX1 and SEX2 must be EQual atoms.

Now we are ready for a definition of EQAL:

```
(EQAL (LAMBDA (SEX1 SEX2)
        (COND ((ATOM SEX1) (EQ SEX1 SEX2))
              ((ATOM SEX2) NIL)
              ((EQAL (CAR SEX1) (CAR SEX2))
               (EQAL (CDR SEX1) (CDR SEX2)))
              (T NIL))
   )))
```

§   *Note:* In all LISP systems there is a function EQUAL which tests the equality of two SEXes.

Perhaps we should look at some alternative ways of defining EQAL, just for additional practice. For example, we may want to express directly the following conditions:

a. If both SEX1 and SEX2 are atoms, then we only need to use EQ.

b. If one but not both of SEX1 and SEX2 are atoms, then SEX1 and SEX2 are not EQAL.

c. If neither SEX1 nor SEX2 is an atom, then they are lists and are equal if both their CAR's and CDR's are equal.

We already have a help function for condition a: It is BOTH. We need to define a function EITHER of two arguments which will be T if either one argument or both arguments are T. So we write somewhere

EITHER: Two args;   T if at least one of the args is T

Now we are ready to define EQAL:

```
(EQAL (LAMBDA (SEX1 SEX2)
         (COND ((BOTH (ATOM SEX1) (ATOM SEX2)) (EQ SEX1 SEX2))
               ((EITHER (ATOM SEX1) (ATOM SEX2)) NIL)
               ((EQAL (CAR SEX1) (CAR SEX2))
                (EQAL (CDR SEX1) (CDR SEX2))    )
               (T NIL)
     ) ))
```

This definition is more symmetric than the previous one. It is also less efficient.

But we still must define EITHER:

```
(EITHER (LAMBDA (ARG1 ARG2)
          (COND (ARG1 T)
                (ARG2 T)
                (T NIL)     )))
```

§   *Note:* In most LISP systems, the function OR does what EITHER does (and some more and some less; see Section 11.1).

So, if ARG1 is T, then EITHER has value T. If ARG1 is NIL, then we check the value of ARG2. If it is T, then so is the value of EITHER. If both ARG1 and ARG2 are NIL, then EITHER has value NIL.

In fact, we can define EITHER more efficiently as follows:

```
(EITHER (LAMBDA (ARG1 ARG2)
          (COND (ARG1 T)
                (T ARG2)    )    ))
```

The value of EITHER will be the same as the value of ARG2 if ARG1 is NIL.

Let us review some of the novelties that we have introduced in this chapter:

a. COND.

b. Functions defined in terms of themselves (recursive definitions).

c.   TRACE and UNTRACE.

d.   Definition of a simple list.

e.   The atom NIL and the list () are identical.

At this point you have the minimal tools to start writing functions on your own. However, some more practice will help, and that is the purpose of the next chapter.

EXERCISE

Compare the definition given for EQSTRUC on page 46 to the following definition:

```
(EQSTRUC1 (LAMBDA (LIS1 LIS2)
           (COND ( (NULL LIS1) (NULL LIS2) )
                 ( (NULL LIS2) NIL)
                 ( (ATOM (CAR LIS1) ) (BOTH (ATOM (CAR LIS2) )
                                          (EQSTRUC1 (CDR LIS1) (CDR LIS2) ) ) )
                 ( (ATOM (CAR LIS2) ) NIL)
                 ( (EQSTRUC1 (CAR LIS1) (CAR LIS2) )
                   (EQSTRUC1 (CDR LIS1) (CDR LIS2) ) )
                 (T NIL)
          )     ))
```

Does this definition give the correct answer for all values of LIS1 and LIS2? If not, for which values of LIS1 and LIS2 will EQSTRUC1 not work? Show that (when and if it works) EQSTRUC1 is significantly less efficient than EQSTRUC.

5

ADDITIONAL RECURSIVE
DEFINITIONS

In this chapter we shall define some additional functions in order to acquire more practice in LISP. We shall use LISP to talk about set theory, lists, arithmetic, and arithmetic properties of lists.

5.1 Sets

A set is a collection of objects. For example, one pear, a black pigeon, and a widow can be viewed as forming a set which consists of the three objects. We shall represent a set by the list of its atomic elements. The above set is (PEAR BLACKPIGEON WIDOW). Another set is (WINE WOMEN SONG). The set (SONG WINE WOMEN) is assumed identical to the set (WINE WOMEN SONG), as we do not care in which order the elements of a set are given. There are six different ways of writing the set (WINE WOMEN SONG). Since we are interested only in the objects of the set, it is meaningless to repeat the same object two or more times in the representation. Thus the list (WINE WOMEN SONG WOMEN) will not be considered a set. Finally, the empty set has no elements and is represented by the empty list ().

The first question to ask about a set is whether it contains some object as an element, i.e., whether that object is in the set. MEMSET is the term used to designate the function of two arguments, an object and a set, which has value T if the object is an element of the set, and NIL

51

otherwise. Since objects are atoms and sets are lists, the definition of MEMSET is the same as the definition of HAS:

```
(MEMSET (LAMBDA (OBJECT SET)
    (COND ((NULL SET) NIL)
          ((EQ (CAR SET) OBJECT) T)
          (T (MEMSET OBJECT (CDR SET))))))
```

```
MEMSET (DOVES (SENATE DOVES WANT A PIECE))
  VALUE IS...
  T
```

5.1.1 UNION

Now, we pass on to something new. The UNION of two sets is a set that contains all the elements of the initial two. For example, the union of the sets (HE PASSED FOR A MAN) and (SHE PASSED FOR A WOMAN) would be the set consisting of the elements A, FOR, HE, MAN, PASSED, SHE, and WOMAN. There are many representations of this set, in fact 7! = 5040. A possible representation could be (SHE MAN PASSED FOR A HE WOMAN).

Let us design a function UNION of two sets SET1 and SET2. The UNION will contain all the elements of SET2. The simplest case occurs when SET1 is the empty set (). Then the union is just SET2. In the next hardest case, SET1 has one element; thus it could be (GLOP). If GLOP is already a MEMSET† of SET2, then the union remains SET2. If GLOP is not a MEMSET of SET2, then it must be made part of the union. In LISP, the union is easily obtained by CONSing GLOP with SET2.

The more complicated case is handled this way. If SET1 is (GLOP GLOB HI), we take the union of SET2 with the set (GLOP), then the union of the result with the set (GLOB), and last the union of this result with the set (HI). Another way of looking at this procedure is as follows: We take the UNION of the set (GLOP) with SET2 and next the union of this result with the set (GLOB HI). Now UNION is becoming clear. We go down SET1 (taking CDR's) and add the leftmost element of SET1 to the partial union.

```
(UNION (LAMBDA (SET1 SET2)
 (COND ((NULL SET1) SET2)
       ((MEMSET (CAR SET1) SET2) (UNION (CDR SET1) SET2))
       (T (UNION (CDR SET1) (CONS (CAR SET1) SET2))))))
```

†The system function MEMQ, although different from MEMSET, could be used to replace it in the various definitions of UNION and INTERSECTION.

```
UNION ( (HE PASSED FOR A MAN) (SHE PASSED FOR A WOMAN) )
   VALUE IS...
   (MAN HE SHE PASSED FOR A WOMAN)
```

By tracing the evaluation of

```
UNION ( (HE PASSED FOR A MAN)(SHE PASSED FOR A WOMAN) )
```

we see that the different values of the partial union are successively

```
(SHE PASSED FOR A WOMAN)
(HE SHE PASSED FOR A WOMAN)
```

and finally

```
(MAN HE SHE PASSED FOR A WOMAN)
```

UNION can be calculated in a different way. Let us return to the union of (GLOP GLOB HI) with some other set SET2. The union will be the union of (GLOP) with the union of (GLOB HI) with SET2. The union of (GLOB HI) with SET2 will be the union of (GLOB) with the union of (HI) with SET2, and we already know how to take the union of a one-element set with another set. So here is another definition UNION1 of union:

```
(UNION1 (LAMBDA (SET1 SET2)
   (COND ( (NULL SET1) SET2)
         ( (MEMSET (CAR SET1) SET2) (UNION1 (CDR SET1) SET2) )
         (T (CONS (CAR SET1) (UNION1 (CDR SET1) SET2) ) ) ) ) )
```

```
UNION1 ( (HE PASSED FOR A MAN) (SHE PASSED FOR A WOMAN) )
   VALUE IS...
   (HE MAN SHE PASSED FOR A WOMAN)
```

You should verify that

```
UNION1 ( (HE PASSED FOR A MAN) (SHE PASSED FOR A WOMAN) )
```

has value

```
(HE MAN SHE PASSED FOR A WOMAN)
```

which is the same set as (MAN HE SHE PASSED FOR A WOMAN) but a different list.

There is a problem with the definition of UNION: The function does more work than is really necessary. Let us see how. Consider another example:

```
UNION  ( (LIE FOR FUN NOT PROFIT) (PROFITEERS PROFIT FROM LAWS) )
   VALUE IS...
   (NOT FUN FOR LIE PROFITEERS PROFIT FROM LAWS)
```

After four passes through the function UNION, we shall wish to calculate

(UNION (QUOTE (PROFIT)) (QUOTE (NOT FUN FOR LIE PROFITEERS PROFIT
FROM LAWS)))

MEMSET is called with arguments PROFIT and the list (NOT FUN FOR LIE PROFITEERS PROFIT FROM LAWS). This list is traversed, and its successive elements are compared to PROFIT. Note, however, that since the original list (LIE FOR FUN NOT PROFIT) was a set, we knew that PROFIT was distinct from each of the elements NOT, FUN, FOR, and LIE that occur in the partial union. Therefore MEMSET is checking unnecessarily that the element PROFIT of SET1 is different from other elements of that set. What needs to be checked is that an element of SET1 is different from elements of SET2.

It is easy to change UNION so as to make it more efficient by introducing the "help" function HUNION.

(UNION (LAMBDA (SET1 SET2) (HUNION SET1 SET2 SET2)))

(HUNION (LAMBDA (SET1 PARUNION SET2)
  (COND ((NULL SET1) PARUNION)
        ((MEMSET (CAR SET1) SET2) (HUNION (CDR SET1) PARUNION SET2))
        (T (HUNION (CDR SET1) (CONS (CAR SET1) PARUNION) SET2)))))

UNION ((HE PASSED FOR A MAN) (SHE PASSED FOR A WOMAN))
  VALUE IS..
  (MAN HE SHE PASSED FOR A WOMAN)

UNION ((LIE FOR FUN NOT PROFIT) (PROFITEERS PROFIT FROM LAWS))
  VALUE IS...
  (NOT FUN FOR LIE PROFITEERS PROFIT FROM LAWS)

An additional argument was introduced in HUNION. PARUNION is the partial union of the sets SET1 and SET2. SET2 is kept unchanged throughout the computation. Notice that in the definition of UNION1, the second argument SET2 does not vary, so that MEMSET does only the work it must do.

5.1.2 INTERSECTION

Let us now define the function INTERSECTION of two sets SET1 and SET2. The intersection of two sets is defined as the set containing all the elements that are members of both sets. For example,

INTERSECTION ((WORK FOR LIVING) (LIVE FOR WORKING))
  VALUE IS...
  (FOR)

and

```
INTERSECTION  ((LIARS FIGURE THAT) (THAT FIGURE LIES))
VALUE IS . . .
(FIGURE THAT)
```

which could also be written as

```
(THAT FIGURE)
```

The simplest case occurs when one of the sets, say SET1, is the empty set (). The intersection is then the empty set. In the next simplest case, SET1 could be a set with only one element, for example, (HAYADOIN). If the element HAYADOIN is a MEMSET of SET2, then the intersection is the set (HAYADOIN). On the other hand, if HAYADOIN is not a MEMSET of SET2, then the intersection is the empty set (). In the general case, we move down SET1 (taking CDR's) and accumulate those elements of SET1 which are also MEMSETs of SET2. The definition is extremely similar to that of UNION1.

```
(INTERSECTION (LAMBDA (SET1 SET2)
   (COND ((NULL SET1) ())
         ((MEMSET (CAR SET1) SET2)
          (CONS (CAR SET1) (INTERSECTION (CDR SET1) SET2)))
         (T (INTERSECTION (CDR SET1) SET2))))))
```

EXERCISES

1. The definition of INTERSECTION is asymmetrical: We test only whether SET1 is the empty set. If SET2 is the empty set, then the INTERSECTION is again (). So a more efficient definition appears to be

```
(INTERSECTION1 (LAMBDA (SET1 SET2)
   (COND ((NULL SET1) ())
         ((NULL SET2) ())
         ((MEMSET (CAR SET1) SET2) (CONS (CAR SET1) (INTERSECTION1 (CDR
                                                          SET1) SET2)))
         (T (INTERSECTION1 (CDR SET1) SET2))
)))
```

Discuss whether this definition is really more efficient by considering the number of operations required to calculate the intersection of two sets.

2. The value of (INTERSECTION SET1 SET2) is the set of all elements in SET1 which are also in SET2. Define in a similar manner a function SETDIFF of two arguments, SET1 and SET2, assumed to be sets. The value of (SETDIFF SET1 SET2) is the set of all elements in SET1 which are not in SET2.

Example: SETDIFF ((GIRLS IN UTAH MARRY YOUNG) (YOUNG OF UTAH WAS POLYGAMOUS)) has value the set (MARRY IN GIRLS).

3. Define a predicate SUBSET of two sets SET1 and SET2. The value of (SUBSET SET1 SET2) is T if SET1 is a subset of SET2; otherwise it is NIL. SET1 is a subset of SET2 if all the elements of SET1 are members of SET2.

Examples: SUBSET ((YOU MUST DIET) (FATSO YOU MUST DYE IT)) has value NIL. SUBSET ((DYE) (FATSO YOU MUST DYE IT)) has value T.

4. Define the POWERSET of a set SETT to be a function that calculates the set of all the subsets of SETT.

Example: (POWERSET (QUOTE (YALL COME BACK))) has as value the set ((YALL COME BACK) (YALL COME) (YALL BACK) (COME BACK) (YALL) (COME) (BACK) ()).

Hint: If a set has N elements, its POWERSET has 2^N elements.

5. Given a simple list (i.e., containing only atomic SEXes), write a function MAKESET which will form a set of the different SEXes of the list (without repetition).

Example: MAKESET ((AN ASS IS AN ASSET)) has value the set (ASSET AN ASS IS).

6. Define a predicate EQSET of two sets, SET1 and SET2, which has value T if the two sets are equal as sets, and value NIL otherwise.

7. (If you have an elegant solution, congratulations!) In a generalized set, we allow some (or all) of the elements of the set to be sets themselves. For example, ((FISH WITHOUT) ((A)) PORPOISE) is a set with three elements: (FISH WITHOUT), ((A)), and PORPOISE. The elements (FISH WITHOUT) and ((A)) are both sets themselves. Write a predicate ISASET which takes a list as argument and has value T if the list is a generalized set, and value NIL otherwise. Study the following examples:

ISASET (((LOVE ((IS) SENTIMENTAL)) (MEASLES) MEASLES)) has value T.

ISASET (((LOVE ((IS) SENTIMENTAL)) (MEASLES) (((IS) SENTIMENTAL) LOVE) MEASLES)) has value NIL, since the set (LOVE ((IS) SENTIMENTAL)) is repeated twice in the list.

√§ 5.1.3 MEMQ and MEMBER

The functions MEMQ and MEMBER are usually system functions and have definitions similar to MEMSET:

```
(MEMQ (LAMBDA (SEX LIS)
        (COND ( (NULL LIS) NIL)
              ( (EQ SEX (CAR LIS) ) LIS)
              (T (MEMQ SEX (CDR LIS)) )    ) ))
```

```
MEMQ (WHAT (DARLING WHAT IS YOUR NAME))
  VALUE IS...
  (WHAT IS YOUR NAME)

MEMQ (PRIME (IN THE (PRIME) OF SENILITY))
  VALUE IS...
  NIL
```

MEMBER is like MEMQ except that is uses EQUAL instead of EQ in its definition:

```
(MEMBER (LAMBDA (SEX LIS)
        (COND ((NULL LIS) NIL)
              ((EQUAL SEX (CAR LIS)) LIS)
              (T (MEMBER SEX (CDR LIS)))))))

MEMBER ((ARE DEAD) (LIVE PERSONS (ARE DEAD) (NUMBERS)))
  VALUE IS...
  ((ARE DEAD) (NUMBERS))

MEMBER (LISP ((LISP PROGRAMMERS) SPEAK CLEARLY))
  VALUE IS...
  NIL
```

5.2 Lists

§ 5.2.1 LAST

In our practice with functions that manipulate lists, we shall start with an easy example. Let us define a function LAST of one argument, a list, which has as value the last SEX of the list.

```
(LAST (QUOTE (MALE CHAUVINISTIC PIG)))
```

has value PIG

```
LAST ((FEMALE (CHAUVINISTIC (SOW))))
  VALUE IS...
  (CHAUVINISTIC (SOW))
```

What shall we do if the argument of LAST is the empty list ()? We could let the value be NIL, but that would conflict with (LAST (QUOTE (NIL))), which also has value NIL. So let us assume that the argument of LAST is a nonempty list. This means, in particular, that we can always take the CDR of the list.

Defining the function should be easy. We go down the list by taking CDR's until the list has only one SEX, and that is characterized by an empty CDR.

```
(LAST (LAMBDA (LIS)
       (COND ( (NULL (CDR LIS) ) (CAR LIS) )
             (T (LAST (CDR LIS) ) )
) ) )
```

§ *5.2.2 APPEND*

One of the most useful functions in LISP is APPEND. APPEND is used for "stringing" two lists back to back:

```
APPEND  ( (THE VICTOR BELONGS) (TO THE SPOILS) )
  VALUE IS . . .
  (THE VICTOR BELONGS TO THE SPOILS)
```

One way of looking at the action of APPEND is to imagine two lists side by side,

```
(COMMUNISTS WEAR)    (IRON CURTAINS)
```

and then grab the rightmost parenthesis of the first list and the leftmost parenthesis of the second list and bury them. The result is

```
(COMMUNISTS WEAR    IRON CURTAINS)
```

and this is exactly what APPEND gives.

If you have a good memory, you will remember that APPEND does almost what UNION1 did. But let us design APPEND from scratch.

```
(APPEND (LAMBDA (LIS1 LIS2)   . . .   ) )
```

Since it is easiest in LISP to add things to the front of a list, instead of to its rear, we shall leave LIS2 fixed and try to add the elements of LIS1 in front of LIS2. The simplest case occurs when LIS1 is (): The result is LIS2. If LIS1 has only one element, we CONS it to LIS2. Let us look at a harder case:

```
APPEND ( (WHIS KEY OPENS) (ALL DOORS) )
```

The value is (WHIS KEY OPENS ALL DOORS). When looking at the first SEX of LIS1, WHIS, it would be nice to have available the list (KEY OPENS ALL DOORS). We could then just CONS WHIS to this list and be through. Now light strikes! (KEY OPENS ALL DOORS) is (APPEND

(QUOTE (KEY OPENS)) (QUOTE (ALL DOORS))). We have found the recursive step:

```
(APPEND (LAMBDA (LIS1 LIS2)
        (COND ( (NULL LIS1) LIS2)
              (T (CONS (CAR LIS1) (APPEND (CDR LIS1) LIS2)))))))
```

By now you will have noticed the similarity between APPEND and UNION1. We shall have numerous occasions to use APPEND.

§

```
Function:  APPEND
Number of arguments:  2
Arguments:  lists
Value:   the list of the SEXes of the two lists
```

The use of APPEND may lead to great inefficiency, as is exemplified in Section 5.2.3.1.

§ *5.2.3 REVERSE*

Another fun function REVERSEs the SEXes of the list it is given as arguments.

```
REVERSE  ((UNITED STATES BONDS))
 VALUE IS...
 (BONDS STATES UNITED)

REVERSE  ((LAW OF GRAVITY))
 VALUE IS...
 (GRAVITY OF LAW)

REVERSE  ((BONDS OF THE UNITED STATES))
 VALUE IS...
 (STATES UNITED THE OF BONDS)

REVERSE  ((BONDS OF THE (UNITED (STATES))))
 VALUE IS...
 ((UNITED (STATES)) THE OF BONDS)
```

The simplest case, the empty list, remains unchanged. Since we are getting more proficient, we jump to the general case. In REVERSEing (UNITED STATES BONDS) we want to move UNITED to the rear. That gives (STATES BONDS) and UNITED. If we had reversed (STATES BONDS) to (BONDS STATES), i.e., if we had solved the simpler case of a list with two SEXes, then we would need only to put together (BONDS STATES) and UNITED to obtain (BONDS STATES UNITED). CONS cannot do the trick immediately, but APPEND can, if we first transform

UNITED into the list (UNITED). Now we have it:

```
(REVERSE (LAMBDA (LIS)
        (COND ( (NULL LIS) ( ) )
             (T (APPEND (REVERSE (CDR LIS) )
                      (CONS (CAR LIS) ( ) ) ) )
        ) ) )
```

5.2.3.1 Potential Inefficiencies in Using APPEND

When APPEND is used in a function definition, as in the above definition of REVERSE, a danger of inefficiency is present. Consider the following example:

REVERSE ((BONDS OF THE UNITED STATES))

APPEND will be called with arguments:

Call of APPEND	Argument 1	Argument 2
[A]	(STATES UNITED THE OF)	(BONDS)
[B]	(STATES UNITED THE)	(OF)
[C]	(STATES UNITED)	(THE)
[D]	(STATES)	(UNITED)
[E]	()	(STATES)

When the first argument of APPEND is a list of n SEXes, APPEND will make n CONSes. When REVERSEing a list of length n, APPEND is called n times, and the total number of CONSes made will be

$$n + (n - 1) + \cdots + 2 + 1 = n \cdot (n + 1)/2$$

where we have included the CONS from the second argument of APPEND. For n large, the number of CONSes is approximately $(1/2)n^2$.

5.2.3.2 Collection Variables

A more efficient definition of REVERSE would apply CONS only n times. We can use a *collection variable*, which is an extra variable introduced to collect partial results.

```
(REVERSE (LAMBDA (LIS) (REVERSE1 LIS NIL) ) )
(REVERSE1 (LAMBDA (LIS COLVARIABLE)
        (COND ( (NULL LIS) COLVARIABLE)
             (T (REVERSE1 (CDR LIS)
                      (CONS (CAR LIS) COLVARIABLE) ) )
) ) )
```

When evaluating

REVERSE ((BONDS OF THE UNITED STATES))

the arguments of REVERSEI will be

Call of REVERSE1	Argument 1	Argument 2
[A]	(BONDS OF THE UNITED STATES)	()
[B]	(OF THE UNITED STATES)	(BONDS)
[C]	(THE UNITED STATES)	(OF BONDS)
[D]	(UNITED STATES)	(THE OF BONDS)
[E]	(STATES)	(UNITED THE OF BONDS)
[F]	( )	(STATES UNITED THE OF BONDS)

5.2.4   SUBSTOP

A manipulation that is often performed in LISP is the replacing of some SEX in some list by another SEX. We shall define a function SUBSTOP of three arguments SEX1, SEX2, and LIS. SUBSTOP will replace every occurrence of SEX1 at the top level of LIS by SEX2.

```
SUBSTOP  (PRESENCE (ABSENCE) (PRESENCE OF BODY PRESENCE OF MIND) )
VALUE IS...
( (ABSENCE) OF BODY (ABSENCE) OF MIND)
```

```
SUBSTOP  (PRESENCE ABSENCE ( (PRESENCE) OF BODY PRESENCE OF MIND) )
VALUE IS...
( (PRESENCE) OF BODY ABSENCE OF MIND)
```

Since the SEX (PRESENCE) of the list is not EQUAL to PRESENCE, it is not replaced.

From our experience with UNION1 and APPEND, it should be clear how we shall proceed. We shall go down the list using CDR, and CONS along the SEXes of the list, but we shall watch out for hitting SEX1, in which case we shall CONS SEX2 instead of SEX1. Therefore we need a conditional:

```
(COND ( (EQUAL SEX1 +++) SEX2)
     (T +++) )
```

where $+++$ will be the SEX of the list that we are considering. We could use a little help function, but we can also dispense with one.

```
(SUBSTOP (LAMBDA (SEX1 SEX2 LIS)
        (COND ((NULL LIS) ())
              (T (CONS (COND ((EQUAL SEX1 (CAR LIS)) SEX2)
                            (T (CAR LIS)) )
                      (SUBSTOP SEX1 SEX2 (CDR LIS)) )))
    ))
```

So you really wish to use a help function? We can do it in two different ways:

```
(HELP1 (LAMBDA (SEX1 SEX2 SEX3)
        (COND ((EQUAL SEX1 SEX3) SEX2)
              (T SEX3)
        )))
```

so that if SEX3 is EQUAL to SEX1, the value of HELP1 is SEX2; otherwise it is SEX3 unchanged. The new version of SUBSTOP becomes

```
(SUBSTOP1 (LAMBDA (SEX1 SEX2 LIS)
         (COND ((NULL LIS) ())
               (T (CONS (HELP1 SEX1 SEX2 (CAR LIS))
                       (SUBSTOP1 SEX1 SEX2 (CDR LIS))))
     )))
```

```
SUBSTOP1  (PRESENCE ABSENCE ((PRESENCE) OF BODY PRESENCE OF MIND))
VALUE IS...
((PRESENCE) OF BODY ABSENCE OF MIND)
```

Notice that in HELP1, SEX1 and SEX2 are fixed and in fact are the same as in SUBSTOP. It is possible to write in such cases a simpler version of HELP which assumes that SEX1 and SEX2 have the values found in SUBSTOP.

```
(HELP2 (LAMBDA (SEX3)
        (COND ((EQUAL SEX1 SEX3) SEX2)
              (T SEX3)
        ) ))
```

With HELP2 we can define

```
(SUBSTOP2 (LAMBDA (SEX1 SEX2 LIS)
        (COND ((NULL LIS) ())
              (T (CONS (HELP2 (CAR LIS))
                      (SUBSTOP2 SEX1 SEX2 (CDR LIS)) ))
            ) ))
```

```
SUBSTOP2  (PRESENCE (ABSENCE) (PRESENCE OF BODY PRESENCE OF MIND))
VALUE IS...
((ABSENCE) OF BODY (ABSENCE) OF MIND)
```

5.2.4.1 Free Variables and Bound Variables

When SUBSTOP2 calls HELP2, the values of SEX1 and SEX2 in SUBSTOP2 are available to HELP2. We say that SEX3 is a variable which is bound in HELP2, while SEX1 and SEX2 are variables which are free in HELP2. SEX1, SEX2, and LIS are bound in SUBSTOP2. When HELP2 is called, all the variables on its list of arguments become bound to their values. The way HELP2 is used, its bound variable SEX3 is bound to the value of (CAR LIS), LIS having been bound in SUBSTOP2. During the evaluation of HELP2, two free variables are encountered, SEX1 and SEX2. HELP2 retrieves the values of the variables from the function that called *it* (i.e., HELP2); or, failing that, from the function that called the function that called it (HELP2); or, failing that, from the function that called the function that called the function that called it (HELP2), etc. . . . Tooph! In our example, the values of SEX1 and SEX2 are found in SUBSTOP2, since that is where SEX1 and SEX2 were bound.

As an application of free variables, it is possible to write yet another version of SUBSTOP. Notice that SUBSTOP2 calls itself recursively: (SUBSTOP2 SEX1 SEX2 (CDR LIS)). The values of SEX1 and SEX2 have not been modified, and it seems a shame to have to keep track of them. We could replace the recursive call of SUBSTOP2 by a call to a function essentially identical to SUBSTOP2 except that SEX1 and SEX2 would be free variables. We call this new version SUBSTOP3:

```
(SUBSTOP3 (LAMBDA (SEX1 SEX2 LIS)
        (COND ((NULL LIS) ())
              (T (COND (HELP2 (CAR LIS))
                        (HELPSTOP3 (CDR LIS)) ))
        ) ) )

(HELPSTOP3 (LAMBDA (LIS)
        (COND ((NULL LIS) ())
              (T (CONS (HELP2 (CAR LIS))
                        (HELPSTOP3 (CDR LIS)) ))
        ) ) )
```

SUBSTOP3 (PRESENCE ABSENCE ((PRESENCE) OF BODY PRESENCE OF MIND))
VALUE IS . . .
((PRESENCE) OF BODY ABSENCE OF MIND)

SUBSTOP3 (PRESENCE (ABSENCE) (PRESENCE OF BODY PRESENCE OF MIND))
VALUE IS . . .
((ABSENCE) OF BODY (ABSENCE) OF MIND)

When HELP2 is called inside HELPSTOP3, it will first search in HELP-STOP3 for the values of SEX1 and SEX2, which are free variables in HELP2. Since SEX1 and SEX2 are not on the list of arguments of HELP-

STOP3, they were not bound by HELPSTOP3. So the function that called HELPSTOP3, namely SUBSTOP3, is interrogated, and the variables SEX1 and SEX2 have indeed been bound in SUBSTOP3. Their values are then utilized by HELP2.

Notice that if we know that LIS will always be a simple list or SEX1 always an atom, then we can replace EQUAL by EQ in all the HELP and SUBSTOP functions. EQ is faster than EQUAL.

5.2.5 LINEARIZE

Given some complicated list, for example, (((EVERY) (((OTHER)) INCH)) (A (GENTLEMAN))), we may wish to delete all the inner parentheses of the list. The function that will do this for us could be called LINEARIZE.

```
LINEARIZE  ( ( ( (EVERY) ( ( (OTHER) ) INCH) ) (A (GENTLEMAN) ) ) )
    VALUE IS...
    (EVERY OTHER INCH A GENTLEMAN)
```

We could try to look at successively more complicated examples, but it sometimes pays to take another approach. The empty list does not need to be LINEARIZEd, or, if you prefer, it has already been LINEAR-IZEd. If the list which is the argument of LINEARIZE is not the empty list, it has a CAR and a CDR. The CDR is always a list. If the CAR is an atom, the answer is clear. (Well, if it is clear, what is it?) Otherwise, we have two lists. *Suppose that each of them had been linearized separately.* How does one get the whole shebang? By APPENDing the two linearized parts. The definition of LINEARIZE is now clear:

```
(LINEARIZE (LAMBDA (LIS)
    (COND ( (NULL LIS) ( ) )
            ( (ATOM (CAR LIS) ) (CONS (CAR LIS) (LINEARIZE (CDR LIS) ) ) )
            (T (APPEND (LINEARIZE (CAR LIS) ) (LINEARIZE (CDR LIS) ) ) ) ) ) )
```

RULE OF THUMB 3:

> *If the value of a function on the CAR and the CDR is known, what would be the value of the function on the whole thing?*

5.2.6 LIST2 and LIST

It is often desirable to make a list of several SEXes. The function LIST2 makes a list of the values of its two arguments. Its definition is

```
(LIST2 (LAMBDA (SEX1 SEX2) (CONS SEX1 (CONS SEX2 ( ) ) ) ) )
```

and a run of the function gives

```
LIST2  ( (REVERE RAN) (FOR HELP) )
VALUE IS . . .
( (REVERE RAN) (FOR HELP) )

LIST2  (MOSQUITOES (LIKE BLUE BLOOD) )
VALUE IS . . .
(MOSQUITOES (LIKE BLUE BLOOD) )
```

§   In LISP there is a very useful function called LIST which has an indefinite number of arguments. The value of LIST is a list of the values of its arguments. If there are no arguments, the value of (LIST) is the empty list (). (LIST SEX) is equivalent to (CONS SEX ()). LIST of two arguments is equivalent to LIST2 defined above. Functions of an indefinite number of arguments are treated specially by LISP. Basically the arguments are evaluated one by one. The function LISTALIST illustrates indirectly the mechanism used to evaluate LIST. (See also Section 11.6.)

The function LISTALIST has one list as argument. LISTALIST evaluates one by one the successive SEXes of its argument and produces a list of these values. Consider the following argument of LISTALIST:

```
( (CAR (QUOTE (BISHOPS SUFFER) ) ) (CONS (QUOTE IN) (QUOTE (TRANSLATION) ) ) )
```

The two SEXes of the list are (CAR (QUOTE (BISHOPS SUFFER))) and (CONS (QUOTE IN) (QUOTE (TRANSLATION))). Their values are, respectively, BISHOPS and (IN TRANSLATION), and a list of these is (BISHOPS (IN TRANSLATION)).

It is easy to take the first SEX of the list to obtain (CAR (QUOTE BISHOPS SUFFER))), but we must further *evaluate* this expression to be able to define LISTALIST. The function which does the evaluation is EVAL. We can now write a definition for LISTALIST:

```
(LISTALIST (LAMBDA (LIS)
        (COND ( (NULL LIS) () )
                (T (CONS (EVAL (CAR LIS) ) (LISTALIST (CDR LIS) ) ) )
        ) ) )

LISTALIST  ( ( (CAR (QUOTE (BISHOPS SUFFER) ) )
            (CONS (QUOTE IN) (QUOTE (TRANSLATION) ) ) ) )
VALUE IS . . .
(BISHOPS (IN TRANSLATION) )
```

Notice that the value of LISTALIST of the single argument ((CAR (QUOTE (BISHOPS SUFFER))) (CONS (QUOTE IN) (QUOTE (TRANSLATION))))) is the same as the value of the list

```
(LIST (CAR (QUOTE (BISHOPS SUFFER) ) ) (CONS (QUOTE IN) (QUOTE (TRANSLATION) ) ) )
```

One way to evaluate the function LIST on its two arguments is to take the CDR of the list we just wrote. The result is precisely the single argument that we need to give to LISTALIST in order to obtain the same answer that the evaluation of LIST would have given. In actual practice, a function such as LISTALIST is not used; instead the arguments of LIST are evaluated one after another and formed into a list.

We shall discuss the function EVAL at greater length in Section 5.3.5.1 and in Chapter 9. For the time being, we stress the importance of the function LIST.

S

| Function: LIST |
| Number of arguments: any |
| Arguments: any SEX |
| Value: a list of the values of the arguments |

EXERCISES

1. Define REMOVELAST, a function of one argument, a list having at least one SEX. REMOVELAST has as value the same list, except that the last SEX has been deleted.

REMOVELAST ((YOU CANNOT SURVIVE DEATH)) has value (YOU CANNOT SURVIVE).

2. Define a function DELETE which removes from a LISt the first occurrence of a SEX. Only the top level of the LISt is processed.
Convention: The LISt is the second argument of DELETE.

DELETE (CANNOT (YOU CANNOT SURVIVE DEATH)) has value (YOU SURVIVE DEATH)
DELETE ((HAVE NO) (MONKEYS (HAVE NO) MONEY (HAVE NO))) has value (MONKEYS MONEY (HAVE NO)).

3. Define DELETETOPS, which is like DELETE except that all top-level occurrences of the first argument are deleted from the second argument. DELETETOPS ((HAVE NO) (MONKEYS (HAVE NO) MONEY (HAVE NO))) has value (MONKEYS MONEY).

4. Define DELETEALL, which removes its first argument, an atom, wherever that atom occurs in the list structure that is its second argument. The structure of the list is otherwise maintained.

DELETEALL (BIP (BIP (BAP ((BIP BIP)) BIP)))
has value   ((BAP ((   ))))
and would print as   ((BAP (NIL))).

5. Define INVERTALL, which is like REVERSE, except that all elements in sublists (and in sublists of these, etc.) are also inverted.

```
INVERTALL ( (SAVINGS (ACCOUNTS ( (ARE (CALLED) ) HUSBANDS) ) ) )
VALUE IS ...
( ( (HUSBANDS ( (CALLED) ARE) ) ACCOUNTS) SAVINGS)
```

6. MEMALL is like MEMSET, except that it tries to find an atom, its first argument, anywhere in the list structure that is its second argument. Write a definition for MEMALL.

```
MEMALL (COUNTERFEIT ( (MISERS) ( ( (LIKE ( (COUNTERFEIT) ) ) (MONEY) ) ) ) )
VALUE IS ...
T
```

7. Define a function ALLPERM which has as value a list of all the ways a given set can be expressed. Assume the set is a simple list.

```
ALLPERM ( (DRINKING IS THINKING) )
VALUE IS ...
( (DRINKING IS THINKING) (DRINKING THINKING IS) (THINKING DRINKING IS)
(THINKING IS DRINKING) (IS DRINKING THINKING) (IS THINKING DRINKING) )
```

The order of the sublists in the result is immaterial.

8. Define a predicate PALINDROME, which has value T if a list is its own inverse, and value NIL otherwise.

```
PALINDROME ( (M A D A M I M A D A M) )
VALUE IS ...
T
```

```
PALINDROME ( (M A D A M I M A D A M O) )
VALUE IS ...
NIL
```

9. Given a set, we can rank the subsets of the set according to a variety of schemes. For example, the 16 subsets of (A B C D) could be ranked

a. In lexicographic (or alphabetical) order:

( )   (A)   (A B)   (A B C)   (A B C D)   (A B D)   (A C)   (A C D)   (A D)
(B)   (B C)   (B C D)   (B D)   (C)   (C D)   (D)

b. In binary order (think of A, B, C, and D as being bit positions). If the rightmost "bit" is the least significant, the ordering would be

( )   (D)   (C)   (C D)   (B)   (B D)   (B C)   (B C D)   (A)   (A D)   (A C)   (A C D)
(A B)   (A B D)   (A B C)   (A B C D)

c. In binary order, but with the leftmost "bit" being the least significant one.

Given a set and one of its subsets, write three functions (NEXTSET (LAMBDA (SUBSET SETT) . . .)) which has as value the next SUBSET according to each of the above schemas. If there is no subset, the value of NEXTSET is T. For example, for scheme b above, NEXTSET ((B) (A B C D)) has value (B D), NEXTSET ((B) (A B C D E)) has value (B E), and NEXTSET ((A B) (A B)) has value T. You certainly should not generate all the subsets of the set to find NEXTSET; that would be very inefficient since there are 2^N subsets of a set of N elements. Nor should you use any explicit arithmetic.

10.   For each of the orderings of sets in Exercise 9, define (PREVIOUSET (LAMBDA (SUBSET SETT) . . .)) which has as value the previous SUBSET according to the ordering considered. If there is no PREVIOUSET, the value of PREVIOUSET is T.

11.   Given a permutation of N elements, the N! permutations of these elements can be ordered according to a variety of schemas. The better known schemas are

a.   Lexicographic ordering. The permutations of (A B C D) would be ordered

```
(A B C D)   (A B D C)   (A C B D)   (A C D B)   (A D B C)   (A D C B)
(B A C D)   (B A D C)   (B C A D)   (B C D A)   (B D A C)   (B D C A)
(C A B D)   (C A D B)   (C B A D)   (C B D A)   (C D A B)   (C D B A)
(D A B C)   (D A C B)   (D B A C)   (D B C A)   (D C A B)   (D C B A)
```

Notice that the rightmost side of the permutation "moves" most.

b.   Ordering with leftmost side "moving" most. The first few permutations are

```
(A B C D)   (B A C D)   (A C B D)   (C A B D)   (B C A D)   (C B A D)
(A B D C)   (A D B C)   (B A D C),  etc.
```

Given the original permutation ORIGINAL and one of its permutations PERM, write two functions (NEXTPERM (LAMBDA (PERM ORIGINAL) . . .)) which have as value the next permutation according to the orderings a and b above. For example, for ordering a we would have NEXTPERMA ((C B A D) (A B C D)) has value (C B D A), and NEXTPERMA ((C B A D) (D C B A)) has value (C A D B). The two examples show the importance of knowing the original permutation, since this permutation determines an order of the elements of the permutation. If there is no next permutation, the value of NEXTPERM is T.

12.   For each of the orderings of permutations in Exercise 11, define PREVIOUSPERM (LAMBDA (PERM ORIGINAL) . . .)), which has as value the previous permutation according to the ordering considered. If there is no PREVIOUSPERM, the value of PREVIOUSPERM is T.

13.   Given a permutation, write programs to

a.   Extract all the disjoint cycles of the permutation.

b. Represent the permutation as a product of transpositions.

Note: Many easy programs can be written to manipulate permutations.

5.3 Arithmetic

Elementary arithmetic is a good area for practice in defining recursive functions. Starting from the functions ADD1 and SUB1 and the predicate ZEROP, we shall build up the elementary arithmetic functions PLUS, TIMES, and DIFFERENCE and the predicate EQUAL. The definitions that we shall give *have no practical value*, since PLUS, TIMES, DIFFER-ENCE, and EQUAL are available in LISP systems and run several orders of magnitude faster than the same functions as we shall define them. Our definitions will be good practice, though, and are quite similar to the axiomatization of arithmetic due to Peano.

Numbers are special atoms in LISP. The predicate ATOM has value T for numbers. Your LISP system will probably permit you to use integers and floating-point numbers, and possibly some more esoteric numbers such as binary, octal, hexadecimal, sexadecimal, duodecimal, and duo-denal numbers. There are such wide differences in the number-crunching possibilities of various LISP systems that we shall wisely restrict ourselves to integers only.

§ 5.3.1 ADD1, SUB1, and ZEROP

The effect of the functions ADD1, SUB1, and ZEROP can be gathered from a few examples.

```
ADD1   (5)
 VALUE IS...
 6

SUB1   (5)
 VALUE IS...
 4

ZEROP   (0)      (here 0 is zero, the number and not the letter)
 VALUE IS...
 T

ZEROP   (2)
 VALUE IS...
 NIL
```

We shall draw boxes for these functions:

§

```
Function:  ADD1
Number of arguments:  1
Argument:  a number
Value:  the argument plus 1
```

§

```
Function:  SUB1
Number of arguments:  1
Argument:  a number
Value:  the argument minus 1
```

§

```
Function:  ZEROP
Number of arguments:  1
Argument:  a number
Value:  T if the argument is zero,
        NIL otherwise
```

5.3.2 PLUS

We shall restrict ourselves to the numbers 0, 1, 2, 3, 4, 5, etc., that is, to the nonnegative integers. We shall assume that to any of these integers we can add 1, using ADD1, and test each of the integers to find out whether it is zero or not, using ZEROP. From any of these integers (except from zero) we can subtract 1, using SUB1. We now wish to define the sum of two nonnegative integers using only ADD1, SUB1, and ZEROP. The function PLUS of two arguments NUM1 and NUM2—both nonnegative integers—will have as value the sum of the values of NUM1 and NUM2.

```
(PLUS (LAMBDA (NUM1 NUM2)   ...   ) )
```

Let us look at some particular cases. In the easiest case, if NUM1 is zero, the sum of NUM1 and NUM2 is the value of NUM2. Consider the next easiest case: NUM1 has value 1. Then the sum is one more than NUM2, i.e., the value of (ADD1 NUM2). If NUM1 has value 2, then the sum is one more than the sum of 1 and NUM2. By now we know how to calculate the sum of 1 and NUM2: It is the value of (ADD1 NUM2). So we need to add 1 to it, i.e., compute the value of (ADD1 (ADD1 NUM2)). The algorithm should become clear: We keep subtracting 1 from NUM1 and adding 1 to NUM2, until NUM1 is zero, at which point we can stop.

```
(PLUS  (LAMBDA  (NUM1  NUM2)
       (COND  ((ZEROP  NUM1)  NUM2)
              (T  (PLUS  (SUB1  NUM1)  (ADD1  NUM2)) )
              )))
```

```
PLUS  (2  3)
 VALUE IS...
 5
```

Another version of PLUS is

```
(PLUS  (LAMBDA  (NUM1  NUM2)
       (COND  ((ZEROP  NUM1)  NUM2)
              (T  (ADD1  (PLUS  (SUB1  NUM1)  NUM2)) )
   )))
```

```
PLUS  (1  2)
 VALUE IS...
 3
```

A trace should make clear the difference between the two versions of PLUS.

5.3.3 TIMES

Given two nonnegative integers NUM1 and NUM2, we wish to calculate their product. We shall use only ADD1, SUB1, ZEROP, and the function PLUS, which can be derived from these three functions, as we have just seen.

```
(TIMES  (LAMBDA  (NUM1  NUM2)   ...   ))
```

If NUM1 is zero, then the product of NUM1 and NUM2 is zero. That was easy. Consider the next simplest case: NUM1 has value 1. Then the product is NUM2. If NUM1 has value 2, which is 1 more than 1, then the product is NUM2 plus the product of 1 with NUM2. The recursive definition becomes clear: We go down NUM1, using SUB1, adding up NUM2's, until NUM1 becomes zero. More precisely, in LISP,

```
(TIMES  (LAMBDA  (NUM1  NUM2)
       (COND  ((ZEROP  NUM1)  0)
              (T  (PLUS  NUM2  (TIMES  (SUB1  NUM1)  NUM2)) )
              )))
```

```
TIMES  (2  3)
 VALUE IS...
 6
```

It is important to notice that *numbers do not need to be QUOTEd*. They evaluate to themselves; i.e., the value of 0 (zero) is 0 (zero); the value of 3 is 3. We had seen that T and NIL also evaluate to themselves and need not be QUOTEd either.

5.3.4 EQUAL

Given two nonnegative integers NUM1 and NUM2, we wish to define a predicate EQUAL which will have value T if the two integers are equal, and otherwise value NIL. We know how to test whether a number is zero using ZEROP; hence we must use ZEROP. What are the simplest cases? If one of the numbers is zero, then the other number must also be zero. If neither of the numbers is zero, then the simplest case occurs when one of the numbers, say NUM1, is 1. Can we get down to the previous case? Yes, by subtracting 1 from NUM1 we obtain zero. But NUM1 and NUM2 are equal if (SUB1 NUM1) and (SUB1 NUM2) are equal. The recursive definition is becoming clear:

```
(EQUAL (LAMBDA (NUM1 NUM2)
       (COND ( (ZEROP NUM1) (ZEROP NUM2) )
             ( (ZEROP NUM2) NIL)
             (T (EQUAL (SUB1 NUM1) (SUB1 NUM2) ) ) ) ) )
```

```
 EQUAL  (2 3)
 VALUE IS...
 NIL

 EQUAL  (2 2)
  VALUE IS...
  T
```

The first left of the conditional tests whether NUM1 is zero. If NUM1 is not zero, then if NUM2 is zero, as is tested in left2, the value of EQUAL must be NIL. If neither NUM1 nor NUM2 is zero, as is the case in the third pair of the conditional, then it is legitimate to SUB1† from both NUM1 and NUM2. Notice how similar this definition of EQUAL for numbers is to the definition of EQUAL that we saw for SEXes in Section 4.4.4.

5.3.5 FACTORIAL

No discussion of recursive functions seems complete without a discussion of FACTORIAL. FACTORIAL has one argument, a nonnegative integer.

†In English, anything can be a verb. For example, "They went on their honeymoon and when they returned, they *he'd* and *she'd* their towels" (A. Perlis, private communication).

If the argument is zero, FACTORIAL has value 1. If the argument NUM has value N > 0, then the value of FACTORIAL is the product of all the integers from 1 to N. For example, FACTORIAL (4) = 1 × 2 × 3 × 4 = 24.

To write a definition of FACTORIAL, it suffices to notice that for all N, the value of FACTORIAL (N + 1) is (N + 1) times the value of FACTORIAL (N).

```
(FACTORIAL (LAMBDA (NUM)
          (COND ((ZEROP NUM) 1)
                (T (TIMES NUM (FACTORIAL (SUB1 NUM))))
          )))

FACTORIAL (4)
VALUE IS...
24
```

In the above definition, we count down from the value of NUM to 0. It is possible to define FACTORIAL by counting up from 1 to NUM. We shall need some additional space to store the original value of NUM, and for this we can use a HELP function. Since NUM will not change, we shall use NUM as a *free variable* in the HELP function.

```
(FACTORIAL (LAMBDA (NUM)
          (COND ((ZEROP NUM) 1)
                (T (HELP 1))
          )))

(HELP (LAMBDA (N)
      (COND ((EQUAL N NUM) N)
            (T (TIMES N (HELP (ADD1 N))))
        )))

FACTORIAL (3)
VALUE IS...
6
```

Since the value of FACTORIAL is obtained progressively by successive multiplications, a definition using a *collection variable* ANSWER and an auxiliary function FACTCOL is immediate:

```
(FACTORIAL (LAMBDA (NUM)
          (COND ((ZEROP NUM) 1)
                (T (FACTCOL NUM 1))  )))

(FACTCOL (LAMBDA (NUM ANSWER)
          (COND ((ZEROP NUM) ANSWER)
                (T (FACTCOL (SUB1 NUM) (TIMES NUM ANSWER))))
     )))
```

A predicate ONEP, which tests whether a number has value 1, could be substituted for ZEROP in FACTCOL.

There is a way to define FACTORIAL (N) in LISP (for $N > 0$) which remains very close to the original definition of FACTORIAL: the product of all integers from 1 to N. In LISP systems, TIMES is usually a function which can take any number of arguments. It is therefore possible to define FACTORIAL directly by using a HELP function which will give us a list of all the numbers from 1 to N (for $N > 0$). The value of HELP will be a set of the numbers from 1 to N. If $N = 4$, the set will be (1 2 3 4). In defining HELP, we could count up from 1 to N or count down from N to 1. In the first case, we would need to keep track of the original value of N by introducing another function with one additional argument.

```
(HELP (LAMBDA (N) (HELPHELP 1 N)))
(HELPHELP (LAMBDA (NUM GOAL)
        (COND ((EQUAL NUM GOAL) (CONS GOAL ()))
              (T (CONS NUM (HELPHELP (ADD1 NUM) GOAL))))
    )))
```

A run of HELP gives

```
HELP  (4)
 VALUE IS...
 (1  2  3  4)
```

Since the goal does not vary, it can be used as a free variable in HELP-HELP. Another definition of HELP would be

```
(HELP (LAMBDA (N) (HELPHELP 1)))
(HELPHELP (LAMBDA (NUM)
        (COND ((EQUAL NUM N) (CONS NUM ()))
              (T (CONS NUM (HELPHELP (ADD1 NUM))) ) )
    )))
```

```
HELP  (4)
 VALUE IS...
 (1  2  3  4)
```

A run of this last HELP would give the same value as the previous HELP function.

If we count down from N to 1, we do not need an additional place to hold the goal, which is always 1. We define a predicate ONEP (found in many LISP systems) which has value T if its numeric argument has value 1, and value NIL otherwise.

```
(ONEP (LAMBDA (NUM) (ZEROP (SUB1 NUM)) ) )
```

Since we have assumed that SUB1 cannot be applied to zero, we must assume that ONEP works only for arguments that are greater than zero, NUM > 0. We can now define another version of HELP:

```
(HELP (LAMBDA (N)
      (COND ((ONEP N) (CONS 1 ()))
            (T (CONS N (HELP (SUB1 N))) )
      )))
```

A run of this version of HELP gives

```
HELP  (4)
 VALUE IS...
 (4 3 2 1)
```

Let us return to FACTORIAL, using one of the versions of HELP, for example, the last one. Taking as an example the computation of FACTORIAL (4), HELP will give the list (4 3 2 1). We would like to evaluate (TIMES 4 3 2 1), to obtain the value 24. CONSing TIMES with the list (4 3 2 1) does indeed give us (TIMES 4 3 2 1), but we must evaluate *that*. There is a function appropriately called EVAL which does evaluate its argument. Therefore (EVAL (QUOTE (TIMES 4 3 2 1))) will have the desired value of 24. We are now ready to define FACTORIAL.

```
(FACTORIAL (LAMBDA (NUM)
           (COND ((ZEROP NUM) 1)
                 (T (EVAL (CONS (QUOTE TIMES) (HELP NUM)))))
  )))

FACTORIAL  (5)
 VALUE IS...
 120
```

The particular case FACTORIAL (0) was treated separately.

5.3.5.1 *Elementary EVAL and EVALQUOTE*

Notice that the value of (CONS (QUOTE TIMES) (HELP NUM)) is a *program*. EVAL evaluates this program. This is another example† of a program that was built by another program. Since programs in LISP are SEXes, it is very easy to have programs build programs in LISP. In most other programming languages, it is impossible (or at least very difficult) to write programs that write other programs that can be evaluated immediately.

Although we shall discuss EVAL in great depth in Chapter 9, we take this opportunity to clarify some of the mysteries of LISP. In EV-

†The first example was seen in Section 5.2.6.

LISP, the function EVAL is listening to you. The LISP monitor calls the function READ, which reads from cards (or tape, disk, or remote console) a SEX. The SEX is given to EVAL, which evaluates the SEX, which is, therefore, considered as a program. The monitor has the value found by EVAL printed by the function PRINT. Control then returns to the monitor, which calls READ once again, then EVAL, then PRINT, etc., until the end of the set of programs submitted by a user is reached.

In EVQ-LISP, the LISP monitor is somewhat different. It calls READ twice, once to obtain, for example, the name of a function, and, the second time, to obtain a list of arguments. Consider, for example,

CONS (A (B))

The two values of READ will be CONS and the list (A (B)). The monitor has each of the arguments of the list of arguments QUOTEd, by a function similar to PUTQUOTES (see Section 6.1.1). This gives ((QUOTE A) (QUOTE (B))) in our example. The name of the function is CONSed in front of the modified list of arguments, giving (CONS (QUOTE A) (QUOTE (B))), and this *program* is given to EVAL to be evaluated. The LISP monitor has the value of EVAL printed, and then loops back to call READ twice. (Actually, some shortcuts are taken in a real system, but the result is the same.)

§ 5.3.6 Some LISP Arithmetic Functions

LISP Function	Number of Arguments	Value of Function
ADD1 (N)	1	$N + 1$
DIFFERENCE (N1 N2)	2	$N1 - N2$
EXPT (N1 N2)	2	$N1^{N2}$
MAX (N1 N2 ... NK)	Any	Maximum of Ni's
MIN (N1 N2 ... NK)	Any	Minimum of Ni's
MINUS (N)	1	$-N$
PLUS (N1 N2 ... NK)	Any	$N1 + N2 + \cdots + NK$
QUOTIENT (N1 N2)	2	$N1/N2$
RECIP (N)	1	$1/N$
REMAINDER (N1 N2)	2	(DIFFERENCE N1 (TIMES N2 (QUOTIENT N1 N2)))
SUB1 (N)	1	$N - 1$
TIMES (N1 N2 ... NK)	Any	$N1 \times N2 \times \cdots \times NK$

✓ Of particular importance is the predicate NUMBERP, which has value T if its argument is a number, and value NIL otherwise.

LISP Predicate	Number of Arguments	Value Is T if
EQUAL (N1 N2)	2	N1 = N2
GREATERP (N1 N2)	2	N1 > N2
LESSP (N1 N2)	2	N1 < N2
MINUSP (N)	1	N < 0
NUMBERP (SEX)	1	SEX is a number
ONEP (N)	1	N = 1
ZEROP (N)	1	N = 0

An error will usually result if an arithmetic function or predicate (except NUMBERP and EQUAL) are given nonnumeric arguments.

EXERCISES

In the following exercises, unless otherwise indicated, we shall assume that the values numbers can take are the nonnegative integers, i.e., 0, 1, 2, 3, 4, etc.

1. Define the predicate LESSP of two numbers NUM1 and NUM2, (LESSP (LAMBDA (NUM1 NUM2) ...)). LESSP is T if the value of NUM1 is less than the value of NUM2; otherwise it is NIL.

2. Define the predicate GREATERP of two numbers NUM1 and NUM2, (GREATERP (LAMBDA (NUM1 NUM2) ...)). GREATERP has value T if the value of NUM1 is greater than the value of NUM2; otherwise the value is NIL. Do not use LESSP.

3. The function DIFFERENCE can be applied to any pair of numbers and has as value their difference. Since we are considering here only nonnegative integers, we shall assume that the value of NUM1 cannot be LESSP than the value of NUM2 for (DIFFERENCE (LAMBDA (NUM1 NUM2) ...)) to make sense. Define DIFFERENCE.

4. If NUM2 is not zero, define (QUOTIENT (LAMBDA (NUM1 NUM2) ...)) as the largest number which when multiplied by NUM2 gives a result that is not greater than the value of NUM1. You can then define the REMAINDER of the division of NUM1 by NUM2.

5. Define the MAXimum of two numbers NUM1 and NUM2 as the value of the largest of the two numbers: (MAX (LAMBDA (NUM1 NUM2) ...)).

6. Define the MINimum of two numbers NUM1 and NUM2 as the value of the smallest of the two numbers: (MIN (LAMBDA (NUM1 NUM2) ...)).

7. We say that NUM1 is a multiple of NUM2 if there is a number which when multiplied by NUM2 yields NUM1. Define a predicate (MULTIPLEP (LAMBDA (NUM1 NUM2) ...)) which has value T if NUM1 is a multiple of NUM2, and otherwise the value is NIL.

8. We say that NUM1 is a divisor of NUM2 if there is a number which when multiplied by NUM1 yields NUM2. Define a predicate (DIVISORP (LAMBDA (NUM1 NUM2) ...)) which has value T if NUM1 is a divisor of NUM2, and otherwise the value is NIL.

9. Given two integers, both greater than zero, the greatest common divisor, or GCD, of the numbers is the largest number that divides both numbers. Define a function (GCD (LAMBDA (NUM1 NUM2) ...)) which has as value the GCD of (the values of) NUM1 and NUM2. You may need to brush up on your arithmetic to find efficient solutions to this exercise and to the next one.

10. Define a function (LCM (LAMBDA (NUM1 NUM2) ...)) which has as value the smallest number that is a multiple of both NUM1 and NUM2. Assume that neither NUM1 nor NUM2 has value zero.

11. Given a list of numbers, the function MAXLIST finds the MAXimum number of the list. Define MAXLIST. MAXLIST ((7 4 2 0 3 7 2)) has value 7.

12. Given a list of numbers, the function MINLIST finds the MINimum number of the list. Define MINLIST. MINLIST ((8 6 3 5 2 3 6)) has value 2.

13. Given a list of numbers, the function SORTUP has as value a list of the same numbers in ascending order. SORTUP ((7 4 2 0 3 7 2)) has value (0 2 2 3 4 7 7). There are some efficient, and some very inefficient, ways of defining SORTUP.

14. Given a list of numbers, the function SORTDOWN has as value a list of the same numbers in descending order. SORTDOWN ((7 4 2 0 3 7 2)) has value (7 7 4 3 2 2 0). Do not use SORTUP.

15. Given ADD1 and EQUAL, use DEFINE to define SUB1. EQUAL is assumed to work for any pair of nonnegative integers.

5.4 Arithmetic and Lists

It is often desirable to obtain numerical information about lists, for example, how long a list is, how many different atoms it has, how many times a sublist is contained in it, etc. In this section we shall describe some functions that have as values arithmetic properties of lists.

§ 5.4.1 LENGTH

The function LENGTH has as value the number of SEXes at the top level of a list. LENGTH is available in most LISP systems.

```
LENGTH   ((VERDI LIKED MASKED BALLS))
   VALUE IS...
   4

LENGTH   ((LISZT WAS (WHITE AS FLOUR)))
   VALUE IS...
   3
```

The length of the empty list is 0. To calculate the LENGTH of any list, we take successive CDR's until we obtain the empty list, and each time we go down the list with CDR, the length increases by 1.

```
(LENGTH (LAMBDA (LIS)
        (COND ((NULL LIS) 0)
              (T (ADD1 (LENGTH (CDR LIS))))
   )))
```

5.4.2 ATOMLENGTH

The function ATOMLENGTH has as value the number of atoms that occur in a list, counting the same atom as many times as it occurs. Before defining ATOMLENGTH, we must agree on what to do with the empty list, which is also the atom NIL. The number of atoms in the list () is clearly 0. Consider, though, the list (()), which can also be represented as (NIL). We shall use the convention that the list (()) has no atoms. Similarly, the list ((())) or ((NIL)) will have no atoms by convention. We do, of course, count the atoms other than NIL.

```
ATOMLENGTH   ((GEOGRAPHY IS ABOUT (MAPS) (BIOGRAPHY (IS ABOUT)) CHAPS))
   VALUE IS...
   8

ATOMLENGTH   ((DIFFERENCE CREATE CREMATE M (((DIFFERENCE RUT)) (GRAVE)
               DIMENSIONS)))
   VALUE IS...
   8
```

To define ATOMLENGTH, it suffices to remember Rule of Thumb 3: The ATOMLENGTH of a list is the sum of the ATOMLENGTH of the CAR of the list and the ATOMLENGTH of the CDR of the list. To satisfy our convention, we must take special care of atoms, and, among atoms, of NIL.

```
(ATOMLENGTH (LAMBDA (LIS)
    (COND ((NULL LIS) 0)
          ((ATOM (CAR LIS)) (COND ((EQ (CAR LIS) NIL) (ATOMLENGTH
                                                         (CDR LIS)))
                                  (T (ADD1 (ATOMLENGTH (CDR LIS))))))
          (T (PLUS (ATOMLENGTH (CAR LIS)) (ATOMLENGTH (CDR LIS))))
          )))
```

1.   Define DIFFERENTATOMS, which has as value the total number of different atoms occurring in a list.

```
DIFFERENTATOMS ( (THINK BEFORE (YOU (THINK) ) ) )
  VALUE IS ...
  3
```

2.   Define OCCURRENCES, which has as value the number of times its first argument, an atom, occurs in the list that is its second argument.

```
OCCURRENCES (TURTLE (TURTLE (WAX FOR (MUD TURTLE) S) ) )
  VALUE IS ...
  2
```

3.   DEPTH counts the depth of a list, which is the number of sublists embedded one in the other in the list.

```
DEPTH ( (SOCRATES DIED OF WEDLOCK) )
  VALUE IS ...
  0

DEPTH ( (SOCRATES ((DIED ((OF) ) WEDLOCK) ) ) )
  VALUE IS ...
  4
```

You must use some convention as to the DEPTH of (()), which is (NIL). Disregarding this convention, the value of DEPTH is equal to the largest number obtained by counting parentheses using algorithm PARENCOUNT2 (see Section A.2 in Appendix A) when we start with 0 instead of 1 for the first left parenthesis.

4.   Define the function COUNTNUMBERS, which sums up the numbers that occur in a list.

```
COUNTNUMBERS ( (FIRST 7 11 (MEDDLE (THEN 13 MUDDLE) ) ) )
  VALUE IS ...
  31
```

5.5   Summary

In this chapter we have seen a large number of functions defined recursively, and the exercises should have given you much additional practice. You may have noticed that, in many cases, there are two parts to the definition of the function. The first part involves bookkeeping, typically going down the CDR of a list, or CAR's and CDR's of a list structure if we wish to access the individual atoms. The second part involves some operation such as counting, comparing, building a structure, etc. For example, in ATOMLENGTH (Section 5.4.2) we access first each atom of the list structure; this is the bookkeeping part. Second, we count the atoms; this is the processing part.

In Chapters 6 and 7, we shall describe some techniques—MAP functions and generators—that allow us to separate the bookkeeping part from the processing part. Such a separation is very convenient for complex programs, since it makes it possible for the programmer to concentrate in turn first on the bookkeeping part and then on the processing part.

6

INTRODUCTION TO
MAP FUNCTIONS AND
LAMBDA EXPRESSIONS

In the definitions of UNION and INTERSECTION (Sections 5.1.1 and 5.1.2) we went down a list—SET1—taking CDR's, and did something for each element of the list. We shall describe a family of functions, called MAP functions, which separates the bookkeeping involved in going down a list and the process that is applied to the various elements and parts of the list or lists considered. The extensive use of MAP functions, property lists (Chapter 8), and generators (Chapter 7) is the sign of mature LISP programming. This chapter opens the doors of puberty. Ready? Blush!

6.1 MAPCAR

§
√O

The function MAPCAR is found in many LISP systems. It has two arguments, a list LIS and a function that is the value of its second argument FUN.†

```
(MAPCAR (LAMBDA (LIS FUN)   ...   ))
```

MAPCAR goes down LIS and picks up each of the SEXes of LIS. Each SEX in turn is given to the value of FUN, a function of one argument, which is applied to the SEX. The value of MAPCAR is a list of the values of the function (which is the value of FUN and which we shall call the

†In some LISP systems, LIS is the second argument and FUN the first.

82

functional argument) applied to the first SEX of LIS, then to the second SEX, then to the third SEX, etc. Here is a slightly different way of saying the same thing. Suppose that the value of LIS has five SEXes,

(SEX1 SEX2 SEX3 SEX4 SEX5)

and that the value of FUN is the function TWICE. Then the value of MAPCAR will be the value of

(LIST (TWICE SEX1) (TWICE SEX2) (TWICE SEX3) (TWICE SEX4) (TWICE SEX5)

where, of course, each expression such as (TWICE SEX2) must be evaluated.

Let us find a definition for MAPCAR. If LIS has value (), the *functional argument* (the value of FUN) cannot be applied to anything, and the value of MAPCAR is the empty list (). If LIS has one SEX, we apply the functional argument to that SEX, and then make a list of that. The easiest way of making a list of some given expression is to CONS it with (). But () is the value of MAPCAR on the CDR of the particular LIS that we are considering. A recursive definition should be clear:

```
(MAPCAR (LAMBDA (LIS FUN)
        (COND ((NULL LIS) ())
              (T (CONS (FUN (CAR LIS))
                       (MAPCAR (CDR LIS) FUN)))
)))
```

Let us consider several examples of the use of MAPCAR.

6.1.1 PUTQUOTES

We saw in Section 5.3.5.1 that EVALQUOTE will want to QUOTE each argument of the list of arguments that it reads before CONSing the list with the name of a function and giving the whole result to EVAL. We shall define a function PUTQUOTES which will take a list as an argument, for example,

(SAMSON BROUGHT DOWN THE HOUSE)

and will have as value

```
PUTQUOTES  ((SAMSON BROUGHT DOWN THE HOUSE))
  VALUE IS...
  ((QUOTE SAMSON) (QUOTE BROUGHT) (QUOTE DOWN) (QUOTE THE) (QUOTE HOUSE))
```

MAPCAR will generate the SEXes SAMSON, BROUGHT, DOWN, THE, and HOUSE one after the other. We shall want to use a function

QUOTEINFRONT, which will make a list of QUOTE and each SEX:

```
(QUOTEINFRONT (LAMBDA (SEX) (LIST (QUOTE QUOTE) SEX) ) )
```

Now we are ready to define PUTQUOTES:

```
(PUTQUOTES (LAMBDA (LIS)
            (MAPCAR LIS (FUNCTION QUOTEINFRONT) )
) )
```

The arguments of MAPCAR *must be evaluated*. We want the *value* of the second argument of MAPCAR to be QUOTEINFRONT. Usually we would write (QUOTE QUOTEINFRONT), which has value QUOTEIN-FRONT. However, for functional arguments, QUOTE is replaced by FUNCTION.†

Let us trace the evaluation of

```
PUTQUOTES ( (ADAM LIKED CIDER) )
```

The value of LIS in PUTQUOTES is (ADAM LIKED CIDER). This argument is passed to MAPCAR as its first argument, the second one being the functional argument QUOTEINFRONT. We are now deep in MAPCAR. LIS has value (ADAM LIKED CIDER). It is not null, so we calculate (QUOTEINFRONT (CAR LIS)), which is QUOTEINFRONT (ADAM) and has value (QUOTE ADAM). This list is kept, and MAP-CAR is called again with arguments (LIKED CIDER) and QUOTEIN-FRONT. Without going into details, it is apparent that the successive values of QUOTEINFRONT are (QUOTE LIKED) and (QUOTE CIDER). After this last list is obtained, MAPCAR is called with argu-ments () and QUOTEINFRONT, and the value of this call to MAPCAR is (). CONSing back all the previous values of MAPCAR gives us the value of PUTQUOTES:

```
PUTQUOTES  ( (ADAM LIKED CIDER) )
 VALUE IS...
 ( (QUOTE ADAM) (QUOTE LIKED) (QUOTE CIDER) )
```

MAPCAR can be viewed as analogous to a party game. MAPCAR throws the successive SEXes of a list to a function. The function covers the successive SEXes, one by one, and slides the resulting values back to MAPCAR. MAPCAR stores these values obtained from the function and,

---

†In some LISP systems QUOTE may work in some cases. FUNCTION is safe in all cases. See Section D.4.11.1 in Appendix D for a discussion of the differences between QUOTE and FUNCTION and of the so-called FUNARG problem.

when it has no additional balls to throw, produces a list of the values received from the function in the order in which they were received. Wah!

6.1.2 SUBSTOP *Revisited*

Defining SUBSTOP (Section 5.2.4) may have seemed complicated. The process becomes almost trivial with MAPCAR. For each SEX that MAPCAR sends, we check whether we should send it back unchanged or replace it with its replacement. The FUNCTION REPLACESEX will be the playmate of MAPCAR.

```
(SUBSTOP (LAMBDA (SEX1 SEX2 LIZ)
                 (MAPCAR LIZ (FUNCTION REPLACESEX) ) ) )
(REPLACESEX (LAMBDA (SEX3)
            (COND ( (EQUAL SEX1 SEX3) SEX2)
                  (T SEX3)
            ) ) )
```

```
SUBSTOP  (PRESENCE ABSENCE ( (PRESENCE) OF BODY PRESENCE OF MIND) )
 VALUE IS . . .
 ( (PRESENCE) OF BODY ABSENCE OF MIND)
```

```
SUBSTOP  (PRESENCE (ABSENCE) (PRESENCE OF BODY PRESENCE OF MIND) )
 VALUE IS . . .
 ( (ABSENCE) OF BODY (ABSENCE) OF MIND)
```

Notice that REPLACESEX has the same definition as HELP2 in Section 5.2.4.

SEX1 and SEX2 are free variables in REPLACESEX and are bound in SUBSTOP. The use of free variables in functional arguments of MAP functions and generators (Section 7.6) is common practice.

An easy way to observe what MAPCAR does is to give it a functional argument that does nothing. Such a function can be defined as

```
(DONOTHING (LAMBDA (SEX) SEX) )
```

Some runs of DONOTHING are

```
DONOTHING  (HAYADOIN)
 VALUE IS . . .
 HAYADOIN
```

```
DONOTHING  ( (THAT IS A DEFINITE MAYBE) )
 VALUE IS . . .
 (THAT IS A DEFINITE MAYBE)
```

```
DONOTHING  ( (HANGOVER IS THE WRATH OF GRAPES) )
 VALUE IS . . .
 (HANGOVER IS THE WRATH OF GRAPES)
```

If DONOTHING is the functional argument of MAPCAR, the value of MAPCAR will be its own first argument, the input list. We can verify this by defining

```
GIVEBACKLIST  ((HOW MANY MEASLES IN BED))
  VALUE IS...
  (HOW MANY MEASLES IN BED)

GIVEBACKLIST  ((WIDOWS PREFER BULL MARKETS))
  VALUE IS...
  (WIDOWS PREFER BULL MARKETS)
```

It is easy to see why GIVEBACKLIST has as value its original argument: DONOTHING sends back to MAPCAR what had been sent to it in the first place.

```
(GIVEBACKLIST (LAMBDA (LIS) (MAPCAR LIS (FUNCTION DONOTHING))))
```

EXERCISE

§ MAPLIST is like MAPCAR, except that its functional argument is given
√O successive CDR's of the list, instead of CAR's of these, as in MAPCAR. Define MAPLIST, and use it to define some interesting or amusing functions.

6.2 LAMBDA Expressions

It seems slightly wasteful to define a new function every time we need a functional argument. There is a LISP construction which we have used all along, the *LAMBDA expression*, which permits us to avoid defining new function names. Considering a very simple example, that of DONO-THING,

```
(DONOTHING (LAMBDA (SEX) SEX))
```

the LAMBDA expression attached to DONOTHING is (LAMBDA (SEX) SEX). (In Chapter 8, we shall see how the attachment is made.) When the function DONOTHING is applied to some arguments, DONO-THING is a convenient abbreviation of the LAMBDA expression (LAMBDA (SEX) SEX). Instead of writing, in EVQ-LISP,

```
DONOTHING ( (HANGOVER IS THE WRATH OF GRAPES) )
```

we could have written

```
(LAMBDA (SEX) SEX)
( (HANGOVER IS THE WRATH OF GRAPES) )
```

with the same effect:

```
VALUE IS...
(HANGOVER IS THE WRATH OF GRAPES)
```

In MAP functions and in generators (Chapter 7), it is often more natural to write the functional argument as a LAMBDA expression, since often there is no compelling reason for giving the functional argument a name. Using LAMBDA expressions, we can redefine PUTQUOTES and SUBSTOP as follows:

```
(PUTQUOTES (LAMBDA (LIS)
 (MAPCAR LIS
  (FUNCTION (LAMBDA (LISELEM) (LIST (QUOTE QUOTE) LISELEM) ) ) ) ) )

(SUBSTOP (LAMBDA (SEX1 SEX2 LIS)
    (MAPCAR LIS
        (FUNCTION (LAMBDA (LISELEM)
            (COND ( (EQUAL SEX1 LISELEM) SEX2)
                  (T LISELEM)
        ) ) )   ) ) )
```

It is good practice to use mnemonics for the names of the variables in the LAMBDA expression used as a functional argument. In both of the above cases, MAPCAR will traverse a list LIS and will send to its functional argument successive elements of this LIS; therefore it is natural to call the *LAMBDA variable* of the functional argument LISELEM (a mnemonic for ELEMent of LIS) or something similar.

As we have just seen, a LAMBDA expression can be used also in place of the name of a function at the top level of EVQ-LISP. A simple example would be the program

```
(LAMBDA (SEX) SEX)
( (ARISTOTLE LIKED THE BOTTLE) )
 VALUE IS...
 (ARISTOTLE LIKED THE BOTTLE)
```

In this program we have clearly separated the LAMBDA expression and its list of arguments. A more complicated program is

```
  (LAMBDA (LIS)
  (MAPCAR LIS
   (FUNCTION (LAMBDA (LISELEM) (LIST (QUOTE QUOTE) LISELEM) ) ) ) )
 ( (LET US BE STRANGERS) )
  VALUE IS...
  ( (QUOTE LET) (QUOTE US) (QUOTE BE) (QUOTE STRANGERS) )
```

The first three lines in the above program could have been replaced by the function name PUTQUOTES. The fourth line is the list of arguments.

The use of LAMBDA expressions is the easiest way of obtaining evaluation in EVQ-LISP. Consider the program

```
CAR  ((CDR (CDR (QUOTE (EINSTEIN HAD RELATIVES)))))
    VALUE IS
    CDR
```

since the argument of CAR is the list

```
(CDR (CDR (QUOTE (EINSTEIN HAD RELATIVES))))
```

and *not* its value. By contrast, the "related" program in EV-LISP is

```
(CAR (CDR (CDR (QUOTE (EINSTEIN HAD RELATIVES)))))
VALUE IS...
RELATIVES
```

The easiest way of obtaining in EVQ-LISP the same result as in EV-LISP is by introducing a dummy LAMBDA expression:

```
(LAMBDA ()
  (CAR (CDR (CDR (QUOTE (EINSTEIN HAD RELATIVES)))))) ()
VALUE IS...
RELATIVES
```

The LAMBDA expression has no variables; hence its list of variables is the empty list (). Therefore the list of arguments given to the LAMBDA expression must be a list of no arguments, or the empty list (). Clearly, the sole purpose of the LAMBDA expression is to provide a framework in which the program

```
(CAR (CDR (CDR (QUOTE (EINSTEIN HAD RELATIVES)))))
```

can be evaluated and its value printed by the LISP system. The above subterfuge of the empty LAMBDA expression (i.e., with no variables and arguments) is quite convenient in EVQ-LISP.

6.3 MAPPENDCAR

Let us return to an old friend, the function INTERSECTION.

```
(INTERSECTION (LAMBDA (SET1 SET2)   ...   ))
```

In a definition of INTERSECTION, we must consider all the elements of one set, for example, SET1, and keep only those elements which are also in SET2. *The fluent LISP speaker always thinks of a MAP function when all the elements of a list are considered one after the other.* The functional argument will throw away the elements of SET1 which are not in SET2 and have the other elements of SET1 kept. The problem with MAPCAR is that there is no way for its functional argument to return *nothing;* NIL, for instance, is definitely not nothing. A solution is not far away, though. Write a MAP function which will discard some special balls returned by the functional argument. APPEND is a good candidate as a help of the MAP function, since it basically disregards NIL if NIL is one of its arguments.

```
(MAPPENDCAR (LAMBDA (LIS FUN)
            (COND ( (NULL LIS) ( ) )
                  (T (APPEND (FUN (CAR LIS) )
                             (MAPPENDCAR (CDR LIS) FUN) ) )
     ) ) )
```

Therefore, MAPPENDCAR is just like MAPCAR, except that it uses APPEND instead of CONS for stringing the various values returned by the functional argument. With MAPPENDCAR it is easy to define INTERSECTION.

```
(INTERSECTION (LAMBDA (SET1 SET2)
     (MAPPENDCAR SET1
             (FUNCTION (LAMBDA (SET1ELEM)
                     (COND ( (MEMBER SET1ELEM SET2) (LIST SET1ELEM) )
                           (T ( ) )
                     ) ) )   ) ) )
```

Let us consider an example:

```
INTERSECTION  ( (SHOT DEAD BY ROTTEN AFFECTION) (DEAD ROTTEN FORGOTTEN) )
VALUE IS . . .
(DEAD ROTTEN)
```

Let us view the elements of SET1 that MAPPENDCAR sends to the functional argument and the values the functional argument sends back to MAPPENDCAR:

Value of SET1ELEM Sent to the Functional Argument	Value Returned by the Functional Argument
SHOT	()
DEAD	(DEAD)
BY	()
ROTTEN	(ROTTEN)
AFFECTION	()

When MAPPENDCAR finally finds the empty list as its first argument, it APPENDs the successive values received from the functional argument, computing

(APPEND () (APPEND (QUOTE (DEAD)) (APPEND () (APPEND (QUOTE (ROTTEN))
(APPEND () ()))))))

which has value (DEAD ROTTEN). Since APPEND takes only lists as arguments, we had to make a list of the elements of SET1 that were to be kept. In Section 8.2 we shall give a more efficient definition of INTER-SECTION.

EXERCISE

1. Using MAPPENDCAR, define SETDIFF of two sets.

2. Using MAPPENDCAR, define UNION of two sets. Do not use SETDIFF.

6.4 MAPPENDLIST

Defining MAKESET is slightly more challenging. Let us consider an example:

MAKESET ((MATERNITY LEAVES FOR MOTHERS PATERNITY LEAVES FOR FATHERS))

We go down the list one by one, and ask whether the element of the list occurs farther down. If it does, we throw it away; if it does not, we keep it so that it can contribute to the set that we are building. A table of the activities is

Element	Action	Reason
MATERNITY	Keep	Not found in (LEAVES FOR MOTHERS PATERNITY LEAVES FOR FATHERS)
LEAVES	Discard	Found in (FOR MOTHERS PATERNITY LEAVES FOR FATHERS)
FOR	Discard	Found in (MOTHERS PATERNITY LEAVES FOR FATHERS)
MOTHERS	Keep	Not found in (PATERNITY LEAVES FOR FATHERS)
PATERNITY	Keep	Not found in (LEAVES FOR FATHERS)
LEAVES	Keep	Not found in (FOR FATHERS)
FOR	Keep	Not found in (FATHERS)
FATHERS	Keep	Not found in ()

We need to keep successive CDR's of the list to implement this algorithm, and we shall use APPEND to discard NIL's. The appropriate MAP function is

```
(MAPPENDLIST (LAMBDA (LIS FUN)
                (COND ( (NULL LIS) ( ) )
                      (T (APPEND (FUN LIS)
                                 (MAPPENDLIST (CDR LIS) FUN) )
              ) ) )
```

and we can define MAKESET as

```
(MAKESET (LAMBDA (LIS)
           (MAPPENDLIST LIS (FUNCTION (LAMBDA (LISCDR)
               (COND ( (MEMBER (CAR LISCDR) (CDR LISCDR) ) ( ) )
                     (T (LIST (CAR LISCDR) ) )
             ) ) ) ) ) )
```

```
MAKESET   ( (MATERNITY LEAVES FOR MOTHERS PATERNITY LEAVES FOR FATHERS) )
VALUE IS . . .
(MATERNITY MOTHERS PATERNITY LEAVES FOR FATHERS)
```

Tracing through an easy example,

```
MAKESET ( (BAD WHISKY IS BAD) )
```

we obtain the following interaction between MAPPENDLIST and its functional argument:

Value of LISCDR Sent to the Functional Argument	Value Returned by the Functional Argument
(BAD WHISKY IS BAD)	( )
(WHISKY IS BAD)	(WHISKY)
(IS BAD)	(IS)
(BAD)	(BAD)

The run of the program gives

```
MAKESET   ( (BAD WHISKY IS BAD) )
VALUE IS . . .
(WHISKY IS BAD)
```

6.5   DOUBLEMAPCAR

MAP functions need not operate on only one list. It is possible to define MAP functions that take several lists and several functions as arguments. A situation that occurs frequently is the following: We wish to apply a function of two arguments to successive SEXes of two lists. We shall assume that the two lists have the same LENGTH, so that we need only check whether one of them has become NULL. The MAP function that does the bookkeeping is

```
(DOUBLEMAPCAR (LAMBDA (LIS1 LIS2 FUN2)
 (COND ( (NULL LIS1) NIL)
       (T (CONS (FUN2 (CAR LIS1) (CAR LIS2) )
               (DOUBLEMAPCAR (CDR LIS1) (CDR LIS2) FUN2) ) ) ) ) )
```

As an application, suppose that we have two lists, (1 2 3 4 5) and (ONE TWO THREE FOUR FIVE), and that we want to set up a dictionary which will tell us that the translation of 1 is ONE; of 2, TWO, etc. One representation of the dictionary could be a list of smaller lists:

((1 ONE) (2 TWO) (3 THREE) (4 FOUR) (5 FIVE))

Each sublist is interpreted as something (the first element of the sublist) and its translation (the second element of the sublist). A function that will build such a dictionary, given the two lists, is BUILDIC:

```
(BUILDIC (LAMBDA (LIS1 LIS2)
        (DOUBLEMAPCAR LIS1 LIS2 (FUNCTION (LAMBDA (LIS1ELEM LIS2ELEM)
                               (LIST LIS1ELEM LIS2ELEM) ) )
) ) )

BUILDIC  ( (ONE TWO THREE FOUR) (UN DEUX TROIS QUATRE) )
 VALUE IS...
 ( (ONE UN) (TWO DEUX) (THREE TROIS) (FOUR QUATRE) )
```

EXERCISE

Two players are playing a stupid game of dice. They each throw a die that can take on values between 1 and 6. If the value thrown by player1 is at least two more or at least three less than the value thrown by player2, then player1 wins a scorpion. Otherwise, it is player2 who wins a scorpion. For example,

Throw by Player1	Throw by Player2	Winner
2	2	2
4	3	2
4	2	1
2	4	2
2	5	1
2	6	1

Assuming that the sequence of throws by player1 is (6 4 4 2 1 1 5 3 2 5 6 4 2 3), while the sequence of throws by player2 is (1 1 2 4 6 3 4 5 5 2 1 4 1 6), how many scorpions will player1 win (or lose)? Write a function that will give the answer, using DOUBLEMAPCAR and EVAL.

6.6   Cascaded MAP Functions

By using MAP functions, it is possible to write some remarkably short programs for processes that are reasonably complicated. As an example of the possibilities, suppose that we are given a list of several dictionaries similar to the dictionary built by BUILDIC,

```
( ( (ONE UN) (TWO DEUX) (THREE TROIS) (FOUR QUATRE) )
  ( (MAN HOMME) (WOMAN FEMME) (PONCE SOUTENEUR) )   )
```

and that we wish to obtain the list of all the things into which we can translate something. For the above example, this list would be

```
(UN DEUX TROIS QUATRE HOMME FEMME SOUTENEUR)
```

Let's break down the problem into subproblems. If we had only one dictionary, for example, the second one,

```
( (MAN HOMME) (WOMAN FEMME) (PONCE SOUTENEUR) )
```

we would obtain the answer (HOMME FEMME SOUTENEUR) by doing

```
(LAMBDA (DIC) (MAPCAR DIC (FUNCTION CADR) ) )
( ( (MAN HOMME) (WOMAN FEMME) (PONCE SOUTENEUR) ) )
VALUE IS . . .
(HOMME FEMME SOUTENEUR)
```

and the function CADR is defined as

```
(CADR (LAMBDA (LIS) (CAR (CDR LIS) ) ) )
```

The function CADR is usually available in LISP systems. In Section 6.6.1 we shall briefly mention some similar functions.

Now, assume that we have a list of several dictionaries. We shall pick up each of the dictionaries, give it to the above LAMBDA expression, and collect the results. Since the LAMBDA expression has a list as value, we shall use MAPPENDCAR to APPEND the various lists together. If we are going to obtain the list of translations only once, we need not write a function definition but could instead use a LAMBDA expression. The complete program would be

```
(LAMBDA (DICLIST)
(MAPPENDCAR DICLIST
 (FUNCTION (LAMBDA (DIC) (MAPCAR DIC (FUNCTION CADR))))))

( ( ((ONE UN) (TWO DEUX)) ((MAN HOMME) (WOMAN FEMME)) ) )

VALUE IS ...
(UN DEUX HOMME FEMME)
```

The LAMBDA expression could also have been written as

```
(LAMBDA (DICLIST)
  (MAPPENDCAR DICLIST (FUNCTION (LAMBDA (DIC)
                 (MAPCAR DIC (FUNCTION (LAMBDA (DICELEM)
                                 (CAR (CDR DICELEM
      )))))))))
((((ONE UN) (TWO DEUX)) ((MAN HOMME) (WOMAN FEMME))))
VALUE IS ...
(UN DEUX HOMME FEMME)
```

The first version of the LAMBDA expression is more efficient and results in far fewer parentheses.

If we process lists of dictionaries several times, it is natural to define a function that will be a shorthand name for (one of) the LAMBDA expressions above.

```
(LISTOFTRANSES (LAMBDA (DICLIST)
        (MAPPENDCAR DICLIST (FUNCTION (LAMBDA (DIC)
                       (MAPCAR DIC (FUNCTION (CADR))))
        )))
```

The program would then be

```
LISTOFTRANSES  ((((ONE UN) (TWO DEUX)) ((MAN HOMME) (WOMAN FEMME))))
VALUE IS ...
(UN DEUX HOMME FEMME)
```

EXERCISE

Without using MAP functions, define LISTOFTRANSES.

§ *6.6.1 Multiple CAR and CDR Functions*

Usually, CADR and similar functions such as CAAR, CADAR, etc., are available in LISP systems. Here are the definitions of these functions up to a "depth" of three for c<u>A</u>r's and c<u>D</u>r's:

Program	Equivalent Program
(CAAR LIS)	(CAR (CAR LIS))
(CADR LIS)	(CAR (CDR LIS))
(CDAR LIS)	(CDR (CAR LIS))
(CDDR LIS)	(CDR (CDR LIS))
(CAAAR LIS)	(CAR (CAR (CAR LIS)))
(CAADR LIS)	(CAR (CAR (CDR LIS)))
(CADAR LIS)	(CAR (CDR (CAR LIS)))
(CADDR LIS)	(CAR (CDR (CDR LIS)))
(CDAAR LIS)	(CDR (CAR (CAR LIS)))
(CDADR LIS)	(CDR (CAR (CDR LIS)))
(CDDAR LIS)	(CDR (CDR (CAR LIS)))
(CDDDR LIS)	(CDR (CDR (CDR LIS)))

6.7 Summary

When the same process is applied sequentially to various parts of a list, for example, to successive SEXes or CDR's of the list, a MAP function may be the natural way to simplify a LISP program. The MAP functions that we have seen are to be used only when all the parts of a list are to be considered. If the process might be discontinued under certain circumstances, before all parts of a list have been given to the process, then another type of function—a generator—may be desirable. Generators and some additional MAP functions are considered in the next chapter.

7

PROG, CONSTANTS
AND GENERATORS

In this chapter, we shall introduce the PROGram function, or PROG. PROG makes it easy to write programs where certain processes are repeated and where the results of some computation can conveniently be stored for subsequent processing.

7.1 Simulation of EV-LISP in EVQ-LISP

Let us assume that you have an EVQ-LISP system running on your computer but would like to run EV-LISP instead. In Section 5.3.5.1, we saw what needs to be done:

1. READ a SEX from some input device such as a card reader, tape, disk, teletype, or display terminal.

2. EVALuate this SEX, using EVAL.

3. PRINT the value of EVAL on some output device such as a line printer, tape, disk, teletype, or display terminal.

4. Go back to step 1.

§ *7.1.1 READ and PRINT*

The functions that we shall use are

§

```
+-------------------------------------------+
| Function:  READ                           |
|                                           |
| Number of arguments:  0                   |
|                                           |
| Value:  the next SEX read from the        |
|         input device                      |
+-------------------------------------------+
```

§

```
+-------------------------------------------+
| Function:  PRINT                          |
|                                           |
| Number of arguments:  1                   |
|                                           |
| Argument:  any SEX                        |
|                                           |
| Value:  the value of the SEX; this        |
|         value is also output to the       |
|         output device                     |
+-------------------------------------------+
```

We can define EVLISP in a somewhat awkward way:

```
(EVLISP (LAMBDA ( )
   (COND ( (PRINT (EVAL (READ) ) ) (EVLISP) )
          (T (EVLISP) ) ) ) )
```

In the above definition, we READ a SEX, EVALuate it, PRINT it, and then, whether the result was NIL or not, we call EVLISP again. Thus, EVLISP calls itself recursively, which is unsatisfactory. In other programming languages, such as FORTRAN, BASIC, ALGOL, and PL/1, we would have used a *go-to* construction for step 4.

EXERCISE

Why is the above definition of EVLISP unsatisfactory?

7.1.1.1 *Debugging with PRINT*

Since the value of PRINT is the value of its argument, PRINT does not change the values of expressions. It does, however, have the side effect of PRINTing its argument. Hence, PRINT statements can be interspersed in functions for debugging purposes.

For example, suppose that we wish to debug LINEARIZE (Section 5.2.5) without using TRACE:

```
(LINEARIZE (LAMBDA (LIS)
   (COND ( (NULL LIS ( ) )
          ( (ATOM (CAR LIS) ) (CONS (CAR LIS)
                                    (LINEARIZE (CDR LIS) ) ) )
          (T (APPEND (LINEARIZE (CAR LIS) ) (LINEARIZE (CDR LIS
) ) ) ) ) ) )
```

Changing the last argument of COND to

```
(T (APPEND (LINEARIZE (PRINT (CAR LIS) ) (LINEARIZE (CDR LIS) ) ) )
```

would PRINT the value of (CAR LIS) every time the recursion goes "left," but the behavior of LINEARIZE is otherwise unchanged. If we are PRINTing several things, we may wish to give a message to keep track of our position:

```
(T (APPEND (LINEARIZE (CDR (PRINT
             (CONS (QUOTE (GOING LEFT IN LINEARIZE) )
                (CAR LIS) ) ) ) )
          (LINEARIZE (CDR LIS) ) ) )
```

We would then obtain

```
LINEARIZE ( ( (HE LIKED (CHILDREN) ) ( (MEDIUM RARE) ) ) )

( (GOING LEFT IN LINEARIZE) HE LIKED (CHILDREN) )
( (GOING LEFT IN LINEARIZE) CHILDREN)
( (GOING LEFT IN LINEARIZE) (MEDIUM RARE) )
( (GOING LEFT IN LINEARIZE) MEDIUM RARE)

VALUE IS . . .
(HE LIKED CHILDREN MEDIUM RARE)
```

Selective PRINTing for debugging purposes should almost always be preferred to TRACEing.

7.1.1.2   Other Print Functions: PRIN1 and TERPRI

PRIN1 is like PRINT, except that it does not do a carriage return.

S

√

Function: PRIN1
Number of arguments: 1
Argument: any SEX
Value: the value of the SEX; this value is also output without carriage return

TERPRI—TERminate PRInt—does a carriage return. Hence PRINT is PRIN1 followed by TERPRI.

S

Function: TERPRI
Number of arguments: 0
Effect: does a carriage return

7.1.1.3 Other Read Functions:
READCH and RATOM

Usually, there are functions that read smaller structures than READ. Two typical examples are READCH and RATOM, although there are many variations from system to system.

RATOM reads the next atom from the input device.

✓

```
Function:  RATOM
Number of arguments:  0
Value:   the next atom read from
         the input device
```

If the input is

(MONTHLY (INSTALLMENTS)(DAILY))

then successive calls to RATOM will have values "(", i.e., the character left parenthesis;

"MONTHLY", "(", "INSTALLMENTS", ")", "(", "DAILY", ")", and ")"

Note that blanks are delimiters and are not read explicitly by RATOM.

READCH reads the next character from the input device.

✓

```
Function:  READCH
Number of arguments:  0
Value:   the next character read
         from the input device
```

If the input is

((MEN)ARE SILLY (AND VAIN) (AND HAVE HAIR ALL OVER THEIR BODIES))

then the first few calls of READCH will have values "(", " ", i.e., the character which is a blank,

"(", " ", "M", "E", "N", ")", "A", etc.

7.1.2 Evaluation of a PROG

We return to the definition of EVLISP (Section 7.1.1). At this point, we do not know how to "go back" anywhere. The solution lies in using a new function, PROG (mentioned above), which has several interesting features:

1. PROG has an indeterminate number of arguments.

2. The first argument of PROG is a list of *PROG variables*. PROG variables are similar to LAMBDA variables. The list of PROG variables may be empty. PROG variables are initialized to the value NIL.

3. The arguments of PROG are evaluated one after the other starting with the second argument of PROG—with the following exceptions:

   a. An atomic argument is not evaluated. It is considered as a *label*. Labels are used in conjunction with the function GO. In most systems, labels must be alpha atoms.†

   b. The evaluation of the function GO makes LISP continue the evaluation of PROG at the argument of PROG following the label that is the argument of GO.

   c. If the function RETURN of one argument is evaluated, then the value of the function PROG is the value of the argument of RETURN.

   d. If the last argument of PROG has been evaluated so that there is no next argument left in PROG, then the value of PROG is NIL.

   e. If an argument of PROG is a COND and if no lefts of the COND are found to be T, then evaluation continues with the next argument of PROG.

We are now almost ready to simulate EV-LISP in EVQ-LISP. The complete program will be‡

```
(EVLISP (LAMBDA NIL
 (PROG (READVAL PROGRAMVAL)
  LOOP (SETQ READVAL (READ))
       (SETQ PROGRAMVAL (EVAL READVAL))
       (PRINT PROGRAMVAL)
       (GO LOOP)))))
```

```
EVLISP ()
```

If the next SEX that is read is

```
(CONS (QUOTE FASHIONS) (QUOTE (IN SIN CHANGE)))
```

then the following will be printed:

```
(FASHIONS IN SIN CHANGE)
```

Let us look at the definition of EVLISP. It is a function of no arguments, since the list of LAMBDA variables is empty. The value of the LAMBDA expression is the value of the function PROG. The PROG has

---

†An alpha atom is an atom which is not a number; see Section 10.2.

‡A more efficient and compact definition of the function EVLISP will be given below.

two PROG variables: READVAL and PROGRAMVAL. Both READ-VAL and PROGRAMVAL (as is the case usually with PROG variables) will be used to store results of computations.

7.1.3 SETQ

The evaluation of PROG begins after the list of PROG variables. The second argument of PROG is LOOP, an atom. LOOP is not evaluated but is considered to be a label. Next the program (SETQ READVAL (READ)) is encountered. SETQ is a function that is used very frequently with PROG. Its box is

```
Function:  SETQ

Number of arguments:  2

Arguments:  first: an alpha atom†;
            second:  any SEX

Value:  the value of the second argument;
        this value becomes the value of
        the first argument
```

(Note that the first argument of SETQ cannot be an atomic number, since it would be absurd to change the value of a number.) So the second argument of SETQ is evaluated: The function READ is called, and the value of (READ) is the next SEX available from the input device. If that SEX is the list

(CONS (QUOTE FASHIONS) (QUOTE (IN SIN CHANGE)))

then the value of the PROG variable READVAL is this list. Moreover, the value of (SETQ READVAL (READ)) is also this list. Notice, however, that nothing is done with the value of SETQ in this case. Quite frequently in a PROG we are more interested in the *effect* of a function than in its *value*. The effect of the SETQ was to change the value of READVAL to the value of (READ). The value of SETQ itself is not utilized.

Evaluation continues with the next SEX of the PROG, namely (SETQ PROGRAMVAL (EVAL READVAL)). We have another SETQ and evaluate its second argument, (EVAL READVAL). First, READVAL is evaluated, and, thanks to the first SETQ, its value is the list (CONS (QUOTE FASHIONS) (QUOTE (IN SIN CHANGE))). EVAL evaluates this program and has value (FASHIONS IN SIN CHANGE). The list (FASHIONS IN SIN CHANGE) becomes the value of the PROG variable PROGRAMVAL. Once again the value of SETQ is not utilized. The

†An alpha atom is an atom which is not a number; see Section 10.2.

next SEX in the PROG, (PRINT PROGRAMVAL), is evaluated. PRINT will cause its argument to be evaluated. The value of PROGRAMVAL is the list (FASHIONS IN SIN CHANGE). PRINT causes this list to be output on an output device, for example, on a line printer. The value of PRINT is the list (FASHIONS IN SIN CHANGE), but once again only the effect of PRINT was used, not its value.

§ 7.1.4 GO

Evaluation of the PROG continues with the SEX (GO LOOP). In most LISP systems, GO is a strange function: if its argument is an alpha atom, then that atom is considered as a label from which evaluation of PROG should continue. If the argument of GO is a numeric atom, an error or garbage result (usually!). If the argument of GO is not an atom, it is evaluated. If the value found is an alpha atom, then that will be the label used by GO; otherwise, another evaluation is made, etc. The value of GO is irrelevant; it could not be used anywhere, since evaluation is transferred elsewhere in the PROG. In our example the argument of GO, LOOP, is an atom. LISP returns evaluation of the PROG to the argument of PROG following the argument LOOP. Therefore, evaluation starts once again at the SEX (SETQ READVAL (READ)).

A more efficient version of EVLISP is the following:

```
(EVLISP (LAMBDA ( ) (PROG ( )
  LOOP (PRINT (EVAL (READ) ) )
       (GO LOOP)
  ) ) )
```

This version uses no PROG variables. Notice that EVLISP goes in an "infinite" loop since there is no RETURN in the PROG. Evaluation would be stopped when READ attempts to read beyond the last SEX in a program.

7.1.5 COND in PROG

If we wish to have EVLISP stop when it READs the SEX STOP, then a version of EVLISP would be

```
(EVLISP (LAMBDA ( ) (PROG (READVAL)
  LOOP (SETQ READVAL (READ) )
       (COND ( (EQ READVAL (QUOTE STOP) )
                           (RETURN (QUOTE (END OF EVLISP) ) ) ) )
       (PRINT (EVAL READVAL) )
       (GO LOOP)
       ) ) )
```

If the value of READ is the atom STOP, then the value of PROG, and hence the value of the LAMBDA expression attached to EVLISP, and the value of EVLISP itself, are each the value of RETURN. The value of RETURN is the value of its argument, and the value of that is the list (END OF EVLISP).

If the first left of COND, (EQ READVAL (QUOTE STOP)), is NIL, then there is no additional left to test in the COND. Inside the PROG it is permissible to have COND's without a True left. Evaluation of the PROG simply continues with the next SEX of the PROG, in this case with (PRINT (EVAL READVAL)).

Notice how important it is to store the value of READ. The following version of EVLISP behaves quite differently from the above versions:

```
(BADEVLISP (LAMBDA ( ) (PROG( )
      LOOP (COND ( (EQ (READ) (QUOTE STOP) ) (RETURN
                                          (QUOTE (END OF EVLISP) ) ) ) )
            (PRINT (EVAL (READ) ) )
            (GO LOOP)
            ) ) )

BADEVLISP ( )
```

The successive values of READ will, in general, be different, and in BADEVLISP only every second SEX will be evaluated. Moreover, only every other SEX is tested to see whether it is the atom STOP.

7.2 SET and Constants

§

The function SET is almost the same as SETQ, except that it evaluates its first argument, and the value of this first argument must be an atom. The value of this atom is changed to be the value of the second argument, and this value is also the value of SET.

§

Function:	SET
Number of arguments:	2
Arguments:	first: must evaluate to an alpha atom; second: any SEX
Value:	value of second argument; the value of the first argument has its value replaced by this value of SET

Consider the following programs in EV-LISP:

```
(SETQ CARESSES (QUOTE CAREERS))
VALUE IS...
CAREERS

(SET CARESSES (QUOTE LUCRATIVE))
VALUE IS...
LUCRATIVE
```

The first program assigns the atom CAREERS as the value of the atom CARESSES. In the second program, CARESSES is evaluated, and its value is found to be CAREERS. The value of CAREERS is replaced by the value of (QUOTE LUCRATIVE), which is LUCRATIVE. Therefore, at the end of the two programs, the value of CARESSES is CAREERS, and the value of CAREERS is LUCRATIVE.

```
CARESSES
VALUE IS...
CAREERS

CAREERS
VALUE IS...
LUCRATIVE
```

SET is often used in PROGs when we wish to change the value of an atom, the name of which we do not know but which can be accessed as the value of some other atom. SET and SETQ are also used to define constants. A constant is an atom which has a value which is rarely changed and which might be used by several functions. For example, if a large list is used repeatedly in a set of LISP programs, it is easier to define a constant to have the value of the large list. Subsequently, whenever we want to use the large list, we have only to evaluate the constant.

Suppose that we wish to use many times the list (A BLUSHING CROW FELL HIM). We might define the constant SPOONER to have this list as value. In EV-LISP, we would execute the program

```
(SETQ SPOONER (QUOTE (A BLUSHING CROW FELL HIM)))
VALUE IS...
(A BLUSHING CROW FELL HIM)
```

If subsequently we execute

```
(CDR SPOONER)
VALUE IS...
(BLUSHING CROW FELL HIM)
```

then the value of this program would be

(BLUSHING CROW FELL HIM)

In EVQ-LISP, we must use SET† at the top level:

```
SET (SPOONER (A BLUSHING CROW FELL HIM))
 VALUE IS...
 (A BLUSHING CROW FELL HIM)
```

Afterwards, we could run the following program:

```
(LAMBDA () (CDR SPOONER))    ()
 VALUE IS...
 (BLUSHING CROW FELL HIM)
```

After a constant has been given a value, its value can be modified by using SET or SETQ. For example, in EVQ-LISP,

```
(LAMBDA () (SETQ SPOONER (CDR SPOONER))) ()
```

will have the effect of changing the value of the constant SPOONER to (BLUSHING CROW FELL HIM). We shall use constants later in this chapter.

7.3 EVQ-LISP in EV–LISP

It is more difficult to simulate EVQLISP in EV-LISP than EVLISP in EVQ-LISP, since certain functions, such as COND, must be treated in a special way. The inputs to an EVQ-LISP system are pairs of SEXes. The first SEX is the name of a function or a LAMBDA expression; the second is a list of arguments. If we exclude special functions as first SEXes to be given to EVQ-LISP, then the following EV-LISP program will do:

```
(DEFINE (QUOTE (
  (EVQLISP (LAMBDA () (PROG ()
    LOOP (PRINT (EVAL (CONS (READ) (PUTQUOTES (READ)))))
        (GO LOOP)
)))
          ))    )
(EVQLISP)
```

If the next line is the EVQ-LISP program

```
CONS (A (BLUSHING CROW FELL HIM))
```

†In some EVQ-LISP systems, CSET and CSETQ must be used for creating and modifying constants, instead of SET and SETQ, which are used solely to modify LAMBDA and PROG variables.

then the function EVQLISP will print the value of the program:

(A BLUSHING CROW FELL HIM)

The first SEX of the EV-LISP program DEFINEs the function EVQLISP. Two SEXes are READ, and we quote the arguments in the list of arguments by using PUTQUOTES (Section 6.1.1). We obtain a program by CONSing the function name or LAMBDA expression in front of the list of QUOTEd arguments, EVALuate the program, PRINT it, and GO back to READing two SEXes. The second SEX of the EV-LISP program, (EVQLISP), evaluates the function EVQLISP on no arguments, thereby causing the start of a pseudo-EVQ-LISP system.

7.4 Some Old Functions Rewritten Using PROG

To get some practice with PROG, we shall give nonrecursive versions of some very simple functions that we have already seen.

7.4.1 UNION

```
(UNION (LAMBDA (SET1 SET2)
 (PROG (PARUNION)
       (SETQ PARUNION SET2)
  LOOP (COND ((NULL SET1) (RETURN PARUNION))
             ((MEMBER (CAR SET1) SET2) (GO DOWN)))
       (SETQ PARUNION (CONS (CAR SET1) PARUNION))
  DOWN (SETQ SET1 (CDR SET1))
       (GO LOOP))))
```

The PROG variable PARUNION is used to hold successive values of the partial union of SET1 and SET2, as more and more elements of SET1 are considered. This example shows that SETQ can be also used to change the values of LAMBDA variables.

7.4.2 LAST

```
(LAST (LAMBDA (LIS) (PROG ()
 LOOP (COND ((NULL (CDR LIS)) (RETURN (CAR LIS))))
      (SETQ LIS (CDR LIS))
      (GO LOOP)
        )))
```

It is assumed that the LENGTH of the LISt that is the argument of LAST is at least 1.

7.4.3 *FACTORIAL*

```
(FACTORIAL (LAMBDA (NUM)
 (PROG (PARVAL)
       (SETQ PARVAL 1)
  LOOP (COND ((ZEROP NUM) (RETURN PARVAL)))
       (SETQ PARVAL (TIMES NUM PARVAL))
       (SETQ NUM (SUB1 NUM))
       (GO LOOP))))
```

It is important to initialize PARVAL, the partial value of FACTORIAL, before we count NUM down to zero.

7.4.4 *LENGTH*

```
(LENGTH (LAMBDA (LIS)
 (PROG (PARCOUNT)
       (SETQ PARCOUNT 0)
  LOOP (COND ((NULL LIS) (RETURN PARCOUNT))
             (T (SETQ PARCOUNT (ADD1 PARCOUNT))))
       (SETQ LIS (CDR LIS))
       (GO LOOP))))
```

Notice that the recursive definitions, for the above four functions, were more compact and elegant, and involved less bookkeeping.

EXERCISE

In some LISP systems, some programs written as loops, using PROG, are executed more efficiently than programs written recursively. Write a function RECTOLOOP which will have as argument a recursive definition of a function (for example, LAST in Section 5.2.1) and will have as value a looping definition of the function, using PROG (for example, LAST in Section 7.4.2). Describe the range of functions that your RECTOLOOP can translate from recursive to looping form. It should work at least on the recursive definitions of the four functions defined, using PROG, in Section 7.4. Run the obtained new definitions using DEFINE and EVAL.

This is not a trivial exercise, but it is not very difficult either. It is an example of a LISP function, RECTOLOOP, taking another LISP function (for example, LAST), producing a new LISP function—call it LAST1—and then running this new function on some arguments.

7.5 MAP and MAPC

Using PROG, it is possible to define two additional MAP functions that are found in many LISP systems: MAP and MAPC.

7.5.1 MAPC

MAPC is like MAPCAR in that successive SEXes of a list are given to a functional argument. MAPC differs from MAPCAR in that MAPC does not return a list of the values of the functional argument on the successive SEXes; instead, in MAPC only the effect of the functional argument counts.

```
(MAPC (LAMBDA (LIS FUN) (PROG ()
        LOOP (COND ((NULL LIS) (RETURN NIL)))
             (FUN (CAR LIS))
             (SETQ LIS (CDR LIS)) (GO LOOP)
           )))
```

With the help of MAPC, it is easy to define COUNTNUMBERS, a function which sums the numbers appearing at the top level of a list:

```
COUNTNUMBERS  ((2 NUDISTS WERE BORN 4 THAT WAY 9))
 VALUE IS...
 15
```

A definition of COUNTNUMBERS is

```
(COUNTNUMBERS (LAMBDA (LIS)
  (PROG (COUNT)
   (SETQ COUNT 0)
   (MAPC LIS
    (FUNCTION (LAMBDA (LISELEM)
      (COND ((NUMBERP LISELEM) (SETQ COUNT (PLUS COUNT LISELEM)))
            (T NIL)))))
   (RETURN COUNT) )))
```

First, COUNT is initialized to zero. Next, the list LIS is traversed, and if an element of the list is a number, it is added to COUNT. If the element of LIS is not a number, nothing is done, and the value of the functional argument has been taken to be NIL. Any other value would be fine. Finally, the value of COUNT is RETURNed as the value of the PROG, and hence of the function COUNTNUMBERS.

7.5.2 MAP

MAP is like MAPC except that the LISt and its successive CDR's are given to the functional argument.

```
(MAP (LAMBDA (LIS FUN) (PROG ()
    LOOP (COND ((NULL LIS ) (RETURN NIL)))
        (FUN LIS)
        (SETQ LIS (CDR LIS)) (GO LOOP)
        )))
```

EXERCISE

Use MAP to give a new version of MAKESET.

We shall see some additional uses of MAPC in the next chapter.

7.6 Generators†

The MAP functions have the common characteristic that the functional argument is applied successively to *all* the parts of a list, these parts generally being either successive SEXes or successive CDR's. In some cases, we wish to apply a functional argument to successive parts of a list (or of several lists), but we may wish to stop after a while. As an example, let us consider the predicate SUBSET of two sets SET1 and SET2. SUBSET has value T if all the elements of SET1 are also elements of SET2; otherwise the value is NIL. One version of SUBSET consists of going down SET1 and, for the successive SEXes of SET1, testing whether the SEX is a MEMBER of SET2. However, as soon as we have found a SEX that is not a member of SET2, there is no need to continue, since the value of SUBSET is known to be NIL.

It is desirable, therefore, to modify the MAP functions. We shall call these modified functions *generators*. In a generator, the functional argument can stop the generator by sending it an appropriate signal. In terms of the party game analogy, the functional argument may tell the generator that it does not wish to receive any further balls to play with. Generators may be built similar to MAPCAR, the generator keeping all the values returned by the playmate (the functional argument), or they may be built

†The influence of IPL (see A. Newell et al. *Information Processing Language-V Manual*, 2nd ed., Prentice-Hall, Inc., Englewood Cliffs, N.J., 1964) is obvious in our description of generators.

similar to MAPC, the generator indicating only whether it has been stopped or not.

7.6.1 GENC

GENC is similar to MAPC in that the effect, and not the value, of the functional argument is important. We shall use the convention that if the functional argument returns T† to the generator GENC, this means that it wants further SEXes of the list to process. Conversely, a value of NIL sent by the functional argument to GENC tells the generator that it should stop sending further SEXes to the exhausted functional argument. Furthermore, we shall use the convention that the value of GENC is T if it has not been stopped, i.e., if it has sent all SEXes, one after the other, to the insatiable functional argument; otherwise, if the generator has been stopped, its value is NIL.

```
(GENC (LAMBDA (LIS FUN) (PROG (FUNVALUE)
      LOOP (COND ((NULL LIS) (RETURN T)))
           (SETQ FUNVALUE (FUN (CAR LIS)))
           (COND ((NULL FUNVALUE) (RETURN NIL)))
           (SETQ LIS (CDR LIS)) (GO LOOP)
      )))
```

If the LISt is empty, or has become empty, then the generator was not stopped, and its value is T. Otherwise, we store the value of the functional argument in FUNVALUE, and check whether it is NIL. If it is NIL, the generator is stopped with value NIL. If the functional argument wants the generator to continue, then the CDR of the LISt is taken, and evaluation returns to LOOP.

EXERCISE

Define GENC without using PROG.

7.6.1.1 SUBSET

With GENC, it is almost trivial to define SUBSET.

```
(SUBSET (LAMBDA (SET1 SET2)
        (GENC SET1 (FUNCTION (LAMBDA (SET1ELEM)
                   (COND ((MEMSET SET1ELEM SET2) T)
                        (T NIL)))))))
```

†Or more generally, not NIL.

If the element of SET1 is found in SET2, the generator is asked to continue; hence the value of the functional argument is T. But as soon as an element of SET1 is not found in SET2, the value of the functional argument is NIL, the generator is turned off, and its value is NIL—which is the value of SUBSET. If the generator was not stopped, its value is T, and that is also the value of SUBSET.

7.6.1.2 MEMSET

It is easy to define MEMSET using GENC, but it is convenient to define first a function NOT:

```
(NOT (LAMBDA (SEX) (COND ( (EQ SEX NIL) T)
                        (T NIL) ) ) )
```

NOT is usually available in LISP systems as a built-in function.

§

```
Function:  NOT
Number of arguments:  1
Argument:  any SEX
Value:  T if SEX has value NIL;
        otherwise NIL
```

Notice that NOT behaves exactly like NULL.

We can now define MEMSET:

```
(MEMSET (LAMBDA (ATM LIS)
    (NOT (GENC LIS (FUNCTION (LAMBDA (LISELEM)
                        (NOT (EQ ATM LISELEM) ) ) ) ) ) ) )
```

If an element of LIS is found EQual to the value of ATM, then the generator should be turned off—hence the NOT in (NOT (EQ ATM LISELEM)). If the generator has been stopped, then the value of GENC is NIL, but the value of MEMSET should be T; therefore another NOT is used to change the value of GENC.

This definition is more complicated than the recursive definition given in Section 5.1, but it serves to illustrate the need for reversing the value of GENC or of its functional argument from T to NIL or from NIL to T.

EXERCISES

1. Define a predicate ALLNUMS, which has value T if all its SEXes are numbers, and otherwise value NIL. Use GENC.

```
ALLNUMS ( (7 4 3 9) )
  VALUE IS...
  T
```

2. Use GENC to define the predicate EQSET, which has value T if two sets are equal, and otherwise value NIL.

```
EQSET ( (INHUMAN ACTS ARE HUMAN MISTAKES)
         (HUMAN ACTS ARE INHUMAN MISTAKES) )
 VALUE IS . . .
 T


EQSET ( (PESSIMISTS KNEW OPTIMISTS) (OPTIMISTS KNOW PESSIMISTS) )
 VALUE IS . . .
 NIL
```

3. Define a generator GEN, which is similar to GENC (except that the functional argument is applied to the list and its successive CDR's—at least until the functional argument is used to stop the generator). Use GEN to define the predicate ISASET, which has value T if a simple list is a set, and otherwise value NIL.

```
ISASET ( (FAIR FAT FORTY AND FORTUNATE) )
 VALUE IS . . .
 T

ISASET ( (HOP ON HOP PORTUNITY) )
 VALUE IS . . .
 NIL
```

4. Define the constant DIC to have as value a fairly large list of several dictionaries (as used in Section 6.6). Using the constant DIC, test your programs for the following functions:
a. Is some atom the translation of anything in one of the dictionaries? Use GENC.
b. What is the translation of some atom according to one of the dictionaries? Modify GENC to answer this question.
c. Is ATM1 the translation of ATM2 in any one of the dictionaries? Use GENC.
d. How many different animals have some given ATM as their translation if all dictionaries are taken into account? (Is it more appropriate to use a generator or a MAP function?)
e. Does some ATM occur more than three times as the translation of something in the dictionaries? (Is it more appropriate to use a generator or a MAP function?)

7.7 FOR and Similar Statements

Languages such as ALGOL, PASCAL, and PL/1 have a control structure very similar to that of the LISP PROG. In addition, they include a variety of statements which permit the repetition of some computation.

The ALGOL FOR statement is of the form

FOR I := FROM **STEP** BY **UNTIL** FINAL **DO** stat;

where I is an integer-valued variable, ':=' is used for assignment statements and is similar to SETQ, and FROM, BY, and FINAL are expressions having numeric values. The statement stat is executed for values of I starting at FROM, incremented in steps of BY until finally the value of I surpasses FINAL. (There are some subtle points to consider if I, FROM, BY, and FINAL can be changed in stat. For the moment, we assume BY to be positive.)

Let us write a function FORSTEP which behaves like the above ALGOL FOR:

```
(FORSTEP (LAMBDA (I FROM BY FINAL STAT)
        (SETQ I FROM)
    LOOP (COND ((GREATERP I FINAL) (RETURN NIL)))
        (STAT)
        (SETQ I (PLUS I BY)) (GO LOOP))))
```

I is initialized to FROM. If FROM is already greater than FINAL, nothing happens. Otherwise, we execute STAT, and I is incremented by BY. Notice that I is a variable global to the functional argument STAT.

EXERCISES

1. Apply FORSTEP to two examples of your own making.

2. Implement FORSTEP without using PROG. Remember that I is a variable the value of which will be used in STAT. Apply FORSTEP to two examples of your own making.

3. The British Computer Programming Language (BCPL) includes the following forms of repeated statements:

Statement	Meaning
a. Stat **REPEAT**	Repeat stat.
b. Stat **REPEATWHILE** bool	Repeat stat while bool is true.
c. Stat **REPEATUNTIL** bool	Repeat stat until bool becomes true.
d. **WHILE** bool **DO** stat	While bool is true, do stat.
e. **UNTIL** bool **DO** stat	Do stat until bool is true.

In the above, stat is a statement (possibly a whole program) in the language, and bool is a Boolean expression; i.e., it has value true or false. Design and program LISP equivalents to the above expressions, giving both recursive and iterative versions of the programs. Apply each version to two examples of your own making.

8

PROPERTY LISTS

The wife of our old friend Phf has become pregnant.† Since she and Phf do not know whether it will be a boy or a girl, they have decided to select a biSEXual first name for their child. Such a name would do equally well for a boy or a girl. It might also do for a dog, but that is beside the point. Phf has forgotten that NIL is biSEXual, so he has borrowed a friend's *Webster Encyclopedic Dictionary of the English Language and Compendium of Usable Knowledge,*‡ which lists about 1000 names for boys and about 1000 names for girls. Phf plans to make a list of all the boys' names and another list of all the girls' names, and then use the LISP function INTERSECTION to find which names are common to both lists.

Happily enough, Phf talked to a student who was learning LISP and was told that his approach would be too time-consuming. Look at the definitions of INTERSECTION and MEMSET:

```
(INTERSECTION (LAMBDA (SET1 SET2)
 (COND ( (NULL SET1) NIL)
       ( (MEMSET (CAR SET1) SET2)
         (CONS (CAR SET1) (INTERSECTION (CDR SET1) SET2)))
       (T (INTERSECTION (CDR SET1) SET2)) )))
(MEMSET (LAMBDA (SEX SETT)
        (COND ( (NULL SETT) NIL)
```

†Phf does not understand how that could have happened. However, since this is a book on LISP, Phf's problems are not within our sphere of interests.

‡Consolidated Book Publishers, Chicago, 1965.

114

```
( (EQ SEX (CAR SETT) ) T)
(T (MEMSET SEX (CDR SETT) ) ) ) )  ) )
```

The student remarked, "In most cases, a boy's name will not be a girl's name; hence the value of MEMSET will be NIL. Since MEMSET has value NIL only if the whole of SET2 has been considered (i.e., if every girl's name was looked at), it follows that for almost every boy's name there will be as many comparisons in MEMSET as there are girls' names. Since there are some 1000 boys' names and some 1000 girls' names, MEMSET will call EQ about 1000 $\times$ 1000 times, or 1 million times. There are more efficient ways of defining INTERSECTION."

8.1 PUTPROP, GET, and REMPROP

The student was referring to the use of property lists. In LISP, it is possible to associate with each atom what is called a property list.[†] Let us assume that Phf has chosen the biSEXual name CAMILLE. With CAMILLE we associate a property list describing some interesting information about CAMILLE. The FATHER of CAMILLE is PHF, and its SIBLINGS are (VIVIAN VIVIEN WYN WYNNE). On the atom CAMILLE we place the *indicator* FATHER with *property* PHF and the indicator SIBLINGS with property the list (VIVIAN VIVIEN WYN WYNNE). The function that places an indicator and its property on an atom is PUTPROP.

§
√o
√n

Function: PUTPROP (ATM INDIC PROP)
Number of arguments: 3
Arguments: first: an atom; second: an atomic indicator; third: a SEX property
Value: the first argument
Effect: the indicator, with its property, is placed on the atom

In some systems the value of PUTPROP is one of the other arguments of PUTPROP.

In EV-LISP, the programs would be

```
(PUTPROP (QUOTE CAMILLE) (QUOTE FATHER) (QUOTE PHF) )
VALUE IS...
CAMILLE
```

†This is a misnomer, since in some systems property lists are not lists.

```
(PUTPROP (QUOTE CAMILLE) (QUOTE SIBLINGS) (QUOTE (VIVIAN
          VIVIEN WYN WYNNE) ) )
 VALUE IS . . .
 CAMILLE
```

Notice that the indicator must be an atom.

　　To find out the property of an indicator, the function GET is used. After the above programs, here are some results of GET in EVQ-LISP:

```
GET  (CAMILLE FATHER)
 VALUE IS . . .
 PHF·
```

```
GET  (CAMILLE SIBLINGS)
 VALUE IS . . .
 (VIVIAN VIVIEN WYN WYNNE)
```

```
GET  (CAMILLE FATHER)
 VALUE IS . . .
 PHF
```

```
GET  (CAMILLE MOTHER)
 VALUE IS . . .
 NIL
```

The third example shows that GET does not modify the property list, while the last example indicates either that no indicator MOTHER was found on the property list of CAMILLE or that the indicator MOTHER was found and had property NIL. It is best never to use the property NIL for an indicator, since GET cannot distinguish this case from the case where no indicator is found.

　　Phf's wife poisons him and then marries Fph, who adopts CAMILLE. A new property for the indicator FATHER is needed. An execution† of PUTPROP will do:

```
PUTPROP  (CAMILLE FATHER FPH)
 VALUE IS . . .
 CAMILLE
```

After this program, we have

```
GET  (CAMILLE FATHER)
 VALUE IS . . .
 FPH
```

　　†Hehe!

S

```
Function:  GET (ATM INDIC)

Number of arguments:  2

Arguments:  an atom and a possible
            indicator (also an atom)

Value:  the property of the indicator, or
        NIL if no such indicator is found
```

Our heroin,† Fph's wife, stabs her new husband to death, leaving CAMILLE without a father. REMPROP will remove an indicator from an atom.

```
REMPROP  (CAMILLE FATHER)
  VALUE IS...
  T


GET  (CAMILLE FATHER)
  VALUE IS...
  NIL


REMPROP  (CAMILLE FATHER)
  VALUE IS...
  NIL
```

REMPROP has value T if the indicator was found; otherwise the value is NIL.

S
✓

```
Function:  REMPROP (ATM INDIC)

Number of arguments:  2

Arguments:  an atom and a possible
            indicator (also an atom)

Value:  T if the indicator is found;
        NIL otherwise

Effect:  the indicator and its property
         are removed from the atom
```

8.1.1 Property List Terminology

The terminology for property lists has some variants. Instead of the pairs indicator-property, the following pairs are also commonly used: attribute-value and property-property value. Moreover, in some LISP systems, the second and third arguments of PUTPROP are reversed. Finally, for those

†Heroine?

systems that have DEFLIST but not PUTPROP, here is a definition of PUTPROP:

```
(PUTPROP (LAMBDA (ATM INDIC PROP)
         (DEFLIST (LIST (LIST ATM PROP)) INDIC)))
```

Some systems have a function called PUT instead of PUTPROP.

8.2 INTERSECTION Revisited

We are now ready to solve Phf's original problem. On each girl's name, we put the indicator SEEN with property T. Then we ask whether any of the boys' names have been SEEN already. If the answer is T, such a name is biSEXual; otherwise it is not. Finally, we remove the indicator SEEN from each of the girl's names, so as not to leave "garbage" behind.

```
(BISEXUAL (LAMBDA (BOYSNAMES GIRLSNAMES)
 (PROG (BISEX)
  (MAPC GIRLSNAMES
   (FUNCTION (LAMBDA (GIRLNAME) (PUTPROP GIRLNAME (QUOTE SEEN) T))))
  (MAPC BOYSNAMES
   (FUNCTION (LAMBDA (BOYNAME)
     (COND ((GET BOYNAME (QUOTE SEEN)) (SETQ BISEX (CONS BOYNAME BISEX)))
           (T NIL)))))
  (MAPC GIRLSNAMES
   (FUNCTION (LAMBDA (GIRLNAME) (REMPROP GIRLNAME (QUOTE SEEN)))))
  (RETURN BISEX))))
```

The third MAPC, which removes indicators that are no longer needed, is very important and is too often forgotten. The function BISEXUAL is really INTERSECTION. If we write a bad version of INTERSECTION, BADIN, without the cleanup of indicators, then funny things happen:

```
(BADIN (LAMBDA (SET1 SET2)
 (PROG (PARINT)
  (MAPC SET2
   (FUNCTION (LAMBDA (SET2ELEM) (PUTPROP SET2ELEM (QUOTE SEEN) T))))
  (MAPC SET1
   (FUNCTION (LAMBDA (SET1ELEM)
     (COND ((GET SET1ELEM (QUOTE SEEN))
                 (SETQ PARINT (CONS SET1ELEM PARINT)))
           (T NIL)))))
  (RETURN PARINT)))

BADIN (() (NOSELESS FISH DONT SMELL))
VALUE IS...
NIL
```

```
BADIN ( (NOSELESS FISH DONT SMELL) () )
    VALUE IS . . .
    (SMELL DONT FISH NOSELESS)
```

During the first call to BADIN, the four atoms NOSELESS, FISH, DONT, and SMELL receive the indicator SEEN with property T. These indicators are not erased by BADIN, and therefore, during the second call to BADIN, each of the elements of SET1, (NOSELESS FISH DONT SMELL), has already been SEEN. Hence the value of BADIN is the list (SMELL DONT FISH NOSELESS), since successive contributions to PARINT are CONSed in front of PARINT. The bad result is that the intersection of a set with the empty set is not necessarily the empty set.

The suspense has been awful. Reader, you must be chewing your wrist by now, waiting for the answer. In about 2 seconds on the CDC 6600, we ascertained that the only biSEXual names were

(WYNNE WYN VIVIEN VIVIAN MERLE MEREDITH MARION LYNN KERETH JEAN GALE GAIL ENDREDE CAROL CAMILLE)

EXERCISES

1. Show that if the INTERSECTION of two sets, having M and N elements, respectively, is computed, then the effort of the above version of INTERSECTION is of the order of M + N, while the effort for the previous definitions of INTERSECTION is of the order of M × N. If M = N = 1000, there is a huge difference between 2000 and 1 million. Obtain more precise estimates.

2. Using property lists, write very efficient versions of

a. UNION

b. SETDIFF

c. SUBSET

d. EQSET

e. MAKESET

Notice that in each case property lists are used to replace calls to MEMBER, or a similar function.

3. Define a function (PUTPROPLIST (LAMBDA (SIMPLELIST INDIC PROP) . . .)) which puts the indicator INDIC with property PROP on each of the atoms of the simple list SIMPLELIST.

4. Define a function (REMPROPLIST (LAMBDA (SIMPLELIST INDIC) . . .)) which removes the indicator INDIC from each of the atoms of the simple list SIMPLELIST.

8.3   EXPR Function Definitions and LABEL

In many LISP systems, when a function is DEFINEd, the LAMBDA expression defining the function becomes the property of the indicator EXPR (for EXPRession) on the property list of the atom naming the function. For example, in EVQ-LISP, the effect of the program

```
DEFINE ( (
(DONOTHING (LAMBDA (SEX) SEX) )
) )
```

is equivalent to the program

```
PUTPROP (DONOTHING EXPR (LAMBDA (SEX) SEX) )
```

Both programs define the function DONOTHING. The values of the programs are different, though. The first value is (DONOTHING); the second is (LAMBDA (SEX) SEX). However, the values are not important here, since presumably we are interested chiefly in defining DONOTHING. Therefore the effect of DEFINE is equivalent to

```
(LAMBDA (LISTOFFUNS)
        (MAPC LISTOFFUNS (FUNCTION (LAMBDA (FUNDEF)
                            (PUTPROP (CAR FUNDEF) (QUOTE EXPR)
                                (CADR FUNDEF) ) ) ) ) )
```

Like DEFINE, the LAMBDA expression takes a list of function definitions as arguments and does a PUTPROP of the LAMBDA expression, defining a function on the name of each function. Again, we notice that the *value* of DEFINE is not the same as that of the above LAMBDA expression.

EXERCISES

1.   Use a single DEFINE to define FIRST, SECOND, and THIRD (see Chapter 2), and then GET the EXPR of each of the atoms FIRST, SECOND, and THIRD to verify the workings of DEFINE.

2.   Assuming that you have PUTPROP but not DEFINE, use PUTPROP to define DEFINE so that your definition OTHERDEFINE will have the same effect and value as the usual DEFINE.

3.   Since the property of the indicator EXPR of an atom that has been DEFINEd as a function is a list, the LAMBDA expression of the definition, the definition of the function can be manipulated. Define the following functions that explicitly change the definition of a function:

a. TRACE takes as argument a list of function names DEFINEd by the user. The behavior of a TRACEd function is shown in Section 4.7.

b. UNTRACE undoes what TRACE has done.

c. TRACESET modifies a list of functions with PROG. Every time a LAMBDA or PROG variable of one of the functions is modified inside the function by SET or SETQ, TRACESET will PRINT something like

```
FUNCTION : BLAH; VARIABLE NAME : GLOOP;
  OLD VALUE : (BE WITH A FOOL); NEW VALUE : (FOOL WITH A BEE);
```

d. UNTRACESET undoes what TRACESET has done.

Since property lists remain on atoms unless they are removed by REMPROP, functions which are no longer used take up space in the memory of the computer. There are several ways to reclaim the space taken up by function definitions. The indicator EXPR of the name of the function can be REMPROPed. Or a LAMBDA expression may have been substituted for the function, as we saw in Section 6.2. In this way the function is never DEFINEd actually. However, if the definition of the function was recursive, the function cannot be replaced by its LAMBDA expression, as is illustrated by the definition of the function LAST:

```
(LAST (LAMBDA (LIS)
      (COND ((NULL (CDR LIS)) (CAR LIS))
            (T (LAST (CDR LIS)))))))
```

The LAMBDA expression defining the function LAST is

```
(LAMBDA (LIS)
       (COND ((NULL (CDR LIS)) (CAR LIS))
             (T (LAST (CDR LIS))))))
```

and this LAMBDA expression contains a reference to the function LAST in the second right of the COND. When the LAMBDA expression is executed, the function LAST will be called, and an error will result if a definition for LAST is not found.

8.3.1 *LABEL and Temporary Function Definitions*

It is possible to write recursive definitions without using DEFINE, by a slight extension of the LAMBDA expression, with the help of the LABEL convention. LAST could be rewritten

```
(LABEL LAST (LAMBDA (LIS)
            (COND ((NULL (CDR LIS)) (CAR LIS))
                  (T (LAST CDR LIS)))))))
```

Let us consider the following program in EVQ-LISP:

```
LAST ( (JUMP A DOWNED MAN) )

(LABEL LAST (LAMBDA (LIS) (COND ( (NULL (CDR LIS) ) (CAR LIS) )
                                (T (LAST (CDR LIS) ) ) ) ) )
( (ORGY IS GROUP THERAPY) )
VALUE IS...
THERAPY

LAST ( (BE GOOD OR CAREFUL) )
```

If we assume that LAST is not a system function,† then the first program, LAST ((JUMP A DOWNED MAN)), will result in an error, since LAST is not a known function to the system. The second program will have as value THERAPY. The third program, LAST ((BE GOOD OR CAREFUL)), will *also* result in an error, since the function LAST has been forgotten by the LISP system. Therefore, LABEL is a way to define recursive functions that will be used only once, while DEFINE assures a more permanent definition of functions.

§ *8.3.2. REMOB*

A drastic way of purging a program of a function that was DEFINEd previously is to remove from the system the atom that is the name of the function. For example, after defining the function DONOTHING and running it in EV-LISP, we may simply delete the atom DONOTHING from the system by using the function REMOB (for REMove OBject):

```
(DEFINE (QUOTE ( (DONOTHING (LAMBDA (SEX) SEX) ) ) ))
VALUE IS...
(DONOTHING)

(DONOTHING (QUOTE (A FIVE CENT SAGA) ) )
VALUE IS...
(A FIVE CENT SAGA)

(REMOB (QUOTE DONOTHING) )
VALUE IS...
NIL
```

At this point, trying to run the program

```
(DONOTHING (QUOTE (NECK OR NOTHING) ) )
```

†If it is, change LAST to LASSST in the above programs.

will result in an error. Previous to this program, the atom DONOTHING was killed and disappeared from the LISP system. It was then read again by READ (remember how EV-LISP works; Section 7.1), but whatever was true of the old, now dead, DONOTHING—in particular that it had an EXPR—is not true of the new DONOTHING. More generally, if an atom which has just been REMOBed is still mentioned in some places, for example, in a list, some real catastrophes may occur, since the atom just does not exist any longer. REMOB should be used with caution. The next exercise should demonstrate how your system reacts.

§

Function: REMOB (ATM)
Number of arguments: 1
Argument: an atom
Effect: the atom is removed from the system
Value: irrelevant, usually NIL

EXERCISE

To test REMOB, do the following operations in succession:

a. SET the constant BAHH to have as value the list

(ANGER HELPS COMPLEXION SAVES PAINT)

b. REMOB two of the atoms of the list, for example, HELPS and SAVES.

c. PRINT the list. How did your LISP react?

d. Run the programs (MEMBER (QUOTE ANGER) BAHH) and (MEMBER (QUOTE HELPS) BAHH). What happened?

8.4 An Application: Substitution Instances

In many applications such as theorem proving, or, more generally, formula manipulation, it is desirable to determine whether some formula SIFORM is a substitution instance of some other formula FORM. We assume that the formulae are written in LISP notation; for example, the formula FORM might be

(TIMES X (PLUS 5 Y X) (MINUS Z) (TIMES 6 X 9))

In this formula, there are the following functions: TIMES, PLUS, and MINUS; constants: 5, 6, and 9; and variables: X, Y, and Z. A substitution instance of the above FORM would be obtained if we replace each of the variables in FORM by formulae. The simplest substitution instance of FORM would replace X by X, Y by Y, and Z by Z, to obtain

(TIMES X (PLUS 5 Y X) (MINUS Z) (TIMES 6 X 9))

which is the original formula. A more complicated substitution would replace X by

(TIMES Y 4), Y by X and Z by (PLUS X Y)

to give

(TIMES (TIMES Y 4) (PLUS 5 X (TIMES Y 4)) (MINUS (PLUS X Y)) (TIMES 6 (TIMES Y 4) 9))

Note that the following are *not* substitution instances of FORM:

1. (TIMES X (PLUS 6 Y X) (MINUS Z) (TIMES 6 X 9)), since we cannot replace a constant by something else;
2. (TIMES (TIMES Y 4) (PLUS 5 Y (TIMES Y 4)) (MINUS Z) (TIMES 6 (TIMES Y 3) 9)), since the first two occurrences of X in FORM were replaced by the formula (TIMES Y 4), while the last occurrence was replaced by (TIMES Y 3).
3. (TIMES X (PLUS 5 X Y) (MINUS Z) (TIMES 6 X 9)), since the first X was replaced by X, but the second X by Y. In arithmetic, the two formulae would have the same value, but neither is a substitution instance of the other.

Now that we understand substitution instances, we shall write a function (SUBINST (LAMBDA (SIFORM FORM) ...)) which will have as value T if (the value of) SIFORM is a substitution instance of (the value of) FORM; otherwise the value will be NIL. We assume that we have a predicate (VARIABLE (LAMBDA (ATM) ...)) which has value T if the value of ATM is a variable, and NIL otherwise.

An easy way to define the function VARIABLE is first to put on all the variables that could occur in a formula the indicator VARIABLE with property T. For instance, if X, Y, Z, U, V, and W are the only expected variables, we could execute the program

(PUTPROPLIST (QUOTE(X Y Z U V W)) (QUOTE VARIABLE) T)

We can now define VARIABLE:

(VARIABLE (LAMBDA (ATM)
          (GET ATM (QUOTE VARIABLE)))))

How could SIFORM fail to be a substitution instance of FORM? This could happen if, in the "corresponding" places,

a.   FORM has a function name but SIFORM does not. Keeping FORM as at the beginning of this section, an example would be

(TIMES X Y (MINUS Z) (TIMES 6 X 9))

b.   FORM has a function name but SIFORM has a different function name:

(TIMES X (TIMES 5 Y X) (MINUS Z) (TIMES 6 X 9))

c.   The function names are the same but the number of arguments are not:

(TIMES X (PLUS 5 Y X 6) (MINUS Z) (TIMES 6 X 9))

    or

(TIMES X (PLUS 5 Y X) (MINUS Z) (TIMES 6 X))

d.   A substitution for a constant is attempted:

(TIMES X (PLUS X Y X) (MINUS Z) (TIMES 6 X 9))

e.   A different substitution for a variable is necessary:

(TIMES (PLUS 5 X) (PLUS 5 Y (PLUS X 5)) (MINUS Z) (TIMES 6 X 9))

The first X in FORM must be replaced by (PLUS 5 X), while the second should be replaced by (PLUS X 5), which is not identical.

In SUBINST, we shall put the indicator SUBVALUE on a variable with property the first substitution that is found to be necessary.

We are now ready to start defining SUBINST. The simplest case occurs when FORM is an atom:

```
(SUBINST (LAMBDA (SIFORM FORM)
    (COND ( (ATOM FORM)
                (COND ( (NUMBERP FORM) (EQUAL FORM SIFORM) )
                      ( (VARIABLE FORM) (CHECKINST SIFORM FORM) )†
                      (T (EQ FORM SIFORM) ) ) )
          ( (ATOM SIFORM) NIL)
```

†On some LISP systems, numbers are atoms without property lists. Hence the function VARIABLE may result in an error message for numbers.

The above code shows that if FORM is an atom, we must distinguish between the possibilities of FORM being a variable or a constant. If a constant, FORM must be EQUAL to SIFORM; if a variable, we use an auxiliary function CHECKINST to verify that either FORM had no substitution for it, in which case SIFORM becomes that new substitution, or if FORM already had a substitution, that this substitution is EQUAL to SIFORM. If FORM is not an atom, but SIFORM is, clearly SUBINST must fail. We continue with the case when both SIFORM and FORM are expressions, i.e., lists of a function name followed by the arguments of the function:

```
( (EQ (CAR SIFORM) (CAR FORM) )
  (GODOWNBOTH (CDR SIFORM) (CDR FORM) (FUNCTION SUBINST) ) )
(T NIL) ) ) )
```

The two functions must, of course, be the same, and when they are, each of the arguments in SIFORM must be a substitution instance of the corresponding argument in FORM. GODOWNBOTH will pick up the arguments one by one and also make sure that the number of arguments is the same in both SIFORM and FORM.

```
(GODOWNBOTH (LAMBDA (SIFORMARGS FORMARGS FUN)
      (COND ( (NULL FORMARGS) (NULL SIFORMARGS) )
            ( (NULL SIFORMARGS) NIL)
            ( (FUN (CAR SIFORMARGS) (CAR FORMARGS) )
             (GODOWNBOTH (CDR SIFORMARGS) (CDR FORMARGS) FUN) )
            (T NIL) ) ) )
```

GODOWNBOTH should have been called DOUBLEGENC for uniformity.

Finally, we need to DEFINE the function CHECKINST:

```
(CHECKINST (LAMBDA (SIFORM VAR)
     (COND ( (NULL (GET VAR (QUOTE SUBVALUE) ) )
           (PUTPROP VAR (QUOTE SUBVALUE) SIFORM) )
          (T (EQUAL (GET VAR (QUOTE SUBVALUE) ) SIFORM) ) ) ) )
```

Another way to define CHECKINST would avoid the two calls to GET:

```
(CHECKINST (LAMBDA (SIFORM VAR) (PROG (PROP)
    (RETURN (COND ( (NULL (SETQ PROP (GET VAR (QUOTE SUBVALUE) ) ) )
                  (PUTPROP VAR (QUOTE SUBVALUE) SIFORM) )
                 (T (EQUAL PROP SIFORM) ) ) ) ) ) )
```

In many systems, though, the second program would run slower, since the bookkeeping associated with PROGs (PROG variables, labels, etc.) is usually expensive.

EXERCISE

Define a function (SOMESUBINST (LAMBDA (FORMONE FORM-TWO) ...)) which has values

Value	Condition
ONE	FORMONE is a SI of FORMTWO but not vice versa
TWO	FORMTWO is a SI of FORMONE but not vice versa
T	FORMONE is a SI of FORMTWO and vice versa
NIL	Neither FORMONE nor FORMTWO is a SI of the other

Do not use SUBINST directly, but modify it.

9

THE LISP INTERPRETER EVAL

In Chapter 7, the function EVALQUOTE was defined in terms of EVAL. Hence we may consider EVAL as the main function in LISP. In this chapter we shall give a restricted definition of EVAL in terms of the elementary functions (multiple) CAR and CDR, CONS, EQ, and ATOM, and the auxiliary functions QUOTE, COND, and DEFINE. Also we shall assume that the definition of a DEFINEd function can be accessed using GET. With the convention that the empty list () and NIL are the same, NULL is no longer an elementary function:

```
(NULL (LAMBDA (SEX)
       (COND (SEX NIL)
             (T     T) )))
```

This restricted EVAL will handle EXPR definitions of functions and LAMBDA and LABEL forms but not other types of functions (for instance, functions with an indefinite number of arguments, such as LIST), constants, and PROG. Moreover, the definition of EVAL and the other functions used in defining it will assume that the programs given have no errors: In this way, we need not concern ourselves with special tests to detect errors.

Thus we are proposing to write a LISP definition of (a restricted) EVAL. Since EVAL is the universal LISP function, we may also consider that we are defining LISP in LISP. This endeavor is not futile, since understanding the rather short definition of EVAL permits us to understand, at

128

least potentially, any LISP function. Moreover, it would be sufficient to implement the definition of EVAL on a particular machine to obtain a LISP system.

The definition of EVAL will make explicit what we already know about the evaluation of elementary functions, DEFINEd functions, COND, LAMBDA expressions, etc. The only novelty will be the description of an explicit method for handling the values of LAMBDA variables, by means of an Association LIST, the ALIST.

9.1 EVAL

EVAL is DEFINEd in terms of EVAL1, so that past bindings can be kept.

```
(EVAL (LAMBDA (FORM) (EVAL1 FORM NIL) ) )
```

The second argument of EVAL1 is the ALIST, which contains the bindings of LAMBDA variables.†

```
(EVAL1 ( LAMBDA (FORM ALIST)
(COND ( (ATOM FORM)
        (COND ( (EQ FORM (QUOTE T) ) T)
              ( (EQ FORM (QUOTE NIL) ) NIL)
              (T (CADR (ASSOC FORM ALIST) ) ) ) )
```

If the atomic form is neither of the built-in constants T or NIL, its value is found by searching the ALIST using ASSOC.

```
      ( (ATOM (CAR FORM) )
        (COND ( (EQ (CAR FORM) (QUOTE QUOTE) ) (CADR FORM) )
              ( (EQ (CAR FORM) (QUOTE COND) )
                (EVCON (CDR FORM) ALIST) )
              ( (GET (CAR FORM) (QUOTE EXPR) )
                (APPLY (GET (CAR FORM) (QUOTE EXPR) )
                    (EVLIS (CDR FORM) ALIST)
                    ALIST) )
              (T (APPLY (CAR FORM) (EVLIS (CDR FORM) ALIST) ALIST) ) )  )
        (T (APPLY (CAR FORM) (EVLIS (CDR FORM) ALIST) ALIST) )
  ) ) )
```

In EVAL1, COND is evaluated using EVCON. If we have a DEFINEd function, then its LAMBDA expression is obtained (it will be the property

†Other mechanisms, besides the ALIST, have been used to keep track of variable bindings.

of the indicator EXPR, of the name of the function), and APPLY is called. In the last case, EVLIS will evaluate, using the ALIST, the arguments of the EXPR·function.

9.2 APPLY

Apply is the main workhorse used by EVAL1. APPLY recognizes the elementary functions CAR, CDR, CONS, ATOM, and EQ as well as LAMBDA and LABEL expressions.

```
(APPLY (LAMBDA (FN LARGS ALIST)
```

FN will usually be a function. LARGS is the List of ARGumentS, the arguments having already been evaluated by EVLIS.

```
(COND ((ATOM FN)
      (COND ((EQ FN (QUOTE CAR))    (CAAR LARGS))
            ((EQ FN (QUOTE CDR))    (CDAR LARGS))
            ((EQ FN (QUOTE CONS))  (CONS (CAR LARGS) (CADR LARGS)))
            ((EQ FN (QUOTE ATOM))  (ATOM (CAR LARGS)))
            ((EQ FN (QUOTE EQ))     (EQ (CAR LARGS) (CADR LARGS)))
            (T (APPLY (EVAL1 FN ALIST) LARGS ALIST))))
      ((EQ (CAR FN) (QUOTE LAMBDA)) (EVAL1 (CADDR FN)
                                    (PAIRLIS (CADR FN) LARGS ALIST)))
      ((EQ (CAR FN) (QUOTE LABEL)) (APPLY (CADDR FN) LARGS
                    (CONS (CONS (CADR FN) (CADDR FN)) ALIST)
  ))))))
```

9.3 ASSOC, PAIRLIS, EVCON, and EVLIS

The auxiliary functions employed by EVAL1 and APPLY are ASSOC, EVCON, EVLIS, and PAIRLIS.

ASSOC finds the value of a variable in the ALIST. The ALIST is a list of sublists of two SEXes each of the form (variable value-of-the-variable).† ASSOC finds the first sublist in the ALIST which has variable as its first SEX.

```
(ASSOC (LAMBDA (VAR ALIST)
  (COND ((EQ VAR (CAAR ALIST)) (CAR ALIST))
        (T (ASSOC VAR (CDR ALIST))) ))))
```

†In actual implementations, a dotted pair (variable · value-of-the-variable) would save memory. See Section 10.7.1 for dotted pairs.

PAIRLIS builds up the ALIST by adding sublists of pairs (variable value-of-the-variable). The new sublists are obtained from a LIST OF VARiableS and a corresponding LIST OF VALUES.

```
(PAIRLIS (LAMBDA (LISTOFVARS LISTOFVALUES ALIST)
 (COND ((NULL LISTOFVARS) ALIST)
       (T (CONS (CONS (CAR LISTOFVARS) (CONS (CAR LISTOFVALUES) NIL))
          (PAIRLIS (CDR LISTOFVARS) (CDR LISTOFVALUES) ALIST))))))
```

EVCON helps to evaluate CONDitional expressions. Its first argument is the list of pairs (left to right) of the CONDitional.

```
(EVCON (LAMBDA (LISTOFPAIRS ALIST)
 (COND ((EVAL1 (CAAR LISTOFPAIRS) ALIST) (EVAL1 (CADAR LISTOFPAIRS) ALIST) )
       (T (EVCON (CDR LISTOFPAIRS) ALIST)))))
```

From a list of nonevaluated arguments NONEVALARGS, EVLIS forms the list of the values of the corresponding arguments.

```
(EVLIS (LAMBDA (NONEVALARGS ALIST)
       (COND ((NULL NONEVALARGS) NIL)
             (T (CONS (EVAL1 (CAR NONEVALARGS) ALIST)
                      (EVLIS (CDR NONEVALARGS) ALIST))))))
```

9.4 A Simulation of EVAL

To illustrate the workings of EVAL, we follow the various functions in the evaluation of

```
(MEMQ (QUOTE AT) (QUOTE (GET UP AT DAWN)))
```

where MEMQ is a function DEFINEd as

```
(MEMQ (LAMBDA (ATM LIS)
 (COND ((EQ LIS NIL) NIL)†
       ((EQ ATM (CAR LIS)) LIS)
       (T (MEMQ ATM (CDR LIS))))))
```

Since MEMQ was DEFINEd, it has an indicator EXPR with property the LAMBDA expression of the definition of MEMQ:

```
(LAMBDA (ATM LIS)
 (COND ((EQ LIS NIL) NIL)
       ((EQ ATM (CAR LIS)) LIS)
       (T (MEMQ ATM (CDR LIS)))))
```

†Equivalent to ((NULL LIS) NIL) but chosen since we assumed that NULL was not an elementary function.

EVAL immediately calls EVAL1 with arguments (MEMQ (QUOTE AT) (QUOTE (GET UP AT DAWN))) and NIL. EVAL1 finds that MEMQ has an EXPR and therefore calls APPLY with the three arguments (1) the LAMBDA expression for MEMQ, (2) the value of EVLIS with arguments ((QUOTE AT) (QUOTE (GET UP AT DAWN))) and NIL, and (3) NIL. EVLIS is entered and calls EVAL1 to evaluate (QUOTE AT). EVAL1 recognizes the QUOTE and returns the value AT. The same process occurs for (QUOTE (GET UP AT DAWN)), and the value of EVLIS is (AT (GET UP AT DAWN)).

So we are back at APPLY with arguments the LAMBDA expression for MEMQ, the list (AT (GET UP AT DAWN)), and NIL. APPLY recognizes the LAMBDA and calls EVAL1 with two arguments: first, the CONDitional expression of MEMQ,

```
(COND ( (EQ LIS NIL) NIL)
      ( (EQ ATM (CAR LIS) ) LIS)
      (T (MEMQ ATM (CDR LIS) ) ) )
```

and second, what will be the new ALIST: the value of PAIRLIS with arguments (ATM LIS), (AT (GET UP AT DAWN)), and NIL. The value of PAIRLIS is the new ALIST: ((ATM AT) (LIS (GET UP AT DAWN))).

Where are we? EVAL1 has been called with arguments

```
(COND ( (EQ LIS NIL) NIL) ...) )
```

and the ALIST

```
( (ATM AT) (LIS (GET UP AT DAWN) ) )
```

EVAL1 recognizes the COND and calls EVCON with arguments the list of pairs of the COND:

```
( ( (EQ LIS NIL) NIL) ( (EQ ATM (CAR LIS) ) LIS)
  (T (MEMQ ATM (CDR LIS) ) ) )
```

and the same ALIST. EVCON calls EVAL1 with arguments (EQ LIS NIL) and the ALIST ((ATM AT) (LIS (GET UP AT DAWN))). EVAL1 immediately passes its work to APPLY with the three arguments (1) EQ, (2) the EVLIS of (LIS NIL) and ((ATM AT) (LIS (GET UP AT DAWN))), and (3) the same ALIST.

EVLIS calls EVAL1† with arguments LIS and ((ATM AT) (LIS (GET UP AT DAWN))). EVAL1 calls ASSOC with arguments LIS and the same ALIST. ASSOC has value (LIS (GET UP AT DAWN)), of which EVAL1 takes the CADR, obtaining (GET UP AT DAWN). Next,

†Nobody seems to rest around here.

EVAL1 finds the value of NIL, which is NIL. At that point, the value of EVLIS is obtained; it is ((GET UP AT DAWN) NIL).

Back to APPLY, which recognizes EQ and decides that (GET UP AT DAWN) and NIL are not the same atom. EVCON failed the first time around, so EVCON calls itself recursively with the new arguments ((((EQ ATM (CAR LIS)) LIS) (T (MEMQ ATM (CDR LIS))) and the ALIST ((ATM AT) (LIS (GET UP AT DAWN))).

Moving a little faster, we see that APPLY will take over with the arguments (1) EQ, (2) the EVLIS of (ATM (CAR LIS)), and (3) the ALIST ((ATM AT) (LIS (GET UP AT DAWN))). The evaluation of ATM from the ALIST will be similar to the previous evaluation of LIS and will yield AT. The EVAL1 of (CAR LIS) and the ALIST will call APPLY with arguments CAR, the EVLIS of LIS and the ALIST, and the ALIST. The value of this APPLY will be GET. The previous APPLY has arguments which are now known to be EQ, (AT GET), and ((ATM AT) (LIS (GET UP AT DAWN))). The value of APPLY will be NIL.

We are back to EVCON, which calls itself recursively again with arguments ((T (MEMQ ATM (CDR LIS)))). The value of T being T, as found by EVAL1, EVCON asks for the evaluation of EVAL1 with arguments (MEMQ ATM (CDR LIS)) and ((ATM AT) (LIS (GET UP AT DAWN))). EVAL1 calls APPLY, as before. The second argument of APPLY, as found by EVLIS, is (AT (UP AT DAWN)). APPLY recognizes the LAMBDA expression, and the CONDitional expression goes to EVAL1 with a *new* ALIST built by PAIRLIS: ((ATM AT) (LIS (UP AT DAWN)) (ATM AT) (LIS (GET UP AT DAWN))). Since ASSOC and EVLIS search the ALIST from left to right, the values of ATM and LIS that will be used will be AT and (UP AT DAWN).

Shall we stop? No, put the rest in an exercise.

EXERCISES

1. Terminate the simulation of EVAL in Section 9.4.

2. Often, in function definitions, the recursive call does not modify some of the arguments of the function. For example, in the definition of MEMQ, the recursive call (MEMQ ATM (CDR LIS)) does not modify the first argument ATM. Modify EVAL so that unmodified arguments of functions can be replaced by *. In the above example, we would write (MEMQ * (CDR LIS)). How is your modified EVAL more efficient?

3. The Hopeless language† is a parenthesized language similar to FOR-TRAN and BASIC. Its features can be guessed from a sample Hopeless program:

†Contributed by R. Duda and designed for pedagogical purposes.

```
( (LET  MAX = 10)
  (LET  SUM = 0.0)
  (LET  I = 1)
  (10 LET  SUM = SUM + I)
  (IF SUM LT 4.0 * I — 0.5 THEN  25)
  (PRINT  I ; SUM ; I ↑ 2 / 2.0 ; SUM / (I + 1) )
  (25 LET  I = I + 1)
  (IF I LE MAX GOTO 10)
  (PRINT)
  (PRINT MAX)
  (PRINT)
  (IF SUM LE 60.0 THEN  12)
  (STOP)
  (12 LET  MAX = MAX + 2)
  (GOTO 10) )
```

Hopeless arithmetic expressions use the standard FORTRAN conventions to avoid parentheses. The various arguments of a PRINT are printed on the same line and separated by two slashes: //.

a. From the example, give the syntax and semantics of Hopeless. (The solution may not be unique.)

b. Write a "compiler" for Hopeless programs which translates a Hopeless program into a LISP program, which can then be executed by EVAL. Try to make few passes over the Hopeless program.

c. Write an interpreter in LISP for Hopeless programs.

Note: The "compiler" takes the Hopeless program, translates it into LISP, and runs the LISP program. The interpreter takes one Hopeless statement at a time, executes the statement, and then looks for the next statement to be executed. Given a sufficiently bad program, the compiler would "die" and no results would be output; on the other hand, the interpreter might be able to execute some statements successfully, producing some output, before "dying" in turn.

An important ingredient in Exercises b and c is a translator from infix to prefix notation:

d. Write a program INFTOPRE which transforms infix notation to LISP prefix notation.

Infix Notation	*LISP Prefix Notation*
(4.0 * I — 0.5)	(DIFFERENCE (TIMES 4.0 I) 0.5)
(I ↑ 2 / 2.0)	(QUOTIENT (POWER I 2) 2.0)
(SUM / (I + 1))	(QUOTIENT SUM (PLUS I 1)) or
	(QUOTIENT SUM (ADD1 I))

4. The interpreter described in this chapter does not recognize PROG. Modify it so that PROG will be recognized and correctly evaluated.

5. In the interpreter described in this chapter, the manipulations of the ALIST are left to the system. During processing, the ALIST will become larger and then will shrink as functions have values and no longer need the binding of their arguments. Modify the interpreter to make explicit the manipulation of the ALIST. *Hint:* You may wish to use a stack for storing lists of pairs for bindings.

10

LISP STORAGE STRUCTURES

10.1 The LISP Cell

What does a LISP SEX look like? This chapter will make us play Peeping Toms with LISP and learn to manipulate directly the storage structures used in LISP.

A nonempty list has a CAR and a CDR. In memory, we deal only with addresses of other cells or atoms. The list (MOURNING) is represented by a cell whose CAR is the address of the atom MOURNING and whose CDR is the address of the atom NIL. Conventionally, a LISP cell is represented as a rectangle with a vertical partition in the middle; see Fig. 10.1.

Figure 10.1

If the word in the memory of the computer is sufficiently large, the CAR and the CDR fields may be packed into a single word. For instance, if the fields each require 16 bits and the computer word is 36 bits long, then one word may be used for one LISP cell, with 4 bits left over. If the computer words have a length of 18 bits, two words would be used for a LISP cell.

136

A field which contains an address is referred to as a *pointer* and is usually diagrammed as an arrow pointing out of the field to the item pointed to; see Fig. 10.2. Traditionally, the atom NIL is not pointed to. Instead, the field is crossed diagonally; see Fig. 10.3. The cell was assumed to be computer word 1732.

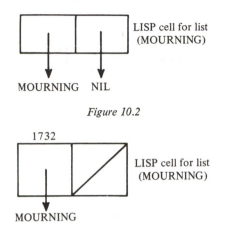

Figure 10.2

Figure 10.3

The memory or *storage structure* for the list (MOURNING IN THE EVENING) is shown in Fig. 10.4, which shows that the CAR of cell 1461 points to the atom MOURNING and that its CDR has value 1914, i.e., points to cell 1914. The car of cell 1914 points to the atom IN, while its CDR points to cell 1918, etc.

The storage structure of the list (((TIME (WOUNDS) ALL) (HEELS))) is shown in Fig. 10.5. Some memory references were given to the various cells. We can better understand the memory structure if we decompose it. The list structure starting at cell 512 would PRINT as (((TIME (WOUNDS) ALL) (HEELS))). Let us list all the structures that can be found in Fig. 10.5:

List Headed by Cell	Would PRINT as
512	(((TIME (WOUNDS) ALL) (HEELS)))
471	((TIME (WOUNDS) ALL) (HEELS))
478	(TIME (WOUNDS) ALL)
7316	((HEELS))
5023	((WOUNDS) ALL)
7317	(ALL)
2574	(HEELS)
441	(WOUNDS)

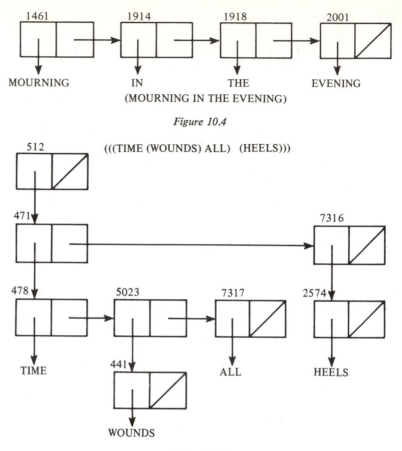

Figure 10.4

Figure 10.5

10.2 Alpha Atoms

Every alpha atom—such as A32G, but not numeric atoms such as 175692—is uniquely remembered by the system. In other words, all pointers to a given atom† point to the same word in memory, as is exemplified in a storage structure for the list (MEAN (MEN MIGHT) (MEAN) MEANS) in Fig. 10.6. Another example is shown in Fig. 10.7. The arrows in Fig. 10.7 show the pointers. For example, the CARs of cells 424 and 103 both point to the atom RIDICULOUS.

The *print name* of an atom is the sequence of characters that "make up" the atom. The print name of A32G is the sequence of the four charac-

†In this section, *atom* will refer to *alpha atom*, i.e., to a nonnumeric atom.

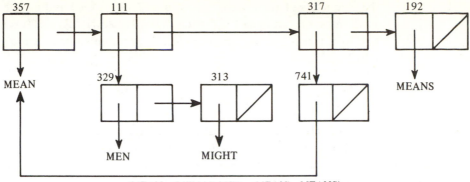

MEAN

MEN   MIGHT

(MEAN   (MEN MIGHT)   (MEAN)   MEANS)

Figure 10.6

(RIDICULOUS   (IN SERIOUS)   THINGS)

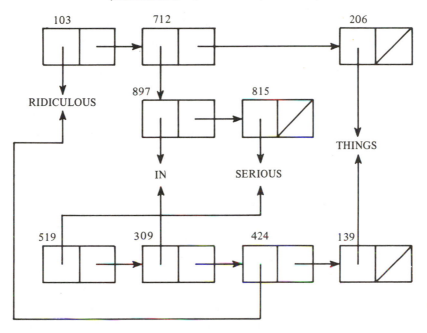

(SERIOUS IN RIDICULOUS THINGS)

Figure 10.7

ters A, 3, 2, and G. When an atom is encountered by the LISP system, generally as the result of an explicit or implicit READ, its print name is compared to the print names of previously encountered atoms which are stored in a special list, the OBLIST. The OBLIST is initialized with all the characters of the system, A through Z, $+$, ., etc., and all the atoms which have a meaning in LISP, such as CAR, LAMBDA, etc. It is instructive to run the following little EV-LISP program to have a look at the OBLIST:

```
EVAL:
OBLIST
```

Generally the OBLIST is a list of sublists, each sublist corresponding to a bucket of the hashing function used to check whether a new print name had been encountered or not.† If a new print name has been encountered, it is assigned a new unique atom cell. Otherwise, if the same atom had already been encountered, its new instance is assigned the same atom cell as when the atom was first encountered. The atom cell is just the address of some cell. When we say, as in Fig. 10.7, that the CAR of cell 103 points to the atom RIDICULOUS, we mean that the CAR of cell 103 has as value some atom cell, say 1455. Every reference to RIDICULOUS will be a pointer to 1455. With 1455 are associated

a. The print name RIDICULOUS of the atom.

b. The property "list" of the atom. Usually, the print name is the property of some indicator, for example, PNAME in some systems.

c. The various values that the atom has if it has been used as a constant or variable, with usually a pointer to the current value.

An atom cell has associated some information indicating that it is an... atom cell, and not, for instance, a number or a list. Some bits in the cell are used for this purpose.

In most LISP systems, numbers have no unique location in memory (except, in some systems, small integers). Instead, when a number is created, for example, as the result of a PLUS, a new number cell is obtained —from available space; see the next section—the number cell is marked, using certain bits, as a number cell and usually as to the type of number (integer, single-precision floating-point, double-precision floating-point, etc.), and one of the fields of the number cell is the address of the binary representation of the number. It should be noted that there is a great variety of implementations of numbers in various LISP systems, and it is difficult to say anything general.

---

†For a discussion of hashing functions, see, for example, M. C. Harrison, *Data-Structures and Programming*, Scott, Foresman and Company, Glenview, Ill., 1973, Chapter 9.

10.3 Available Space and the Garbage Collection

When LISP is called to run a program, the memory space not taken up by the LISP system itself is linked together—for example, by using the CDR's of the cells—into a list, or several lists, making up what is called the available space. As cells are needed, for example, to make a new number, atom, or list, they are taken from available space. As computation goes on, some cells become "garbage," in the sense that they can no longer be accessed by the programmer. For example, suppose that the list (MEAN (MEN MIGHT) (MEAN) MEANS) of Fig. 10.6 was created as the result of

(SETQ MMM (QUOTE (MEAN (MEN MIGHT) (MEAN) MEANS)))

If we now do

(SETQ MMM (CDDR MMM))

the value of MMM will point to cell 317, which, as a list, would PRINT as

((MEAN) MEANS)

However, cells 357, 111, 329, and 313 are no longer accessible from the value of MMM. These four cells represent "garbage".

When available space is exhausted, a special program, named the garbage collector, is executed. The garbage collector starts with the OBLIST and marks as accessible all the cells that are directly or indirectly accessible from the OBLIST. This would include all the atoms in the program, their values, property lists, etc. In the above example, if the garbage collector is called after the program

(SETQ MMM (CDDR MMM))

has been evaluated, then cells 317, 192, and 741 would be marked accessible. After all accessible cells have been marked, the garbage collector traverses memory (at least the memory not taken up by the LISP system, and perhaps some special memory areas) and

a. Unmarks the cells that had been marked.
b. Links all cells that had been left unmarked to form the new available space.

If the new available space is sufficiently large, the program continues. Otherwise, an error resulting from insufficient space results, and either the program stops or more memory is granted the program.

It is a paradox of garbage collection that as memory becomes more and more crowded (i.e., as an increasing fraction of memory is being used for accessible cells), more and more time is spent on a garbage collection to recuperate smaller and smaller amounts of available space. The reason is that additional time will be needed to mark the additional accessible cells and to unmark them subsequently.

We are now ready to understand some of the functions we have used in terms of their effect on memory cells.

10.4   REMOB

(REMOB atom), for example, (REMOB (QUOTE RIDICULOUS)), removes the atom cell corresponding to "atom" from the OBLIST. If some structure, for example, a list cell, still points to this atom cell, unpredictable results may occur, since the cell that had been used as the atom cell of "atom" may now be used for quite different purposes. If "atom" is READ again, or recreated by a program, it will usually be assigned a different atom cell from the one previously used.

10.5   Cell Values

When one starts to consider actual memory structures used in LISP, it should be remembered that LISP deals only with cell addresses. Referring to Fig. 10.7, the program

```
(SETQ LIST1 (QUOTE (RIDICULOUS (IN SERIOUS) THINGS)))
```

would have built the list structure for (RIDICULOUS (IN SERIOUS) THINGS), using cells 103, 712, 897, 815, and 206. The value of LIST1 is (RIDICULOUS (IN SERIOUS) THINGS), but, internally, from LIST1 one accesses only cell 103. Since it is possible to change parts of a memory structure, we must distinguish between the value of a structure, as given by PRINT, and the cell from which we access the structure. We shall use the term *cell value* to denote the cell from which a structure is accessed (by some variable, say.) In the above example, the cell value of LIST1 is 103. Functions also have cell values. The cell value of the above SETQ is 103. The cell value of (CDR LIST1) is 712, and its value ((IN SERIOUS) THINGS).

If we now evaluate

(SETQ LIST2 (QUOTE (SERIOUS IN RIDICULOUS THINGS)))

the cell value of LIST2 is 519, and 519 is also the cell value of this last SETQ.

10.6   EQ

The function EQ checks whether the cell values of its two arguments are identical: (EQ LIST1 LIST2) would result in comparing the cell value of LIST1, 103, to the cell value of LIST2, 519. Since 103 is not equal to 519, the value of EQ is NIL (and its cell value is the atom cell of NIL). When we evaluate

EQ (MEAN MEAN)

the address of the atom cell of the atom MEAN is compared to the address of the atom cell of the same atom MEAN. Since the atom cell of an atom and hence its address are unique, the two addresses are the same, and the value of EQ (MEAN MEAN) is T.

On the other hand, with LIST1 and LIST2 as in the above section, the program

(EQ (CDDR LIST1) (CDDDR LIST2))

would compare the cell value of (CDDR LIST1), which is 206, to the cell value of (CDDDR LIST2), which is 139. Hence the value of the program is NIL, even though both arguments of EQ have the same value (THINGS).

In Section 10.8, we shall give an example of a little program where the value of EQ is T, although its two arguments have different values (but the same cell value). We shall also see structures which have cell values (as they must) but no value, in the sense that PRINT cannot print the structure.

10.7   CONS

CONS evaluates the cell values of its two arguments and takes a new cell from available space. The CAR of this new cell is replaced by the cell value of the first argument, and the CDR of the new cell is replaced by the cell value of the second argument. If we evaluate the programs

(SETQ LIST3 (QUOTE (CANNIBALS EAT)))
(SETQ LIST4 (QUOTE (WITH FISH FORKS)))

the cell values might be 757 and 430, as in Fig. 10.8(a). (SETQ LIST5 (CONS LIST3 LIST4)) will result in a new cell being taken from available space, for example, cell 544. The address 757 is placed in the CAR of cell 544 and address 430 in its CDR, as shown in Fig. 10.8(b). The value of cell 544 considered as a list is ((CANNIBALS EAT) WITH FISH FORKS).

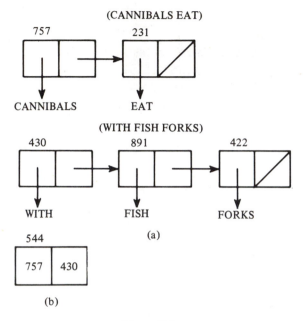

Figure 10.8

Unlike CAR and CDR, which access only addresses of LISP cells, CONS is an expensive operation since it eats up some of the available space and therefore makes memory more crowded. It is sometimes possible to avoid explicit or implicit uses of CONS, as will be seen in Section 10.9, which compares APPEND with NCONC.

10.7.1 Dotted Pairs

When the second argument of CONS is an atom different from NIL, CONS will still work, although the result will not be the type of list which we have considered until now. Instead, we obtain a *mixed list*. The result of the program

```
(SETQ WILLIAM (CONS (QUOTE THE) (QUOTE CONQUEROR)))
```

is illustrated in Fig. 10.9. The new cell, 327, obtained by CONS from available space has its CAR pointing to the atom cell of THE and its CDR

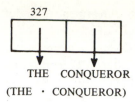

THE   CONQUEROR

(THE · CONQUEROR)

Figure 10.9

pointing to the atom cell of CONQUEROR. The value of WILLIAM
would PRINT in the notation

(THE . CONQUEROR)

and is called a *dotted pair*. LISP systems allow mixed lists to be created,
using CONS, as in the above example. Mixed lists may also be input. The
programs

(SETQ MAXIMS (QUOTE (((CHORUS . GIRLS) ARE) . KEPT)))

or equivalently

(SETQ MAXIMS ((CHORUS . GIRLS) ARE . KEPT)))

would give MAXIMS the same value as

(SETQ MAXIMS (CONS (LIST (CONS (QUOTE CHORUS) (QUOTE GIRLS)) ARE)
          (QUOTE KEPT)   ))

The PRINT function would print the value of MAXIMS as

((CHORUS . GIRLS) ARE . KEPT)

The memory structure is shown in Fig. 10.10.

    Note that as the right-hand side of a dotted pair, the atom NIL

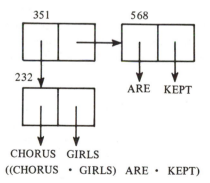

((CHORUS · GIRLS) ARE · KEPT)

Figure 10.10

receives a special treatment. The dotted pair (RATTLE . NIL) is always PRINTed (RATTLE).

Dotted pairs are sometimes useful to save memory. The list (PROTECT YOUR HONOR) requires three cells, while the mixed list ((PROTECT . YOUR) . HONOR), usually written (PROTECT YOUR . HONOR), requires only two cells.

EXERCISES

1. Write a print function (MYPRINT (LAMBDA (LIS) ...)) which will print mixed lists and dotted pairs in the format ((CHORUS . GIRLS) ARE . KEPT). The value of MYPRINT is its argument LIS; the printing is a side effect.

Notes:

a. You should use the function PRIN1 (available in most systems), which prints an atom without doing a carriage return.

b. The values of the atoms LPAR, RPAR, PERIOD, and BLANK are, respectively, a left parenthesis "(," a right parenthesis ")," a period ".," and a blank " ". (These atoms are usually available.)

c. Assume that MYPRINT wants to print the structure whose cell value is 351 in Fig. 10.10. 351 is not an atom, so it uses PRIN1 to print a LPAR. Taking the CAR of 351, it reaches 232, again not an atom, so it prints another LPAR. Taking the CAR of 232, it reaches an atom, CHORUS, which is printed using PRIN1. The CDR of 232 is taken. It is not NIL, so a BLANK is inserted. It is an atom, though, so a PERIOD, BLANK, the atom GIRLS, and a RPAR are inserted. MYPRINT returns to 351, takes the CDR, which is neither NIL nor an atom, so a space is inserted, etc.

d. At the end of the list, the function TERPRI of no arguments TERminates the PRInting for MYPRINT.

2. Write a function (MYCOPY (LAMBDA (LIS) ...)) which makes a copy of the list LIS. The value of MYCOPY will be EQUAL to LIS, but the storage structures of the two lists will consist of two disjoint sets of LISP cells (except for atom cells). *Hint:* CONS utilizes a new cell from available space.

Note: A function COPY is usually available in LISP systems.

10.8 RPLACA and RPLACD

It is possible to change the CAR and CDR of a LISP cell using the functions RPLACA (an acronym for RePLACe the cAr) and RPLACD (an acronym for RePLACe the cDr).

10.8.1 RPLACA

RPLACA replaces the CAR of the cell value of its first argument by the cell value of its second argument. The cell value of RPLACA is the (original) cell value of the first argument, but generally the *value* of this cell has been modified. Consider the programs

```
(SETQ LIST6 (QUOTE (CIGARETTES CAUSE STATISTICS) ) )
(SETQ LIST7 (QUOTE (STATISTICIANS ALSO) ) )
```

Possible storage structures are shown in Fig. 10.10(a). The cell values of LIST6 and LIST7 are cells 937 and 805, respectively. After the program (SETQ LIST8 (RPLACA LIST6 LIST7)), the storage structure is as shown in Fig. 10.10(b). The cell value of LIST8 is the same as the cell value of LIST6—the first argument of RPLACA—i.e., cell 937. The *value* of LIST6, however, has been changed. It is now

```
( (STATISTICIANS ALSO) CAUSE STATISTICS)
```

Since EQ checks only for the equality of addresses, it is now possible to obtain a value of T for EQ with two arguments which have different values. Indeed, the program

```
(EQ (SETQ LIST6 (QUOTE (CIGARETTES CAUSE STATISTICS) ) )
    (RPLACA LIST6 (QUOTE (STATISTICIANS ALSO) ) ) )
```

would have value T, since the cell values of the two arguments of EQ are one and the same address: the cell value of LIST6, 937. When the second argument of EQ is EVALuated, the value of LIST6 changes to ((STATISTICIANS ALSO) CAUSE STATISTICS).

10.8.2 RPLACD

RPLACD replaces the CDR of the cell value of its first argument by the cell value of its second argument. Starting with the example in Fig. 10.10(a), the program

```
(SETQ LIST9 (RPLACD (CDR LIST6) LIST7) )
```

gives LIST9 the cell value 46. The value of LIST6 has been changed to (CIGARETTES CAUSE STATISTICIANS ALSO), as shown in Fig. 10.11. Note that cell 322 has become garbage.

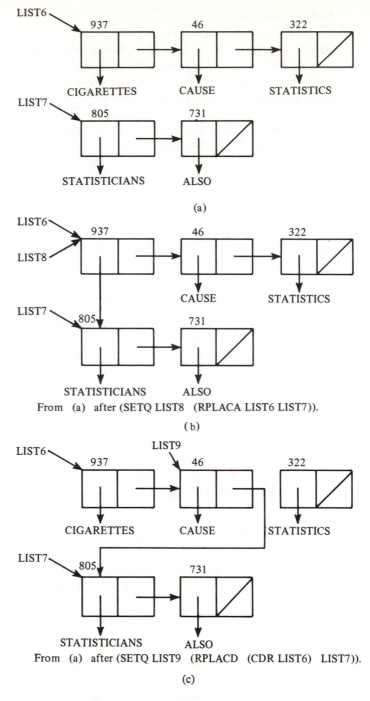

From (a) after (SETQ LIST8 (RPLACA LIST6 LIST7)).

(b)

From (a) after (SETQ LIST9 (RPLACD (CDR LIST6) LIST7)).

(c)

Figure 10.11

10.8.3   Caution: Handle with Care

Using RPLACA or RPLACD, it is possible to create memory structures that are not "regular" lists and which can easily get various system functions into infinite loops, or cause other difficulties. Such structures have no value in the sense that they cannot be PRINTed. For example,

```
(SETQ HORROR1 (CONS NIL NIL))
```

is shown in Fig. 10.12(a), while Fig. 10.12(b) shows what happens after (RPLACA HORROR1 HORROR1). The CAR of HORROR1 is

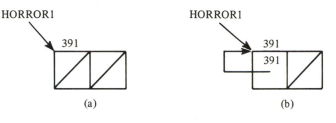

Figure 10.12

HORROR1 itself. The functions which go down CAR's of lists, such as MEMALL and PRINT, would get into an infinite loop on HORROR1. When attempting to PRINT HORROR1, PRINT would produce a stream of left parentheses that would be cut off only by limits put on computer time or output length.

RPLACD also makes it easy to build "irregular" lists. (SETQ HORROR2 (LIST (QUOTE YAK))) is shown in Fig. 10.13(a). After (RPLACD HORROR2 HORROR2) [see Fig. 10.13(b)], we obtain a circular list. An attempt to PRINT HORROR2 would result in (YAK YAK YAK YAK

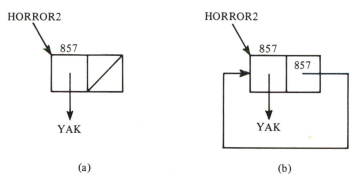

Figure 10.13

YAK YAK YAK YAK YAK YAK. . .† until limits on computer time or output length saves us.

HORROR2 is an example of a circular list, since taking CDR after CDR would not result in obtaining NIL. Many functions—EQUAL, MEMBER, LAST, LENGTH, etc.—would not terminate on infinite lists. Circular lists have their utility, though, as shown in Section 12.1.

The moral (and also the immoral) of the story is that the RPLAC functions are potentially dangerous and should be used with utmost care. They can lead to nonstandard structures which may not be processable by standard LISP functions. However, judiciously used, they can help to build very efficient programs.

EXERCISES

1. Without using CONS, i.e., without creating new memory structures, write programs for

a. SUBSTOP

b. REMOVELAST

c. DELETE

d. DELETETOPS

e. DELETEALL

f. (SUBSALL (LAMBDA (SEX1 SEX2 LIS) . . .)), which replaces SEX1 by SEX2 everywhere in LIS and not just at its top level.

2. Define a predicate (GOODLIST (LAMBDA (ANIMAL) . . .)) which has value T if the ANIMAL that is its argument is a GOODLIST. A GOODLIST is either an atom or the CONS of two GOODLISTs. Many memory structures that can be built using RPLACA and RPLACD are not GOODLISTs. Many system functions expect GOODLISTs as arguments.

3. A NODOTLIST is a GOODLIST which will PRINT with no dot. Define a predicate NODOTLIST which has value T if its argument is a NODOTLIST.

4. Even a GOODLIST may have common sublists, as in the example

```
(SETQ LISONE (QUOTE (THE POLICE FARCE)))
(SETQ LISTWO (CONS LISONE (APPEND (QUOTE (PROTECTS YOU FROM))
                                  LISONE)))
VALUE IS...
((THE POLICE FARCE) PROTECTS YOU FROM THE POLICE FARCE)
```

†A feeble attempt at imitating your neighbour.

which has a memory structure of the form

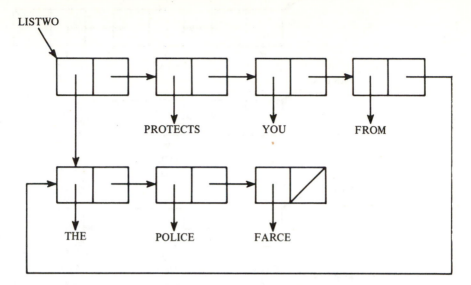

Define a predicate NOCOMSUB which has value T if a GOODLIST has no two common substructures (except, of course, atoms). *Hint:* Use EQ.

5. Build a simple structure which would PRINT as an infinite number of right parentheses (and nothing else).

10.9 APPEND and NCONC

Remembering the function APPEND,

```
(APPEND (LAMBDA (LIS1 LIS2)
        (COND ( (NULL LIS1) LIS2)
              (T (CONS (CAR LIS1) (APPEND (CDR LIS1) LIS2)) ) ) ))
```

we see that CONSes are used for all the SEXes of LIS1. Hence, LIS1 is essentially copied. For example, the results of the programs

```
(SETQ PART1 (QUOTE (EIGHT MEN DEAD) ) )
(SETQ PART2 (QUOTE (TWO SERIOUSLY) ) )
```

are shown in Fig. 10.14(a). After

```
(SETQ PART3 (APPEND PART1 PART2) )
```

the storage structures are as shown in Fig. 10.14(b). Note that PART1 is left unchanged.

By comparison, the function NCONC, usually available in LISP sys-

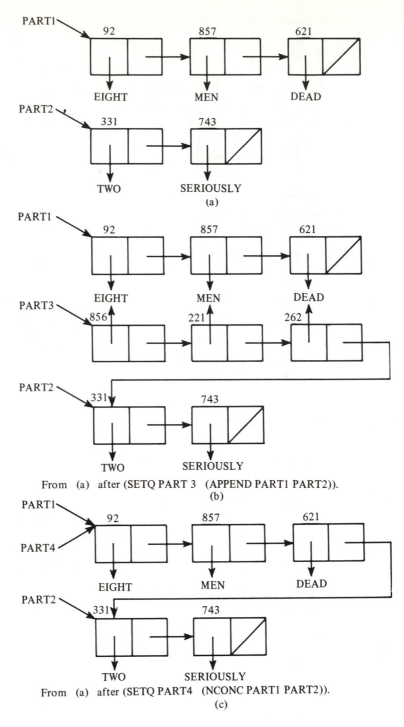

From (a) after (SETQ PART 3 (APPEND PART1 PART2)).

(b)

From (a) after (SETQ PART4 (NCONC PART1 PART2)).

(c)

Figure 10.14

tems, links the last cell of PART1 to the first cell of PART2. Figure 10.14(c) shows what would happen to Fig. 10.14(a) after the program (SETQ PART4 (NCONC PART1 PART2)) is evaluated. No new cells were introduced, but the value of PART1 has been changed.

A program for NCONC could be

```
(NCONC (LAMBDA (LIS1 LIS2)
        (COND ( (NULL LIS1) LIS2)
            (T (PROG (TEMP)
                    (SETQ TEMP LIS1)
                LOOP (COND ( (NULL (CDR TEMP) ) (GO EXIT) ) )
                    (SETQ TEMP (CDR TEMP) ) (GO LOOP)
                EXIT (RPLACD TEMP LIS2)
                    (RETURN LIS1) ) ) ) )
```

Unless LIS1 is NIL, the pointer of LIS1 will be the cell value returned by NCONC, but, unless LIS2 is NIL, the value of LIS1 will have changed.

EXERCISES

1. Given two lists of numbers in nondecreasing order, write a function (MERGE (LAMBDA (LISNUM1 LISNUM2) ...)), which is a list of all the numbers in both LISNUM1 and LISNUM2 in nondecreasing order. Repetitions are kept.

```
MERGE ( (5 7 11 11 15 62 97) (2 4 6 9 10 11 17 23 62 83) )
    VALUE IS ...
    (2 4 5 6 7 9 10 11 11 11 15 17 23 62 62 83 97)
```

MERGE should not use new cells from available space but instead should RPLACD (some) cells in the two lists to form a new list utilizing the cells of LISNUM1 and LISNUM2.

2. With two lists as in Exercise 1 above, write a function (MERGESET (LAMBDA (LISNUM1 LISNUM2) ...)) which has as value all the numbers in both LISNUM1 and LISNUM2 in nondecreasing order, but without repetitions.

```
MERGESET ( (5 7 11 11 15 62 97) (2 4 6 9 10 11 17 23 62 83) )
    VALUE IS ...
    (2 4 5 6 7 9 10 11 15 17 23 62 83 97)
```

Again, no new cells should be introduced. Do not just "clean up" the result given by MERGE; instead, write MERGESET directly.

3. It is sometimes desirable to divide a list into two sublists of almost equal length (within one). Write a function (SPLITMIDDLE (LAMBDA (LIS) ...)) which divides a list in the middle. The value of SPLITMIDDLE is a list of two

sublists, the first of which is the left-hand half of the list and the second of which is the right-hand half of the list. If the list has an odd length, the left-hand half is one longer than the right-hand half.

```
SPLITMIDDLE ( (ETERNITY IS STILL WITH US) )
 VALUE IS...
 ( (ETERNITY IS STILL) (WITH US) )

SPLITMIDDLE ( (INTEREST YES PRINCIPLE NO) )
 VALUE IS...
 ( (INTEREST YES) (PRINCIPLE NO) )
```

SPLITMIDDLE may not use more than two new cells from available space but must utilize the cells from the original LIS.

    4.   Another way to divide a list into two sublists of equal length (within one; see Exercise 3 above) is to form two sublists, one sublist of the odd SEXes of the list and one of the even SEXes. Write a function SPLITODDEVEN which makes such a division of a list.

```
SPLITODDEVEN ( (PUT WHISKEY IN YOUR TANK) )
 VALUE IS...
 ( (PUT IN TANK) (WHISKEY YOUR) )
```

SPLITODDEVEN should use as few new cells as possible.

    5.   Compare the efficiencies of your (or someone else's) versions of SPLITMIDDLE and SPLITODDEVEN.

    6.   Given a list of unordered numbers, we wish to sort them in nondecreasing order. Using MERGE and SPLIT, write a SORT.

```
SORT ( (27 15 22 34 8 15 6 75 34) )
 VALUE IS...
 (6 8 15 15 22 27 34 34 75)
```

Hint: A list of one number is already sorted. Two sorted lists can be MERGEd to form a sorted list. This SORT is interesting since (if SORT, MERGE, and SPLIT are well written) it is of cost n $\times$ log(n), for a list of length n.

10.10 Self-Modifying Functions

Since function definitions are lists and are accessible as the property of the atom EXPR of the function name, it is possible to change the list which defines a function. The change may be made by the function itself. We shall now give a very simple example of a self-modifying function.

    It is not uncommon for a function to have a certain first behavior.

However, after some time or after some result has been obtained, the function switches to a second behavior without ever returning to the first behavior. The usual way of treating this problem is as follows: Let us assume that the change of behavior is caused when some INPUT which is READ satisfies the function CHANGEPROPERTY. A variable SWITCH is initialized to NIL and set to T when (CHANGEPROPERTY INPUT) becomes T. The outline of a function BEFOREAFTER would be

```
(BEFOREAFTER (LAMBDA (...) (PROG (INPUT SWITCH...)
LOOP (SETQ INPUT (READ))
     (COND (SWITCH (GO SECONDBEHAVIOR))
           ((CHANGEPROPERTY INPUT) (GO CHANGESWITCH)))
FIRSTBEHAVIOR    ‹program for first behavior›
(GO LOOP)
CHANGESWITCH (SETQ SWITCH T)
SECONDBEHAVIOR    ‹program for second behavior›
(GO LOOP)    )))
```

Once the SECONDBEHAVIOR starts being observed, SWITCH is still tested. Moreover, the CONDitional and the code describing the FIRST-BEHAVIOR take up memory space, although they correspond to programs that will no longer be executed. What would be desirable is to transform the code, after (CHANGEPROPERTY INPUT) becomes T, to something like

```
(BEFOREAFTER (LAMBDA (...) (PROG (INPUT SWITCH...)
LOOP (SETQ INPUT (READ))
‹program for second behavior›
(GO LOOP)    )))
```

Moreover, we might want to delete the function CHANGEPROPERTY (if it is not used elsewhere) and perhaps even go to the luxury of deleting SWITCH from the list of PROG variables.

An example will help to clarify the matter and motivate the technique. Let us assume that we want to simulate—in a rather coarse way—the playing activities of Phf. As a child, he participates in child play, when he encounters a child's toy. Examples of child toys could be DOLL or LOLLIPOP. However, as soon as he encounters SEX, he switches forever to adult play, playing with adult toys, of which SEX, LADY, GENTLE-MAN, and BOOZE are examples. Only DEATH will stop his activities.

The toys are assumed to be data that are READ by the program. When a child's toy is encountered, the function PLAYCHILD PRINTs (toy IS CHILD PLAY).

```
(PLAYCHILD (LAMBDA (PLAYTOY) (PRINT (CONS PLAYTOY (QUOTE (IS CHILD PLAY) ) ) ) ) )
```

In the second stage, when an adult toy is encontereed, the function PLAYADULT PRINTs (toy IS ADULT PLAY).

```
(PLAYADULT (LAMBDA (PLAYTOY) (PRINT (CONS PLAYTOY (QUOTE (IS ADULT PLAY) ) ) ) ) )
```

We are now ready to define a first version of PLAY:

Line	Program
1	(PLAY (LAMBDA () (PROG (PLAYTOY SWITCH)
2	LOOP (SETQ PLAYTOY (READ))
3	(COND ((EQ PLAYTOY (QUOTE DEATH))
	(RETURN (QUOTE (DEAD HAHA))))
4	(SWITCH (GO ADULT))
5	((EQ PLAYTOY (QUOTE SEX))
	(GO CHANGESWITCH)))
6	(PLAYCHILD PLAYTOY) (GO LOOP)
7	CHANGESWITCH (SETQ SWITCH T)
8	ADULT
9	(PLAYADULT PLAYTOY) (GO LOOP))))

If the input to LISP is

PLAY ()

followed by the data

DOLL LOLLIPOP SEX LADY GENTLEMAN BOOZE DEATH

the output will be

(DOLL IS CHILD PLAY)
(LOLLIPOP IS CHILD PLAY)
(SEX IS ADULT PLAY)
(LADY IS ADULT PLAY)
(GENTLEMAN IS ADULT PLAY)
(BOOZE IS ADULT PLAY)
VALUE IS...
(DEAD HAHA)

Our goal is to write a self-modifying function that would not use the SWITCH and would eliminate its CHILD phase (line 6) and intermediary tests and modifications (lines 4, 5, 7, and 8) from the program. A possible solution is as follows:

Line	Program
1	(PLAY (LAMBDA () (PROG (PLAYTOY)
2	LOOP (SETQ PLAYTOY (READ))
3	(COND ((EQ PLAYTOY (QUOTE DEATH))
	(RETURN (QUOTE (DEAD HAHA)))))
4	(COND ((EQ PLAYTOY (QUOTE SEX)) (GO ADULT)))
5	(PLAYCHILD PLAYTOY) (GO LOOP)
6	ADULT (REMOB (QUOTE PLAYCHILD))
7	(RPLACD (CDR (NEXT (QUOTE LOOP))
	(CADDR (GET (QUOTE PLAY) (QUOTE EXPR)))))
	(CDDR (NEXT (QUOTE ADULT)
	(CADDR (GET (QUOTE PLAY) (QUOTE EXPR))))))
8	(PLAYADULT PLAYTOY) (GO LOOP))))

Once the ADULT phase is reached, we REMOB the atom PLAYCHILD
since PLAYCHILD will no longer be used and do a RPLACD to link the
end of line 3 with the beginning of line 8, thereby effectively removing
lines 4, 5, 6, and 7 from the program. The function NEXT is used to locate
the appropriate cells in the storage structure of the function definition.

```
(NEXT (LAMBDA (ATM LIS)
      (COND ((NULL LIS) NIL)
            ((EQ ATM (CAR LIS)) (CDR LIS))
            (T (NEXT ATM (CDR LIS))) )))
```

If NEXT finds the atom ATM at the top level of a LISt, its value is what
is left of the LISt after the occurrence of ATM. If ATM is not found, the
value of NEXT is NIL.

```
(NEXT (QUOTE WHILE) (QUOTE (WHILE YOU ARE A HEAD)))
VALUE IS...
(YOU ARE A HEAD)

(NEXT (QUOTE FAILURE) (QUOTE (SUCCESS SPOILS FAILURE)))
VALUE IS...
NIL

(NEXT (QUOTE TIDE) (QUOTE (IT WISHES THE DIRT AWAY)))
VALUE IS...
NIL
```

A few additional explanations: (GET (QUOTE PLAY) (QUOTE
EXPR)) is the LAMBDA expression (LAMBDA () (PROG (PLAYTOY)

. . .)) which defines the function PLAY. Its CADDR is (PROG (PLAY-TOY) . . .). With the same input as in the previous case, the output would be identical. However, at the end of the run of the self-modifying PLAY, the function definition of PLAY has changed. To check this, we do

```
GET (PLAY EXPR)
  VALUE IS...   (output edited by hand for easier comparison)
  (LAMBDA () (PROG (PLAYTOY)
  LOOP (SETQ PLAYTOY (READ))
  (COND ( (EQ PLAYTOY (QUOTE DEATH) ) (RETURN (QUOTE (DEAD HAHA) ) ) ) )
  (PLAYADULT PLAYTOY) (GO LOOP) ))
```

We can also check that PLAYCHILD no longer has a function definition:

```
GET (PLAYCHILD EXPR)
  VALUE IS...
  NIL
```

EXERCISES

1. Certain functions may run correctly, even though they have useless code, i.e., code that is not accessed. For example, a pair of a COND may never be reached as in

```
(STUPID1 (LAMBDA (X)
        (COND ( (NULL X) T)
              (T (QUOTE (IT WAS NOT NIL) ) )
              ( (NULL (CAR X) ) (QUOTE (THE CAR WAS NULL) ) )  )))
```

The third pair of the COND in STUPID1 is never reached. Another possibility is a label in a PROG which is never reached. In STUPID2, the label USELESS is an example:

```
(STUPID2 (LAMBDA (X) (PROG (HELLO)
        (RETURN (QUOTE (THIS FUNCTION ALWAYS SAYS HI) ) )
  USELESS (RETURN (QUOTE (THAT WAS A USELESS LABEL) ) )  )))
```

A related problem is that of "incomplete" tests of a function. If the (not very good) definition of LAST

```
(UGLYLAST (LAMBDA (LIS)
    (COND ( (NULL (CDR LIS) ) (CAR LIS) )
          ( (NULL (CDDR LIS) ) (CADR LIS) )
          ( (NULL (CDDDR LIS) ) (CADDR LIS) )
          (T (UGLYLAST (CDR LIS) ) )  )))
```

is tested only against the test cases (GRINN), (GRINN AND), and (GRINN AND BARRETT), then the last pair of the CONDitional is never reached and therefore is never tested. Write a function (CHECKWASTE (LAMBDA (FUN-

NAME LISTOFTESTS) ...)). The first argument is the name of a function defined as an EXPR. The second argument is a list of test cases. CHECKWASTE checks whether the tests in the list of test cases leave any part of the function definition wasted. A possible approach would be to modify the function definition, inserting behind each label and each left of a COND a different marker. When the label is reached, or the left of the COND is not NIL, the marker is modified. For example, its value may be changed from NIL to T, and the test case which made this change can be placed on the property list of the marker. After all the test cases have been run, the unchanged markers point to untried code.

2. Sometimes incorrect function definitions cause errors because some (auxiliary) function was given incorrect arguments. For example, an attempt may have been made to evaluate (PLUS 5 7 NIL 6). However, if the function definition includes several occurrences of PLUS, it is not generally known which particular PLUS went wrong. Write a function FINDTHEBEAST which will modify a function definition so that occurrences of errors in auxiliary functions can be detected precisely.

3. Another cause of errors in programs is due to "infinite" loops. The loops may be recursive, as in

```
(RECURSIVELOOP (LAMBDA (X) (RECURSIVELOOP X) ) )
```

where the function is entered again and again. The loop may also be caused by successive GOs in a PROG, as in

```
(ITERATIVELOOP (LAMBDA (X) (PROG (Y)
                LOOP (GO LOOP) (RETURN X) ) ) )
```

Write a function CHECKINFINITY which will modify a function definition in an attempt to locate possibly infinite loops. A possible approach would be to insert a counter at the entrance of functions and behind labels. When any counter becomes too large, the program is stopped and a diagnostic given as to the location of "high" counters.

Note: Sometimes a high number of loops are legitimate, so that the limits on the counters may have to be reset depending on the test cases given to the (modified) function definition.

4. Give one or more essentially different examples of LISP functions which get into some form of infinite loop but where the infinity would not be discovered by the counter technique outlined in Exercise 3 above.

11

MISCELLANEOUS FUNCTIONS AND FEATURES

In this chapter we shall regroup a number of useful functions and features found in many LISP systems. These features did not find a convenient niche in the previous chapters.

11.1 Boolean Functions: AND, OR, and NOT

In Section 4.4.2, we introduced the auxiliary function BOTH. A similar system function is AND. AND, like LIST, is a function of an indefinite number of arguments. Its arguments are evaluated left to right. If an argument is found to have value NIL, the value of AND is NIL and no additional arguments are evaluated. If no argument with value NIL was encountered, the value of AND is T. (In some systems, the value of AND is then the value of the last argument, or T if there were no arguments. In some other systems, all the arguments must evaluate to either T or NIL.)

Function:	AND
Number of arguments:	any
Arguments:	any SEXes
Value:	NIL if some argument is NIL; otherwise T

160

It is interesting to compare AND and BOTH:

```
(BOTH (LAMBDA (ARG1 ARG2)
      (COND (ARG1 ARG2)
            (T NIL) ) ) )
```

BOTH has two arguments, while AND could have any. In particular, AND (), i.e., AND of no arguments, has value T since no NIL argument was found. Even in the case of two arguments, AND and BOTH can behave differently if the second argument has no value. For example, consider the infinitely recursive function FOREVER:

```
(FOREVER (LAMBDA ( ) (FOREVER) ) )
```

The value of (AND NIL (FOREVER)) is NIL, since the first argument of AND is NIL, and the evaluation of further arguments is terminated, while (BOTH NIL (FOREVER)) results in an error. Before evaluating BOTH, LISP wants to find the values of the two arguments of BOTH. When evaluating the value of the second argument, ARG2, which is the value of (FOREVER), an infinite recursion is entered, and usually an error—recursion stack overflow—will result.

Very similar to AND is the function OR of any number of arguments. OR evaluates its arguments left to right. When a non-NIL argument is encountered, the evaluation of the arguments stops. The value of OR is T in some systems; in others, it is the value of this non-NIL argument. If no non-NIL argument was encountered, the value of OR is NIL. Hence, in particular, OR () has value NIL.

§
✓

Function: OR
Number of arguments: any
Arguments: any SEXes
Value: NIL if no argument is non-NIL; otherwise T

A third common Boolean function, NOT, is identical to NULL.

§

Function: NOT
Number of arguments: 1
Argument: any SEX
Value: T if argument is NIL; otherwise NIL

1. Assuming that the value of OR is the value of the first non-NIL argument encountered (from left to right), compare it to a function EITHER of two arguments (EITHER (LAMBDA (ARG1 ARG2) . . .)), which behaves like OR of two arguments on well-behaved arguments but might behave differently on ill-behaved arguments. Characterize the cases and give two examples when OR and EITHER have different values.

2. Define the function (EQUIVALENT (LAMBDA (ARG1 ARG2) . . .)), which is T if the arguments are both NIL or both non-NIL. Otherwise, the value of EQUIVALENT is NIL.

3. Define the function (IMPLY (LAMBDA (ARG1 ARG2) . . .)), which is NIL if ARG1 is non-NIL and ARG2 is NIL; otherwise IMPLY has value T.

4. Define the function exclusive-or XOR, (XOR (LAMBDA (ARG1 ARG2) . . .)), which is T if one of the arguments is NIL, while the other one is not. In other cases, XOR has value NIL.

5. If A and B have the values T or NIL, show that the three evaluations

(SETQ A (XOR A B)) (SETQ B (XOR A B)) (SETQ A (XOR A B))

"permute" the values of A and B, without using a temporary variable. That is, the effect of the above program is equivalent to

(SETQ TEMP A) (SETQ A B) (SETQ B TEMP)

6. It was mentioned that in some implementations, the values of AND and OR are the values of one of the non-NIL arguments of the function. Since COND checks only for NIL, AND and OR would appear the same to COND under either implementation. Try to redefine XOR for any two SEX arguments so that the values of two arguments can be permuted using only XOR and no temporary storage variable, in a manner similar to Exercise 5.

11.2 Commas and Unusual Characters in Input Lists

Usually, a comma "," is READ as a space by LISP. For example, the two lists

(A BIRD IN (THE HAND (SHOWS)) POOR MANNERS)

and

(A,BIRD,IN(THE,HAND(SHOWS)))POOR,MANNERS)

are EQUAL. Each would PRINT in the format of the first list.

If one wishes to PRINT the list (FAMILY TREES , PRODUCE NUTS), then the input format could be (FAMILY TREES $$$,$

PRODUCE NUTS) or (FAMILY TREES $$B,B PRODUCE NUTS) for systems using the $$ convention, or (FAMILY TREES /, PRODUCE NUTS) for systems using the slash "/" convention for unusual characters.

11.2.1 The $$ Convention

Any string of characters that starts with $$ must be of the form

```
$$c<any string of charcters>c
```

where <any string of characters> is a string of characters not containing the character "c" which follows $$. LISP then creates (if necessary) an atom with print name the <any string of characters>.

For example, an atom with print name))(),.(would be $$A))(),.(A. The *atom* $$B(GARTER SNAKE)B has as print name (GARTER SNAKE) but is *not* EQUAL to the *list* (GARTER SNAKE). It is EQual to the atom $$$(GARTER SNAKE)$.

11.2.2 The | Convention

In other systems, a slash "/" is used to signify unusual characters which otherwise have a meaning for LISP. The character that follows a slash is taken literally.

For example, the atom /)/)/(/)/,/./(has))(),.(as its print name. The atoms /(GARTER/ SNAKE/) and /(/GAR/TER/ S/NAKE/) are EQual *atoms*, and PRINT as (GARTER SNAKE).

Note: The length in characters of an atom is usually limited.

11.2.3 Character Atoms

LISP systems often include some constants that have special characters as print names. Examples are

Constant	Print Name
DOLLAR	$
LPAR	(
RPAR	)
COMMA	,
PERIOD	.

Therefore, (EQ PERIOD $$$.$) has value T.

11.3 PROG2 and PROGN

PROG2 and PROGN are functions similar to, but more restricted than, PROG. When they can be used, PROG2 will be more efficient than PROGN, which in turn will be more efficient than PROG.

$\sqrt[n]{\text{S}}$

```
Function:  PROG2

Number of arguments:  2

Arguments:  any SEXes

Value:  value of the
          second argument

Side effect:  the arguments are
               evaluated left to right
```

S

```
Function:  PROGN

Number of arguments:  any

Arguments:  any SEXes

Value:  value of the last
          (rightmost) argument

Side effect:  the arguments are
               evaluated left to right
```

PROG2 and PROGN are used to "do several things on the side." They do not allow labels, as does PROG.

11.4 Extended COND

In some LISP systems, COND is a function of several arguments, each argument being a nonempty list of arbitrary length—instead of a length of 2.

```
(COND (arg11 arg12 arg13 . . . arg1N1)
       (arg21 arg22 arg23 . . . arg2N2)
         .
         .
         .
       (argM1 argM2 argM3 . . . argMNM)  )
```

If N1 and NM are both greater than 1 and if N2 = 1, the above COND can be written in a more familiar form, using a temporary TEMP:

```
(COND  (arg11 (PROGN arg12 arg13 . . . arg1N1) )
        ( (SETQ TEMP arg21) TEMP)
            .
            .
            .
        (argM1 (PROGN argM2 argM3 . . . argMNM) )  )  )
```

That is, the leftmost element of the list, which is the argument of COND, is evaluated. If it is not NIL, the other elements are evaluated left to right, and the value of COND is the value of the rightmost element. (If the list has only one element, the value of COND is the non-NIL value of the single element.) If the first element of the list is NIL, evaluation continues with the next argument of COND, which is also a list. If no further lists exist, either the value of COND is NIL or an error is generated, depending on the implementation.

An extended COND makes programming simpler by eliminating the use of PROGN. On the other hand, the programs are less uniform and could therefore be more liable to contain errors.

11.5 GENSYM

There are a variety of implementations of gensym, all having as purpose the generation of *new atoms*. GENSYM is often a function of no arguments:

| Function: GENSYM |
| Number of arguments: none |
| Value: a new atom cell, with print name Gn on the n-th call |

Hence, the four programs

```
(GENSYM) (GENSYM) (GENSYM) (GENSYM)
```

would evaluate as

```
(GENSYM)
VALUE IS . . .
G00001

(GENSYM)
VALUE IS . . .
G00002
```

```
(GENSYM)
  VALUE IS...
  G00003

(GENSYM)
  VALUE IS...
  G00004
```

The next time GENSYM is called, its value would be G00005. But something strange happens:

```
(EQ (SETQ HOLDGENSYM (GENSYM)) (QUOTE G00005))
  VALUE IS...
  NIL
```

even though

```
HOLDGENSYM
  VALUE IS...
  G00005
```

and

```
(QUOTE G00005)
  VALUE IS...
  G00005
```

The explanation is tricky: GENSYM does not place the newly created atom in the OBLIST (Section 10.2). Hence two different atom cells coexist, even though they have the same PRINT name. There are two consequences. First, once created, a GENSYM atom can be accessed only indirectly: as the value of a variable—hence our use of HOLDGENSYM —or as some element of an accessible list. Second, GENSYM atoms that are no longer accessible will become garbage that can be reclaimed by the garbage collector (Section 10.3).

GENSYM is a remarkably useful function in programs that build or modify structures. In particular, numerous properties can be attached on the GENSYM atom, using property lists.

11.6   FEXPR: Functions of Many Arguments

LIST, AND, and OR are functions of any number of arguments. Moreover, in AND and OR, some of the arguments may not be evaluated. The usual DEFINE yields functions with fixed numbers of arguments which are all evaluated when the function is called and before execution of the function. FEXPR definitions overcome the limitations of DEFINE.

We saw (Section 8.8) that DEFINE was equivalent to

```
PUTPROP (function-name EXPR LAMBDA-expression)
```

FEXPR functions are built similarly:

```
PUTPROP (function-name FEXPR LAMBDA-expression)
```

The LAMBDA-expression has a unique LAMBDA variable whose value is *not* evaluated. Therefore, the programmer must control the evaluation of the variable and the sequencing through the implied list of arguments, as a few examples will show.

11.6.1 MULTAPPEND

We wish to define a function MULTAPPEND of any number of arguments which will APPEND its arguments left to right. The definition will be

```
PUTPROP (MULTAPPEND FEXPR (LAMBDA (FEX) ... ) )
```

In a typical call,

```
(MULTAPPEND (QUOTE (LEFT PARENTHESES) ) (LIST (QUOTE (LOOKING) ) )
            (QUOTE (FOR) ) (QUOTE (A SEX) ) )
VALUE IS...
(LEFT PARENTHESES (LOOKING) FOR A SEX)
```

the value of FEX will be the CDR of the program starting with MULTAPPEND, namely

```
( (QUOTE (LEFT PARENTHESES) ) (LIST (QUOTE (LOOKING) ) ) (QUOTE (FOR) )
(QUOTE (A SEX) ) )
```

We must sequence through the elements of FEX, EVALuate them, and APPEND them left to right. The sequencing suggests using MAPC:

```
(LAMBDA (FEX) (PROG (RES)
    (MAPC FEX (FUNCTION (LAMBDA (FEXPART)
             (SETQ RES (APPEND RES (EVAL FEXPART) ) ) ) ) )
             (RETURN RES) ) )
```

EXERCISES

1. Explain why the above definition of MULTAPPEND is inefficient. Rewrite MULTAPPEND more efficiently under the conditions

a. The values of the arguments of MULTAPPEND may be changed in memory, for example, by the RPLAC functions.

b. They may not be changed.

2. Give FEXPR definitions of

a. AND

b. OR

c. LIST

d. PLUS, given a function SUM of two arguments which adds two numbers

e. TIMES, given a function MULT of two arguments which multiplies two numbers

f. DIFFERENCE, where (DIFFERENCE A1 A2 A3 ... AN) equals A1 − A2 − A3 − ··· − AN

11.7   The LISP Compiler

Most LISP systems include a compiler. Functions defined as EXPR and FEXPR functions are translated by the compiler into machine code. Compiled functions usually run faster and take less memory. On the other hand, errors in compiled functions are harder to detect, and compiled functions are almost impossible to examine and manipulate since they are no longer lists. Consult your user manual for the ways to access, and the limitations of, your LISP compiler.

12

SOME LARGER EXAMPLES

In this chapter we shall outline some possible LISP programs for examples that are somewhat larger than the small ones that we have considered previously. Complete programs will seldom be given. Instead, we shall discuss various ways of structuring data, of writing partial programs to manipulate the data, etc. You should try to complete the proposed solutions, or alternative ones of your own design, and run them on your favorite computer—or the one that happens to be available.

12.1 Monopoly†

Monopoly is a game for two or more players. Since a partner is not always available, it is a good idea to program a computer to play the game. In this way, a partner is always available, as long as the computer is not down—which it tends to be when one wants to play Monopoly with it. In fact, the computer can be programmed to play Monopoly all by itself, and then *she* does not have to look for partners. One can certainly do wonders with electricity.

In the discussion that follows, a knowledge of Monopoly is not essential. In fact, some of the programs discussed—how to build circular lists, shuffle a deck, throw dice, etc.—might be used in many other systems.

†Sold by Parker Brothers.

12.1.1   The Board

The Monopoly board consists of 40 consecutive spaces. It could be represented by a list of 40 atoms† :

```
(GO MEDITERRANEAN–AV COMMUNITY–CHEST BALTIC–AV . . .
        PARK–PLACE LUXURY–TAX BOARDWALK)
```

These places are traversed sequentially by the players, according to the combined throw of two dice. Hence, GO follows BOARDWALK. Therefore a circular structure is more desirable. The function CIRCULAR will make any nonempty list circular by changing the CDR of the last cell of the list to point to the first cell of the list.

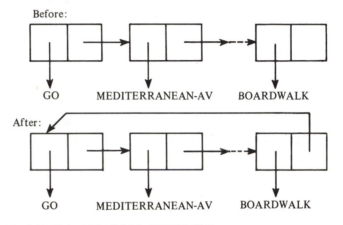

```
(CIRCULAR (LAMBDA (LIS) (PROG (BEGINNING)
      (SETQ BEGINNING LIS)
LOOP (COND ((NULL (CDR LIS)) (RETURN (RPLACD LIS BEGINNING)) ) )
      (SETQ LIS (CDR LIS)) (GO LOOP) )))
```

In CIRCULAR, BEGINNING holds the beginning of the list, which must be nonempty. We take successive CDR's of the LISt, and when the last cell is encountered—whose CDR is NIL—we RPLACD the cell to the BEGINNING. The value of CIRCULAR is the new circular list beginning at the last cell. Note that this circular list should not be printed, either explicitly or by running, for example, the program

```
CIRCULAR ((SEX LIVES HAVE UPS AND DOWNS))
```

since EVALQUOTE would attempt to print forever the circular list that results:

```
(DOWNS SEX LIVES HAVE UPS AND DOWNS SEX LIVES HAVE UPS AND ... )
```

†We assume that a dash "–" is allowed when writing atoms.

12.1.2 Rolling Dice

We now wish to simulate the throwing of a die. The function DIE will have one of the values 1, 2, 3, 4, 5, or 6 with equal probability. To define DIE, we use a pseudo-random number generator, which, under the name RANDOM (or some other name; check your LISP system), is usually available. RANDOM is a function of no arguments, and its value is a floating-point number between 0 and 1: $0 \leq$ (RANDOM) < 1.

The values of RANDOM are scattered between 0 and 1 in a manner which seems random. To simulate the effect of throwing a die and to help shuffle decks (of CHANCE and COMMUNITY–CHEST), we shall define a function (RANDOMINT (LAMBDA (LOW HIGH) ...)) which has as value an integer between LOW and HIGH in such a way that these values appear to be randomly distributed between LOW and HIGH. Both LOW and HIGH are possible values of (RANDOMINT LOW HIGH).

LOW $\leq$ (RANDOMINT LOW HIGH) $\leq$ HIGH

Starting with (RANDOM), we can obtain floating-point numbers in the range 0 to (HIGH $-$ LOW $+$ 1):

$0 \leq$ (TIMES (RANDOM) (ADD1 (DIFFERENCE HIGH LOW))) $<$ (HIGH $-$ LOW $+$ 1)

Adding LOW we obtain

LOW $\leq$ (PLUS LOW (TIMES (RANDOM) (ADD1 (DIFFERENCE HIGH LOW)))) $<$ (HIGH $+$ 1)

Finally, we transform the floating-point number into an integer by truncating; the usual function to be used is FIX:

LOW $\leq$ (FIX (PLUS LOW (TIMES (RANDOM) (ADD1 (DIFFERENCE HIGH LOW))))) $\leq$ HIGH

Throwing a die can now be simulated by successive evaluations of (RANDOMINT 1 6), where

```
(RANDOMINT (LAMBDA (LOW HIGH)
      (FIX (PLUS LOW (TIMES (RANDOM) (ADD1 (DIFFERENCE HIGH LOW) ) ) ) ) ) )
```

If we are interested only in random integers between 1 and HIGH, a simpler definition for a function RANDOMINTFROMONE would be

```
(RANDOMINTFROMONE (LAMBDA (HIGH)
      (FIX (ADD1 (TIMES (RANDOM) HIGH) ) )
      ) )
```

and the evaluations of (RANDOMINTFROMONE 6) would simulate

the throwing of a perfect die. Two definitions of DIE could be

```
(DIE (LAMBDA ( ) (RANDOMINTFROMONE 6) ) )
```

or

```
(DIE (LAMBDA ( ) (RANDOMINT 1 6) ) )
```

12.1.3 Shuffling a Deck

There are two decks of cards in Monopoly, the CHANCE and COM-MUNITY–CHEST decks. When a player falls on a CHANCE space he will draw the top card of the CHANCE deck. We first wish to shuffle the decks. The CHANCE deck might have been initialized as a list:

```
SETQ (CHANCE ( ( (ADVANCE ILLINOIS–AV) (ADVANCE TO ILLINOIS AVE) )
              ( (PAY 15) (PAY POOR TAX OF 15 DOLLARS) )
                ...
              ) )
```

where each card is represented by a list of two sublists. The second sublist is the verbatim description of the card; the first sublist is its telegraphic style description that will indicate to the Monopoly-playing program what must be done.

Perhaps the easiest way to shuffle a deck is to use an array. We first place the elements of a LISt into an ARRaY that has been previously defined, starting at the first index of the array:

```
(PUTINARRAY (LAMBDA (LIS ARRY) (PROG (INDEX)
     (SETQ INDEX 0)
TEST (COND ( (NULL LIS) (RETURN INDEX) )
     (SETEL ARRY (LIST (SETQ INDEX (ADD1 INDEX) ) ) (CAR LIS) )
     (SETQ LIS (CDR LIS) ) (GO TEST) ) ) )
```

The value of PUTINARRAY is the value of the INDEX of the last array element that was filled. (SETEL array-name list-of-indices value-of-slot) makes the appropriate array assignment.

If one evaluates the program

```
PUTINARRAY ( (TOMMORROW WE SHALL POSSESS YESTERDAY)
            SOMEARRAY)
```

where SOMEARRAY is some previously defined one-dimensional array, then the value of PUTINARRAY will be 5, and

1. SOMEARRAY(1) will be TOMORROW,

2. SOMEARRAY(2) will be WE,

3. SOMEARRAY(3) will be SHALL,

4. SOMEARRAY(4) will be POSSESS, and finally

5. SOMEARRAY(5) will be YESTERDAY,

where SOMEARRAY(n) is used to denote the value of the n-th element of the array SOMEARRAY.

We now wish to shuffle the elements of the original LISt. We first put the elements of LISt in an array, using PUTINARRAY. The last element of the shuffled LISt will be found by taking a random number between 1 and the original length of the LISt. This element is deleted from the LISt, which is made one shorter. A new random number, obtained using RANDOMINT, selects the second to the last element of the shuffled list. (Because we shall CONS elements in the shuffled list, we first obtain the last element, then the second to the last element, etc.) The function SHUFFLE is now clear; we assume that a one-dimensional array SOME-ARRAY has been previously defined and that its size is not less than the LENGTH of LIS.

```
(SHUFFLE (LAMBDA (LIS) (PROG (HIGH INDEX)
        (COND ( (NULL LIS) (RETURN NIL) ) )
        (SETQ HIGH (PUTINARRAY LIS (QUOTE SOMEARRAY) ) )
        (SETQ LIS NIL)
  LOOP (COND ( (EQUAL HIGH 1)
                  (RETURN (CONS (GETEL (QUOTE SOMEARRAY) (LIST 1) ) LIS) ) )
        (SETQ INDEX (RANDOMINTFROMONE HIGH) )
        (SETQ LIS (CONS (GETEL (QUOTE SOMEARRAY) (LIST INDEX) ) LIS) ) )
        COND ( (EQUAL INDEX HIGH) NIL)
              (T (SETEL (QUOTE SOMEARRAY) (LIST INDEX)
                            (GETEL (QUOTE SOMEARRAY) (LIST HIGH) ) ) ) )
        (SETQ HIGH (SUB1 HIGH) ) (GO LOOP) ) ) )
```

✓ where (GETEL array-name list-of-indices) accesses the value of an array element. To understand SHUFFLE, let us see what happens on a small example:

SHUFFLE ((TWINS NEVER COME SINGLY))

The first CONDitional in SHUFFLE would eliminate the empty list. After PUTINARRAY is completed, HIGH has value 4, and the picture of SOMEARRAY is

INDEX	1	2	3	4
CONTENTS	TWINS	NEVER	COME	SINGLY

↑ HIGH

LIS is reset to NIL. Let us assume that the evaluation of (RANDOMINT-FROMONE 4) gives us 3. LIS becomes (COME), we move SOMEAR-RAY(4) to SOMEARRAY(3), and decrease HIGH by 1. The array configuration is

INDEX	1	2	3	4
CONTENTS	TWINS	NEVER	SINGLY	SINGLY

$\uparrow$ HIGH

Assuming that the evaluation of (RANDOMINTFROMONE 3) is 3, the new value of LIS is (SINGLY COME); the contents of SOMEARRAY are not touched, since INDEX and HIGH are EQUAL; and HIGH is decremented by 1 to 2.

Again (RANDOMINTFROMONE 2) is called; assume that it gives us 1. The new value of LIS is (TWINS SINGLY COME); SOMEARRAY is modified to

INDEX	1	2	3	4
CONTENTS	NEVER	NEVER	SINGLY	SINGLY

and HIGH is decremented by 1 to 1. At LOOP, we stop, and the final value of SHUFFLE is (NEVER TWINS SINGLY COME). What a ball!

Some LISP systems do not allow arrays, and therefore another definition of SHUFFLE, SHUFFLE2, will be given for such systems. Again, we shall pick out elements at random from a shorter and shorter list. To move down the list, we need a function that takes a given number of CDR's: The function

```
(FINDNTHCDR (LAMBDA (N LIS) ... ))
```

will take N successive CDR's of LIS. N is assumed to be a nonnegative integer.

```
(FINDNTHCDR (LAMBDA (N LIS)
            (COND ( (EQUAL N 0) LIS)
                  (T (FINDNTHCDR (SUB1 N) (CDR LIS)) ) ) )
            ) )
```

Although this definition is very simple, it will result in N auxiliary calls to FINDNTHCDR, which is expensive in terms of time and space. A more efficient definition is

```
(FINDNTHCDR (LAMBDA (N LIS) (PROG ()
LOOP (COND ((EQUAL N 0) (RETURN LIS)))
        (SETQ N (SUB1 N)) (SETQ LIS (CDR LIS)) (GO LOOP) )))
```

Here, no recursive calls to FINDNTHCDR are made; efficiently we CDR down LIS, while decreasing N, until N reaches the value zero.

We are now ready to write SHUFFLE2:

```
(SHUFFLE2 (LAMBDA (LIS) (PROG (HOLDBEGINNING HIGH WHERE TEMP)
      (COND ((NULL LIS) (RETURN NIL)))
      (SETQ HOLDBEGINNING LIS) (SETQ HIGH (LENGTH LIS))
 LOOP (COND ((NULL (CDR LIS)) (RETURN HOLDBEGINNING)))
      (SETQ WHERE (FINDNTHCDR (SUB1 (RANDOMINTFROMONE HIGH)) LIS))
      (COND ((EQ WHERE LIS) (GO DOWN)))
      (SETQ TEMP (CAR LIS)) (RPLACA LIS (CAR WHERE)) (RPLACA WHERE TEMP)
 DOWN (SETQ LIS (CDR LIS)) (SETQ HIGH (SUB1 HIGH)) (GO LOOP) )))
```

Let us partially go through an example:

```
SHUFFLE2 ( (RELIGIONS IMPROVE WITH BURNINGS) )
```

The original LIS is

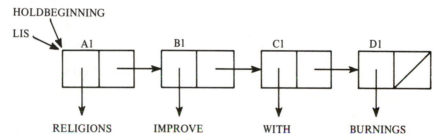

A1, B1, C1, and D1 are the addresses of the cells whose CAR's point to the atoms RELIGIONS, IMPROVE, WITH, and BURNINGS. The original values of LIS and HOLDBEGINNING are A1. HIGH starts with value 4. The test at LOOP fails; it could also have been

```
LOOP (COND ((EQUAL HIGH 1) (RETURN HOLDBEGINNING)))
```

Let us assume that (RANDOMINTFROMONE 4) gives us 4. WHERE points to cell D1, and its value is (BURNINGS). Since WHERE and LIS do not point to the same cell, we flip the contents of their CARs, using a TEMPorary and two RPLACAs. The result before reaching the

label DOWN is

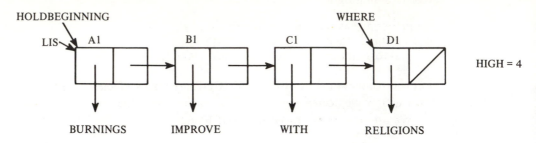

HOLDBEGINNING

WHERE

LIS   A1   B1   C1   D1   HIGH = 4

BURNINGS   IMPROVE   WITH   RELIGIONS

It should be easy to verify that if the subsequent calls to RANDOMINT-FROMONE give the values

1. (RANDOMINTFROMONE 3) gives 1,

2. (RANDOMINTFROMONE 2) gives 2,

then at the last LOOP we reach the configuration

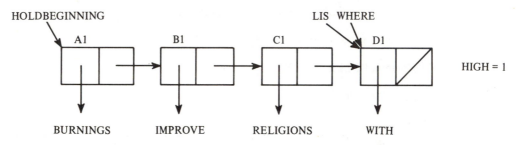

HOLDBEGINNING

LIS WHERE

A1   B1   C1   D1   HIGH = 1

BURNINGS   IMPROVE   RELIGIONS   WITH

and at LOOP we exit with the value of HOLDBEGINNING, which is the same cell as it was originally; however, some of the CARs of the LISt have been changed.

12.1.4 Adding and Deleting Cards from a Deck

When a player takes a CHANCE card, he usually reads it, follows the instructions on the card, and replaces the card at the bottom of the CHANCE deck. Hence, the CHANCE deck should be considered CIRCULAR and made so by using the function CIRCULAR. Some variable, CHANCE–POINTER, for example, points to a cell in the circular list. This cell can be considered as being the "top" of the deck; that is, (CAR CHANCE–POINTER) would be the card drawn by the next player who lands on a CHANCE place. After this card has been processed, doing (SETQ CHANCE–POINTER (CDR CHANCE–POINTER)) has the effect of "moving" the top of the deck to the bottom.

Sometimes a CHANCE card, such as a "Get out of jail, free" card, may be held by a player for later use. It must then be removed from the deck. So suppose that (CAR CHANCE–POINTER) is such a card:

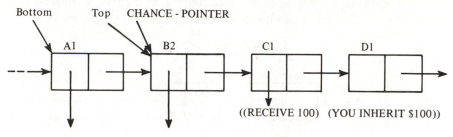

Again, A1, B1, and C1 are just arbitrary addresses of the LISP cells shown. Assume that the name of the player, PLAYER2, who drew the card is accessed as the value of a variable PRESENT–PLAYER and that we wish to add the card to PLAYER2 on a list that is the property of the indicator CARDS–HELD of PLAYER2. We do†

```
(PUTPROP PRESENT–PLAYER (QUOTE CARDS–HELD)
      (CONS (CAR CHANCE–POINTER) (GET PRESENT–PLAYER (QUOTE CARDS–HELD) ) ) )
```

and must now "delete" this card from the deck. The following sequence of programs accomplishes our goal:

```
(RPLACA CHANCE–POINTER (CADR CHANCE–POINTER) )
(RPLACD CHANCE–POINTER (CDDR CHANCE–POINTER) )
```

At this point, the situation is as follows:

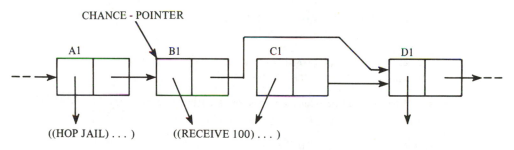

†Some care must be taken to distinguish cards from CHANCE or COMMUNITY–CHEST so as to be able to replace them in the appropriate deck. One could have two CARDS–HELD lists, either separated as properties of two indicators CARDS–HELD–CHANCE and CARDS–HELD–COMMUNITY or combined in one list ((list of cards from CHANCE) (list of cards from COMMUNITY)). Another solution is to mark each card as to its origin: (CHANCE (RECEIVE 100) . . .) before adding it to the CARDS–HELD list—perhaps the easiest solution.

Notice that the top of the deck is indeed the card ((RECEIVE 100) . . .) and that the one below is (CAR D1), as it should be. Moreover, cell C1 is no longer accessible—there is nothing pointing to it—and is therefore garbage. C1 will be collected during the next garbage collection.

Let us now assume that when the CHANCE deck looks like

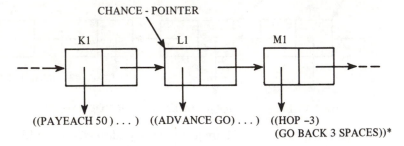

CHANCE - POINTER

K1   L1   M1

((PAYEACH 50) . . .)   ((ADVANCE GO) . . .)   ((HOP –3)
                                          (GO BACK 3 SPACES))*

we wish to place on the bottom of the deck the first card in the CARDS–HELD list of PRESENT–PLAYER (actually, the value of PRESENT–PLAYER, as before). We assume that we have the use of a TEMPorary variable. Onward LISPers! Grab the card (SETQ TEMP (CAR (GET PRESENT–PLAYER (QUOTE CARDS–HELD)))). Update the CARDS–HELD list:

```
(PUTPROP PRESENT-PLAYER (QUOTE CARDS-HELD)
         (CDR (GET PRESENT-PLAYER (QUOTE CARDS-HELD) ) ) )
```

Place the card in the CAR of a cell:

```
(SETQ TEMP (CONS TEMP NIL) )
```

Now insert this new cell. We can use another temporary, TEMPSTORE:

```
(RPLACD TEMP (CDR CHANCE-POINTER) )
(RPLACD CHANCE-POINTER TEMP)
(SETQ TEMPSTORE (CAR TEMP) )
(RPLACA TEMP (CAR CHANCE-POINTER) )
(RPLACA CHANCE-POINTER TEMPSTORE)
```

We can also be tricky and dispense with the temporary TEMPSTORE, using instead the CDR of TEMP:

```
(RPLACD TEMP (CAR TEMP) )
(RPLACA TEMP (CAR CHANCE-POINTER) )
(RPLACA CHANCE-POINTER (CDR TEMP) )
(RPLACD TEMP (CDR CHANCE-POINTER) )
(RPLACD CHANCE-POINTER TEMP)
```

†It is awkward to move backward in the circular list that represents the board. Replacing the command (HOP −3) by (HOP 37) solves the problem. For a definition of HOP, see Section 12.1.7.

We notice that the first of these last five operations, (RPLACD TEMP (CAR CHANCE–POINTER)), could have been omitted by replacing the earlier (SETQ TEMP (CONS TEMP NIL)) by (SETQ TEMP (CONS TEMP TEMP)). In either case, we finish by placing the top of the deck in the right place, (SETQ CHANCE–POINTER (CDR CHANCE-POIN-TER)), to obtain

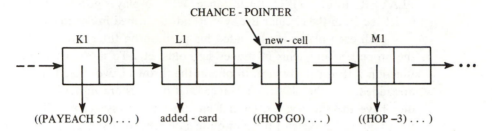

For clarity, the above-suggested programs are repeated separately: Program1 uses a second temporary TEMPSTORE:

```
(SETQ TEMP (CAR (GET PRESENT–PLAYER (QUOTE CARDS–HELD) ) ) )
(PUTPROP PRESENT–PLAYER (QUOTE CARDS–HELD)
        (CDR (GET PRESENT–PLAYER (QUOTE CARDS–HELD) ) ) )
(SETQ TEMP (CONS TEMP NIL) )
(RPLACD TEMP (CDR CHANCE–POINTER) )
(RPLACD CHANCE–POINTER TEMP)
(SETQ TEMPSTORE (CAR TEMP) )
(RPLACA TEMP (CAR CHANCE–POINTER) )
(RPLACA CHANCE–POINTER TEMPSTORE)
(SETQ CHANCE–POINTER (CDR CHANCE–POINTER) )
```

Program2 does not use a second temporary and is more efficient:

```
(SETQ TEMP (CAR (GET PRESENT–PLAYER (QUOTE CARDS–HELD) ) ) )
(PUTPROP PRESENT–PLAYER (QUOTE CARDS–HELD)
        (CDR (GET PRESENT–PLAYER (QUOTE CARDS–HELD) ) ) )
(SETQ TEMP (CONS TEMP TEMP) )
(RPLACA TEMP (CAR CHANCE–POINTER) )
(RPLACA CHANCE–POINTER (CDR TEMP) )
(RPLACD TEMP (CDR CHANCE–POINTER) )
(RPLACD CHANCE–POINTER TEMP)
(SETQ CHANCE–POINTER (CDR CHANCE–POINTER) )
```

12.1.5 Advancing the Players

The players in Monopoly play in turn, one after the other. Therefore, it appears best to make the list of players, for example,

```
(PLAYER1 PLAYER2 PLAYER3 PLAYER4 PLAYER5)
```

CIRCULAR, with a variable PLAYERS pointing to the cell whose CAR is the PRESENT–PLAYER. To move to the next player in turn, it suffices to do

```
(SETQ PLAYERS (CDR PLAYERS) ) (SETQ PRESENT–PLAYER (CAR PLAYERS) )
```

In this way the value of PRESENT–PLAYER would change from PLAYER5 to PLAYER1, for instance. When a player goes bankrupt, he is deleted from the circular list by methods described in Section 12.1.4.

With each player is associated his position on the board, the cards, the properties and sums of money he holds, etc. To move a player, the function DIE is called twice, to obtain the throw of two dice. The results are added, and the player is advanced. (If doubles are thrown, i.e., both dice have the same value, special handling is necessary; it will not be discussed in this sketch.) It is not quite sufficient to advance the player by the DICE–THROW he just made, using, for instance,

```
(SET PRESENT–PLAYER (FINDNTHCDR DICE–THROW (EVAL PRESENT-PLAYER) ) )†
```

since the PRESENT–PLAYER must collect $200 when passing GO, and the above program is unaware of the player passing GO. So instead of just CDRing down the board, we must also check about passing GO. To maintain some generality, we define a function FINDNTHFUNCTION which will apply its third argument, a functional argument, N times to its second argument. N is assumed to be a nonnegative integer, and the computation should make sense; i.e., the N applications of FUN should be possible.

```
(FINDNTHFUNCTION (LAMBDA (N LIS FUN) (PROG ( )
LOOP (COND ( (ZEROP N) (RETURN LIS) ) )
       (SETQ N (SUB1 N) ) (SETQ LIS (FUN LIS) ) (GO LOOP) ) ) )
```

Note that FINDNTHCDR is a particular example of FINDNTHFUNC-TION:

```
(FINDNTHCDR (LAMBDA (N LIS)
                (FINDNTHFUNCTION N LIS (FUNCTION CDR) ) ) )
```

To move the token of a player, we would evaluate

```
(SET PRESENT–PLAYER (FINDNTHFUNCTION DICE–THROW (EVAL PRESENT–PLAYER)
                (FUNCTION MOVE–AND–CHECK) ) )
```

†Note that SET and EVAL must be used, since the value of PRESENT–PLAYER is, say, PLAYER4 and the value of PLAYER4 is a cell in the circular board.

where

```
(MOVE–AND–CHECK (LAMBDA (BOARD–POSITION–CELL)
        (COND ( (EQ BOARD–POSITION–CELL (EVAL PRESENT–PLAYER) )
                (CDR BOARD–POSITION–CELL) )
              ( (NOT (EQ (QUOTE GO) (CAR BOARD–POSITION–CELL) ) )
                (CDR BOARD–POSITION–CELL) )
              ( (PUTPROP PRESENT–PLAYER (QUOTE WORTH) (PLUS 200
(GET PRESENT–PLAYER (QUOTE WORTH) ) ) (CDR BOARD–POSITION-CELL) ) ) ) ) )
```

The first test of MOVE–AND–CHECK is to avoid the case when the token of PRESENT–PLAYER was on GO at the time he threw the dice; in this way, he will not collect twice. If an intermediary place of the player is not GO, he continues; otherwise, his WORTH is increased by $200. The last pair of the CONDitional shows a standard trick: The left of the pair will never be NIL, it has the desired side effect of increasing the WORTH, and the right is then evaluated. We have assumed that the WORTH of a player is the property of the indicator WORTH of the player. This property would be initialized at the start of the game.

Notice that MOVE–AND–CHECK checks only intermediate positions of the player. If the player lands on GO at the end of his throw of dice, MOVE–AND–CHECK does not increase his worth. Final positions of a player are treated uniformly, as described in the next section.

12.1.6 *Information on Places and Cards*

We need to associate information with each place on the board. The majority of places are properties, and the information on a property can be easily stored using indicator-property pairs. For example, at one point in the game, the property PACIFIC–AV might have the following information:

Indicator	*Property*
COLOR	GREEN
COST	300
MORTGAGE	150 (always one half of COST, so may be ignored)
OWNER	PLAYERS
HOUSES	2
HOTEL	0
HOUSE–COST	200
RENT	26
RENT–HOUSE	(130 390 900 1100)
RENT–HOTEL	1275
PROPERTY	T

The existence of a color indicates that houses and hotels may be built on the property. The formula for rent is more complicated for other types of properties, such as the railroads and water–works.

We need to consider now the case of places which are not properties, such as INCOME–TAX, CHANCE, GO–TO–JAIL, etc. We propose to treat all such places in a uniform way. They are recognized by the absence of the indicator PROPERTY; i.e., (GET (QUOTE CHANCE) (QUOTE PROPERTY)) would have value NIL. With each nonproperty place we associate the indicator ACTION with property a little program to be evaluated. The different cases are the following:

Place	Indicator	Property
GO	ACTION	(RECEIVE 200)
COMMUNITY–CHEST	ACTION	(COMMUNITY–CHEST)
INCOME–TAX	ACTION	(PAY 200)†
CHANCE	ACTION	(CHANCE)
VISITING–JAIL	ACTION	NIL‡
FREE–PARKING	ACTION	NIL‡
GO–TO–JAIL	ACTION	(HOP JAIL)
LUXURY–TAX	ACTION	(PAY 75)

After the throw of dice, a player will be resting at a place on the board or will be in JAIL. A uniform treatment is afforded if we agree that the value of PRESENT–PLAYER, for example, PLAYER2, is a cell on the board, for example, the cell

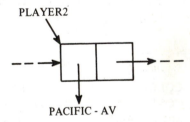

JAIL is handled uniformly with other places if we make it the CAR of a cell, the CDR of the cell being the next place the player would go when getting out of JAIL. If PLAYER3 is now in JAIL, the information would

†Here, as in other places, some simplifications will be made to the rules of Monopoly.

‡Which would be implemented by placing no indicator ACTION on VISITING–JAIL and FREE–PARKING.

be represented as

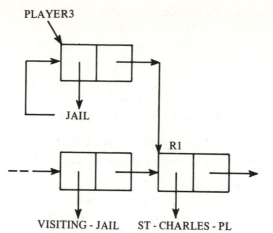

The above configuration is easily obtained. We first need to obtain the cell whose CAR is ST–CHARLES–PL. The function HOP—described in Section 12.1.7—will have as value this cell, arbitrarily labeled R1 in the diagram. Since the cell whose CAR is JAIL is not in the circular board, let us decide to access it as the *value* of . . . JAIL. Hence, it suffices to do

(SETQ JAIL (CONS (QUOTE JAIL) (HOP (QUOTE ST–CHARLES–PL))))

Now, if the PRESENT–PLAYER is PLAYER2, PLAYER2 will always be at the place which is the value of PLAYER2. We can check whether this place is a property or not by doing

(COND ((GET (CAR (EVAL PRESENT–PLAYER)) (QUOTE PROPERTY))
          (appropriate action about the property))
(T (EVAL (GET (CAR (EVAL PRESENT–PLAYER)) (QUOTE ACTION)))))

In the first case in the CONDitional, the player has landed on a property which may belong to him, to another player, or to the bank. If on his own property, he has nothing to do. If on another player's property, he may have to pay rent, and if the property is not owned, he may decide to purchase it. How he will pay the rent or make the purchase, or whether he will purchase at all, would depend on the strategy of play of the particular player. In fact, it is possible to program various strategies for various players and compare them in a variety of games.

In the second case of the conditional, the action associated with the place is evaluated. That is, one of the programs (RECEIVE 200), (COMMUNITY–CHEST), (HOP JAIL), etc., will be evaluated.

The information on CHANCE and COMMUNITY–CHEST cards could also be handled in exactly the same way: Each card could be a list of two SEXes. The second SEX is a verbatim description of the card, used for printing purposes only. The first SEX is a small program to be evaluated. Some examples of cards would be

```
((HOP JAIL) (GO TO JAIL GO DIRECTLY TO JAIL ... ))
((PAY 100) (PAY HOSPITAL 100))
((RECEIVE 200) (BANK ERROR IN YOUR FAVOR COLLECT 200))
```

Hence, when the player lands on a CHANCE card, the function CHANCE is executed. The outline of the function CHANCE is

```
(CHANCE (LAMBDA ()
(COND ((EQUAL (CAR CHANCE–POINTER) (QUOTE (OUT JAIL)))
              (remove this card from deck and give it to PRESENT–PLAYER))
         (T (PROG2 (EVAL (CAR CHANCE–POINTER))
                   (SETQ CHANCE–POINTER (CDR CHANCE–POINTER)))))))
```

and similarly for the function COMMUNITY–CHEST.

We need to describe some of the auxiliary functions that have been mentioned: HOP, ADVANCE, PAY, RECEIVE, etc.

12.1.7 Auxiliary Functions

12.1.7.1 HOP and ADVANCE

Two functions will make a player move to a new place on the board: HOP and ADVANCE. These functions differ in only one respect: When a player ADVANCES, if he passes GO, he collects money; when he HOPs, he "flies" directly to the place where he should go. Although one never has an opportunity to ADVANCE to JAIL, both functions wiil be written to take this possibility into account.

```
(HOP (LAMBDA (WHERE) (SET PRESENT–PLAYER
   (COND ((NUMBERP WHERE) (COND ((MINUSP WHERE) (HOP (PLUS WHERE 40)))
                           (T (FINDNTCHCDR WHERE (EVAL PRESENT–PLAYER)))))
         ((EQ WHERE JAIL) JAIL)
         (T (MOVE–TO–FIND (CDR (EVAL PRESENT–PLAYER))
                   WHERE
                   (FUNCTION CDR))))))))
```

In HOP, we first check whether WHERE is a number. Since it is not possible to go back in the circular list that represents the board, a negative number, such as -3, has the number of places on the board—40—added to it. Then an appropriate number of CDR's are taken, and the position of the PRESENT–PLAYER, for example, PLAYER3, is reset.

JAIL is treated specially. The value of JAIL is a cell whose CAR is JAIL, so it suffices to reset the value of PLAYER3 (for example) to this cell. Finally, in the general case, we look for a cell whose CAR is the value of WHERE. The function MOVE–TO–FIND is utilized, starting with the next place on the board after the value of PLAYER3.

```
(MOVE–TO–FIND (LAMBDA (INITIAL–CELL FINAL–CAR HOW) (PROG ()
LOOP (COND ( (EQ (CAR INITIAL–CELL) FINAL–CAR) (RETURN INITIAL–CELL) ) )
     (SETQ INITIAL–CELL (HOW INITIAL–CELL) ) (GO LOOP) ) ) )
```

The function ADVANCE is essentially similar to HOP, except that as we move around the board, if we pass GO then the WORTH of PRE-SENT–PLAYER is increased by 200. Hence, instead of just CDRing down the circular list representing the board, we have to use MOVE–AND–CHECK.

```
(ADVANCE (LAMBDA (WHERE) (SET PRESENT–PLAYER
   (COND ( (NUMBERP WHERE (COND ( (MINUSP WHERE) (HOP (PLUS WHERE 40) ) )
                            (T (FINDNTHFUNCTION WHERE
                                  (EVAL PRESENT–PLAYER)
                                  (FUNCTION MOVE–AND–CHECK) ) ) )
      ( (EQ WHERE JAIL) JAIL)
      (T (MOVE–TO–FIND (CDR (EVAL PRESENT–PLAYER) )
                         WHERE
                         (FUNCTION MOVE–AND–CHECK) ) ) ) ) ) )
```

In both HOP and ADVANCE, PRESENT–PLAYER is used as a global variable. In this way, the cards can be written without reference to the player who draws them.

12.1.7.2 RECEIVE

The PRESENT–PLAYER will have his WORTH increased by the SUM he RECEIVEs:

```
(RECEIVE (LAMBDA (SUM)
    (PUTPROP PRESENT–PLAYER (QUOTE WORTH)
        (PLUS SUM (GET PRESENT–PLAYER (QUOTE WORTH) ) ) ) ) )
```

EXERCISES

1. Define the function (PAY (LAMBDA (SUM) . . .)) which decreases the WORTH of PRESENT–PLAYER by SUM. Assume that his WORTH is at least SUM. (If his WORTH is less than SUM, a strategy must be followed to obtain money from the bank by mortgaging property, etc.)

2. Define the function (PAYEACH (LAMBDA (SUM) . . .)) by which PRESENT–PLAYER increases the WORTH of each of the other players by SUM, thereby, of course, decreasing his WORTH by as many times SUM as

there are other players. Assume that he is sufficiently rich to PAYEACH other player. Remember that PLAYERS points to the circular list of players and that PRESENT–PLAYER is (CAR PLAYERS).

3. Define the function (RECEIVE–FROM–EACH (LAMBDA (SUM) . . .)) by which PRESENT–PLAYER receives SUM from each of the other players.

There are a few additional functions that need to be defined, but they will be left to the Monopoly buff. It is time to have a look at the total picture.

12.1.8 The Monitor and Review

It is now possible to outline the complete Monopoly playing program. First, a certain number of actions must be taken to initialize the game:

a. Make the board circular; attach JAIL off the board.

b. Make PLAYERS circular and initialize PRESENT–PLAYER.

c. Shuffle the CHANCE and COMMUNITY–CHEST decks, make them circular, and initialize pointers to the tops of the decks.

d. Initialize all information about properties.

e. Program strategies for each player. The player has the option of buying or not, of trading, of maintaining large amounts of cash or building houses, of selling houses or mortgaging property when short of cash, of choosing between various alternatives for getting out of JAIL, etc.

f. If you are playing with the computer, it will throw dice, but you can decide your own strategy.

During play, the monitor program will throw dice, advance the players in turn, and handle the bookkeeping of their wealth and the funds and properties that are exchanged among players and between players and the bank. When necessary, the monitor will invoke the strategy program of a particular player.

That's almost it. Soon, you will be ready for an opportunity to ruin your best friend through bloodthirsty, sadistic, capitalistic machinations.

12.2 Pig Latin

We have considered atoms as being indivisible. That is, such questions as "Does the atom THYMES end in S?" did not make any sense. In most LISP systems, though, it is possible to break atoms apart. The function to

√n   be used does not have an accepted name. It is sometimes called **EXPLODE**:

```
EXPLODE ( THYMES )
 VALUE IS ...
 (T H Y M E S)
```

As the example shows, EXPLODE takes an atom as argument and has as value a list of all the atomic characters of the atom. The list (T H Y M E S) has a length of 6.

Of interest is the particular case of digits in an atom.

```
(EXPLODE (QUOTE THYMES9) )
 VALUE IS ...
 (T H Y M E S 9)

(LAST (EXPLODE (QUOTE THYMES9) ) )
 VALUE IS ...
 9

(EQUAL 9 (LAST (EXPLODE (QUOTE THYMES9) ) ) )
 VALUE IS ...
 NIL
```

√   What has happened? When an atom is exploded, the digits become *characters*, not numbers. The value of (LAST (EXPLODE (QUOTE THYMES9))) is the character 9, and not the number 9. It happens that both the character 9 and the number 9 PRINT the same way, and thus the confusion. The treatment of characters in LISP is not uniform. Some
√   systems would recognize $$$9$ as the character 9; others, /9. Consult your local LISP reference manual.

To reconstruct an atom from its characters, a function, sometimes
√n   called **COMPRESS**, is usually available.

```
(COMPRESS (QUOTE (T H Y M E S) ) )
 VALUE IS ...
 THYMES
(EQ (QUOTE THYMES) (COMPRESS (QUOTE (T H Y M E S) ) ) )
 VALUE IS ...
 T
```

However, the program

```
(COMPRESS (QUOTE (T H Y M E S 9) ) )
```

may result in an error, since 9 is not a character. On the other hand,

```
(COMPRESS (QUOTE (T H Y M E S $$$9$) ) )
 VALUE IS ...
 THYMES9
```

We are now ready to program a function PIGLATIN which takes an English sentence as argument, in the form of a list, and turns it into PIGLATIN. Each word is transformed according to the rules

a. If a word begins with a vowel, add "way" to the word.

b. If the word does not start with a vowel, take all the consonants of the beginning of the word up to the first vowel, move them to the back of the word, and add "ay." First (SETQ VOWELS (QUOTE (A E I O U Y)))†; then DEFINE:

```
(PIGLATIN (LAMBDA (SENTENCE)
   (MAPCAR SENTENCE (FUNCTION PIGWORD) ) ) )
(PIGWORD (LAMBDA (WORD) (PROG (EXPL FRONT)
        (SETQ EXPL (EXPLODE WORD) )
        (COND ( (MEMBER (CAR EXPL) VOWELS) NIL)
              (T (GO NOTFIRSTVOWEL) ) )
   FIRSTVOWEL
        (RETURN (COMPRESS (APPEND EXPL (QUOTE (W A Y) ) ) ) )
   NOTFIRSTVOWEL
        (SETQ FRONT (CONS (CAR EXPL) FRONT) )
        (SETQ EXPL (CDR EXPL) )
        (COND ( (NULL EXPL) (RETURN (PRINT (LIST (QUOTE ERROR) WORD) ) ) )
              ( (MEMBER (CAR EXPL) VOWELS) (GO END) ) )
        (GO NOTFIRSTVOWEL)
   END (RETURN (COMPRESS (APPEND EXPL
                                 (APPEND (REVERSE FRONT) (QUOTE (A Y) ) ) ) ) )
       ) ) )
```

The label FIRSTVOWEL is not used but makes the program easier to follow. If the argument of PIGWORD has no vowel, for example, SHRDL, then the value of PIGWORD would be (ERROR SHRDL), and this list is also PRINTed. We shall now show some examples:

```
(PIGWORD (QUOTE ACTIVITY) )
VALUE IS...
ACTIVITYWAY

(PIGWORD (QUOTE CONTAGIOUS) )
VALUE IS...
ONTAGIOUSCAY

(PIGLATIN (QUOTE (ACTIVITY IS CONTAGIOUS) ) )
VALUE IS...
(ACTIVITYWAY ISWAY ONTAGIOUSCAY)
```

†Why is "y" a vowel?

```
(PIGLATIN (QUOTE (AT THYMES THE SAGE ROSEMARY EATS PARSLEY)))
VALUE IS...
(ATWAY YMESTHAY ETHAY AGESAY OSEMARYRAY EATSWAY ARSLEYPAY)
```

Isntway isthay unfay?

Compressing and exploding constantly is fairly expensive in terms of computer time. If your planned program is mainly concerned with the manipulation of words, or strings of characters, you may wish to investigate a programming language, such as SNOBOL,† which is specifically designed for string manipulation.

EXERCISES

1. Write a function KILLPIGGY which takes as argument a sentence in pig Latin, in the form of a list, and transforms it into English. Are there any difficulties?

```
KILLPIGGY ( (ATWAY YMESTHAY ETHAY AGESAY OSEMARYRAY EATSWAY ARSLEYPAY) )
VALUE IS...
(AT THYMES THE SAGE ROSEMARY EATS PARSLEY)
```

2. Write a function ARAGUE which transforms English to the ARAGUE language.

```
ARAGUE ( (TO BED SAYS SLEEPY HEAD) )
VALUE IS...
(TARAGO BARAGED SARAGAYS SLARAGEEPY HARAGEAD)
```

Other variations consist of putting "ag" or "eg" before each vowel of a word, resulting in the well-known Aygo-Paygo and Eggy-peggy languages.

12.3   Common Substitution Instance

In Chapter 8, the question was asked whether one formula F1 is a substitution instance of another formula F2. In this section, we shall ask a related question: If F1 and F2 are two formulae, is there a formula F3 such that F3 is a substitution instance of both F1 and F2? F3 is then called a *common substitution instance*, or CSI, of F1 and F2. Finding a CSI for two formulae is frequently necessary in programs that try to prove theorems.

†R. E. Griswold, J. F. Poage, and I. P. Polonsky, *The SNOBOL4 Programming Language*, 2nd ed., Prentice-Hall, Inc., Englewood Cliffs, N.J., 1971.

12.3.1 The Unification Algorithm

To find a CSI for F1 and F2 is often called to *unify* F1 and F2. The unification algorithm that we shall implement is due to J. A. Robinson.†

The algorithm as considered here assumes that the variable names of F1 are disjoint from the variable names of F2. To unify F1 with F2,

Loop 1: If F1 is a variable, and F1 is bound to F1', replace F1 by F1' and go to loop 1.

Loop 2: If F2 is a variable, and F2 is bound to F2', replace F2 by F2' and go to loop 2.

(Now neither F1 nor F2 is a variable bound to an expression.)

If F1 is a variable, then if F1 occurs in F2 fail-to-unify else bind F2 onto F1 and succeed.

If F2 is a variable, then if F2 occurs in F1 fail-to-unify else bind F1 onto F2 and succeed;

If neither F1 nor F2 are variables,

```
F1 = (G1 arg11 arg12 ... arg1n)
F2 = (G2 arg12 arg22 ... arg2m)
```

then to unify we must have G1 = G2, and arg1i must unify with arg2i, for i = 1, 2, . . . , m = n. During these unifications, the previously built bindings are kept.

We still need to describe "occurs."

Loop: To find out whether F1 (an unbound variable) occurs in F2:

a. If F2 is a variable and is bound to F2', replace F2 by F2' and go to loop.

b. If F2 is an unbound variable, if F1 = F2, then F1 occurs in F2 else F1 does not occur in F2.

c. If F2 is not a variable, it is of the form (G2 arg1 . . . argn) and we check whether F1 occurs in any of arg1, . . . , argn.

Some examples will help to understand the algorithm:

a. (FF X) and (GG Y) do not unify since FF and GG are different function names.

†J. A. Robinson, "A Machine-Oriented Logic Based on the Resolution Principle," *J. ACM 12*, (1) (1965), 23–41.

b. (FF X1 (FG X1)) and (FF (GG Y1) Y1) do not unify. First, X1 is bound to (GG Y1). Next, trying to bind Y1 to (FG X1), we must check that Y1 does not occur in (FG X1). In fact, Y1 occurs in the binding of X1, so the unification fails.

12.3.2 A LISP Program for Unification

The unification algorithm is translated into the function CSI. Constants are represented as functions of no arguments. Bindings will be properties of the indicator BOUND. We shall use generators for bookkeeping. Since both in CSI and in "occurs" we chase down the bindings of atoms, we define a function LASTBIND which chases the bindings of an atom until an expression is found which is either nonatomic (and hence not a variable) or a variable with nothing BOUND to it:

```
(LASTBIND (LAMBDA (EXP) (PROG (TEMP)
     (SETQ TEMP EXP)
LOOP
     (COND ((AND (ATOM (SETQ EXP TEMP))
                 (SETQ TEMP (GET EXP (QUOTE BOUND)))))
            (GO LOOP))
           (T (RETURN EXP)))
   )))
```

Since generators are conventionally stopped by NIL values of their functional argument, it is slightly more practical to ask whether variable EXP1 does *not* occur in EXP2:

```
(NOCCUR (LAMBDA (EXP1 EXP2) (NOCCUR1 EXP2)))

(NOCCUR1 (LAMBDA (EXP2)
   (AND (NOT (EQ EXP1 (SETQ EXP2 (LASTBIND EXP2))))
        (OR (ATOM EXP2) (GENC (CDR EXP2) (FUNCTION NOCCUR1))))
 )))
```

When we unify two nonvariable expressions, we use DOUBLEGENC to go down the arguments of the two expressions:

```
(DOUBLEGENC (LAMBDA (LIS1 LIS2 FUN2)
    (COND ((NULL LIS1) (NULL LIS2))
          ((NULL LIS2) NIL)
          ((FUN2 (CAR LIS1) (CAR LIS2))
               (DOUBLEGENC (CDR LIS1) (CDR LIS2) FUN2))
          (T NIL)
   )))
```

191   Section 12.3   Common Substitution Instance

We are now ready for CSI:

```
(CSI (LAMBDA (EXP1 EXP2)
    (PROG2
        (SETQ  EXP2 (LASTBIND EXP2))
        (COND ( (ATOM (SETQ EXP1 (LASTBIND EXP1)))
                (AND (NOCCUR EXP1 EXP2)
                    (PUTPROP EXP1 (QUOTE BOUND) EXP2)))
              ( (ATOM EXP2)
                (AND (NOCCUR EXP2 EXP1)
                    (PUTPROP EXP2 (QUOTE BOUND) EXP1)))
              ( (EQ (CAR EXP1) (CAR EXP2))
                (DOUBLEGENC (CDR EXP1) (CDR EXP2) (FUNCTION CSI)))
              (T NIL) )
    )))
```

Note that CSI does not clean the properties of the indicator BOUND since they may be used to find the common substitution instance, as in Exercise 2 below.

EXERCISES

1.   Before a binding is set in CSI, NOCCUR is called. However, for the first time a binding is considered, NOCCUR must fail; hence the call to NOCCUR is useless. Change CSI to make use of this observation. Give examples where these changes result in savings in computation.

2.   Given that (CSI EXP1 EXP2) has value T, write a function GETCSI which has as value the common substitution instance of EXP1 and EXP2. *Hint:*   Assume that CSI has been run and that all the bindings have been set.

3.   If F1 and F2 have variable names in common, CSI will not work. So, before calling CSI, F1 and F2 should be transformed into formulae FONE and FTWO, by some function DIFFVARIABLES which guarantees that FONE and FTWO have no variables in common and are isomorphic to F1 and F2, respectively. Define DIFFVARIABLES. Should it be a function of one or two variables? *Hint:*   GENSYM (Section 11.5) may be appropriate.

12.4   A Shortest Path Algorithm

Suspense! You have been notified that your beloved cat has been poisoned. You rush to your 200-room palace. You enter the door, and although you know where the cat is, you pause for a millisecond to ask yourself, "What is the shortest path to my beloved cat?" It is just for such emergencies that shortest path algorithms have been designed.

Let us consider a small example. Let the plan of the floor be

1	2	3	4	5	6								
7	8	9	10	11	12								
13	14	15	16	17	18								
19	20	21	22	23	24								
25	26	27	28	29	30	43	44	45	46	47	48	49	50
31	32	33	34	35	36								
37	38	39	40	41	42								

Any wall common to two rooms has a door joining the two rooms. Let us assume that you are in room 28 and want to make sure that you do find the shortest path from room 28 to room 48.

12.4.1 Breadth-first Search from the Start

One method would be to see where you can go crossing only one door. You could then reach rooms 22, 27, 29, and 34. Crossing yet another door, you can reach further into rooms 16, 21, 23, 26, 30, 33, 35, and 40. Progress would be shown by the table

In N, but Not in N — 1 Steps	You Can Reach Rooms
N = 0	28
N = 1	22 27 29 34
N = 2	16 21 23 26 30 33 35 40
N = 3	10 15 17 20 24 25 32 36 39 41 43
N = 4	4 9 11 14 18 19 31 38 42 44
N = 5	3 5 8 12 13 37 45
N = 6	2 6 7 46
N = 7	1 47
N = 8	48. Success!

To find the cat, and to make sure that you have taken the shortest path, you considered 46 rooms besides the initial and final ones.

12.4.2 Breadth-first Search from the Goal

If instead of advancing from your position in room 28, you had imagined *backing from* room 48, the situation would have been

In N, but Not in N − 1 Steps	You Can Reach Rooms
N = 0	48
N = 1	47 49
N = 2	46 50
N = 3	45
N = 4	44
N = 5	43
N = 6	30
N = 7	24 29 36
N = 8	18 23 28 35 42. Success!

In this way you would have explored only a maximum of 15 intermediary rooms.

12.4.3 Bidirectional Search with Equal Speed in Both Directions

Of course, since you don't know the solution, you cannot predict that moving backwards would necessarily be better. In fact, think of the situation when you are in room 48 and the cat is in room 28. So, to have the best of both worlds, let us see what happens when one moves alternately forward from the start and then backward from the goal.

After N Steps	From the Start	From the Goal
0	28	48
1	22 27 29 34	47 49
2	16 21 23 26 30 33 35 40	46 50
3	10 15 17 20 24 25 32 36 39 41 43	45
4	4 9 11 14 18 19 31 38 42 44	44

At this point we stop since the path from the start and the path from the goal have a common room, 44. The number of intermediary rooms is 39, which is better than the first solution but worse than the second.

12.4.4 Weighted Bidirectional Search

In the previous case, it would have been better to grow the search space mostly from the goal. But how were we to know?

We first introduce some terminology. We call the *frontier from the start* or the *forward frontier after N steps*, the set of rooms that can be reached from the start in N but not in N − 1 steps. Similarly, we define the frontier from the goal, or the backward frontier after N steps. The total number of rooms visited is the sum of the frontiers, both forward and backward. If we assume that the frontiers grow about regularly, which is not quite true, then we shall limit the number of rooms considered by growing always from the smallest frontier.

In our example, we would proceed as follows:

Frontier	Rooms	Size	Choice to Grow Next
Forward N = 0	28	1	
Backward N = 0	48	1	Tossup; pick forward
Forward N = 1	22 27 29 34	4	Backward N = 1
Backward N = 1	47 49	2	Backward N = 2
Backward N = 2	46 50	2	Backward N = 3
Backward N = 3	45	1	Backward N = 4
Backward N = 4	44	1	Backward N = 5
Backward N = 5	43	1	Backward N = 6
Backward N = 6	30	1	Backward N = 7
Backward N = 7	24 29 36	3	Success; stop

The two *search spaces*, the forward space and the backward space, met in room 29, so the procedure stops. If it had not, the next choice to grow from would have been backward frontier N = 7, since its size, 3, was smaller than the forward frontier N = 1. The number of intermediary rooms was 14, counting the common room 29 only once. We shall now describe an implementation of this algorithm as the FINDPATH function.

12.4.5 FINDPATH

In FINDPATH we make the following assumptions:

a. The starting room is the value of ROOMST.

b. The goal room is the value of ROOMGO.

c. The OPENINGS from a room are the value of the function OPENINGS applied to the room; it is assumed to be in the form of a list of dotted pairs (room . passage). For example, in our example, OPENINGS (ROOM28) would have value

((ROOM22 . DOOR22–28) (ROOM27 . DOOR27–28) (ROOM 29 . DOOR28–29)
(ROOM34 . DOOR28–34))

d. To add more generality, each passage is checked for feasibility, by the functional argument FEASIBLE of FINDPATH. For example, a closed door may not be FEASIBLE, or if a person is too fat, he may not go through some tiny doors, etc.

e. Growing the forward and growing the backward frontiers are essentially similar processes. In FINDPATH only one process is used, which accesses either frontier *indirectly*. Assuming that ROOMST is down and ROOMGO is up, the PROG variable DIR indicates which frontier is being considered. The names used for each case are

	DIR Has Value T	*DIR Has Value NIL*
Frontier being grown	From ROOMST	From ROOMGO
Direction of growth	UP	DOWN
Frontier	FRONUP	FRONDOWN
New frontier	NEWFUP	NEWFDOWN
Starting room	ROOMST	ROOMGO
Door considered	DOORUP	DOORDOWN

A set of very simple functions translate the above dictionary:

```
(UP      (LAMBDA (B) (COND (B (QUOTE UP))      (T (QUOTE DOWN))))))
(FRONUP  (LAMBDA (B) (COND (B (QUOTE FRONUP))  (T (QUOTE FRONDOWN))))))
(NEWFUP  (LAMBDA (B) (COND (B (QUOTE NEWFUP))  (T (QUOTE NEWFDOWN))))))
(ROOM    (LAMBDA (B) (COND (B (QUOTE ROOMST))  (T (QUOTE ROOMGO))))))
(DOORUP  (LAMBDA (B) (COND (B (QUOTE DOORUP))  (T (QUOTE DOORDOWN))))))
```

Property lists will be used on encountered rooms. These property lists must be cleaned up. The rooms encountered in the UP space of rooms will be stored in the list CLEANUP, while the rooms encountered in the DOWN space of rooms will be stored in CLEANDOWN:

```
(CLEANUP (LAMBDA (B) (COND (B (QUOTE CLEANUP)) (T (QUOTE CLEANDOWN))))))
```

We are now ready to get going:

```
(FINDPATH (LAMBDA (ROOMST ROOMGO FEASIBLE) (PROG (NEWROOM DIR
NEWFUP NEWFDOWN UP DOWN DOORUP DOORDOWN CLEANUP CLEANDOWN)
```

We first check whether there is any path to be found:

```
(COND ((EQ ROOMST ROOMGO) (RETURN ROOMST)))
```

Then we initialize the clean-up lists and frontiers and mark the initial and final rooms as having been encountered:

```
(MAPC (LIST T NIL) (FUNCTION (LAMBDA (BOOL)
(PROG2 (PUTPROP (EVAL (ROOM BOOL)) (UP BOOL) T)
       (SET (FRONUP BOOL) (SET (CLEANUP BOOL) (LIST (EVAL (ROOM BOOL)))))))
 ))))
```

If, as in the example, ROOMST is ROOM28 and ROOMGO is ROOM48, then after initialization, ROOM28 has indicator UP with value T, and the forward frontier FRONUP and CLEANUP have value (ROOM28). Similarly, ROOM48 has indicator DOWN with value T; FRONDOWN and CLEANDOWN have value (ROOM48). Now we select from which frontier we shall grow. If FRONUP is smaller than or equal in LENGTH to FRONDOWN, we grow UP and DIR has value T.

```
SELECT (SETQ DIR (COND ((GREATERP (LENGTH FRONDOWN) (LENGTH FRONUP)) T)
                       (T NIL) ))
```

For each room on the chosen frontier we find all its OPENINGS, which is a list of dotted pairs ((newroom . passage) ... (newroom . passage)). We discard new rooms that can be reached through passages that are not FEASIBLE. For new rooms that can be reached, we ask

a. Is NEWROOM in the *other* space? If so, a path has been found.

b. Has NEWROOM already been met from (ROOM DIR)? If so, since we are only interested in one path; the NEWROOM is discarded. If the NEWROOM has not been encountered yet, it becomes part of the new frontier. Moreover, on the property list of NEWROOM we add the indicator DOORUP with property the passage and the indicator (UP DIR) with value the room NODE from which NEWROOM was reached.

To lighten FINDPATH, the last pieces of processing are carried out in the bookkeeping function BOOKPG:

```
(COND ((GENC (EVAL (FRONUP DIR))) (FUNCTION (LAMBDA (NODE)
 (GENC (OPENINGS NODE) (FUNCTION (LAMBDA (PAIR)
  (COND ((GET (SETQ NEWROOM (CAR PAIR)) (UP DIR)) T)
```

This eliminated a NEWROOM that had already been encountered.

```
        ((NOT (FEASIBLE (CDR PAIR))) T)
```

This eliminated a passage that was not FEASIBLE.

```
        ((GET NEWROOM (UP (NOT DIR))) (PROG2 (BOOKPG) NIL))
```

We just found a common room; the generators are stopped.

```
(T PROGN (BOOKPG)
        (SET (NEWFUP DIR) (CONS NEWROOM (EVAL NEWFUP DIR
) ) ) ) ) ) ) ) ) ) (GO TRYAGAIN) ) )
```

At TRYAGAIN we look at the new frontier; here, we obtain the path—
using FRONUP and FRONDOWN to hold the paths—and clean up:

```
(MAPC (LIST T NIL) (FUNCTION (LAMBDA (BOOL) (PROG (HOLD NEXT)
 (SET (FRONUP BOOL) (LIST (SETQ HOLD NEWROOM) ) )
 CHECK (COND ( (EQ (SETQ NEXT (GET HOLD (UP BOOL) ) ) T) (RETURN NIL) )
             (NEXT (PROGN (SET (FRONUP BOOL) (CONS NEXT (CONS (GET HOLD
                                 (DOORUP BOOL) ) (EVAL (FRONUP BOOL) ) ) ) )
             (SETQ HOLD NEXT) (GO CHECK) ) ) ) ) ) )
```

In the above, we start from NEWROOM, which is common to both paths.
We build a list, stored in (FRONUP BOOL), of the sequence of passages
and rooms leading to NEWROOM. For example, in our example, the
value of NEWROOM would be ROOM29. At the end of the above
MAPC, the value of FRONUP would be (ROOM28 DOOR28–29
ROOM29), while the value of FRONDOWN would be (ROOM48
DOOR47–48 ROOM 47 DOOR46–47 ROOM46 DOOR45–46 ROOM45
DOOR44–45 ROOM 44 DOOR43-44 ROOM43 DOOR30–43 ROOM30
DOOR29–30 ROOM29). We put the whole path in NEWROOM:

```
(SETQ NEWROOM (NCONC FRONUP (CDR (REVERSE FRONDOWN) ) ) )
```

Then clean up:

```
CLEANUP (MAPC (LIST T NIL) (FUNCTION (LAMBDA (BOOL)
               (MAPC (EVAL (CLEANUP BOOL) )
               (FUNCTION (LAMBDA (NODE)
                (PROG2 (REMPROP NODE (UP BOOL) )
                       (REMPROP NODE (DOORUP BOOL) ) ) ) ) ) ) )
(RETURN NEWROOM)
TRYAGAIN
```

We come here if no common room was found. To continue, we must make
sure that the new frontier is not NIL, which would indicate that *no* path
can be found†:

```
(COND ( (NULL (EVAL (NEWFUP DIR) ) ) (PROG2 (SETQ NEWROOM NIL) (GO CLEANUP) ) ) )
```

Otherwise, we rename the new frontier as the frontier, and again select
the direction of growth:

†Assuming that there are no one-way passages.

```
(SET (FRONUP DIR) (EVAL (NEWFUP DIR)))
(SET (NEWFUP DIR) NIL) (GO SELECT) )))
```

We must still define

```
(BOOKPG (LAMBDA () (PROGN
 (SET (CLEANUP DIR) (CONS NEWROOM (EVAL (CLEANUP DIR)))))
 (PUTPROP NEWROOM (DOORUP DIR) (CDR PAIR))
 (PUTPROP NEWROOM (UP DIR) NODE)    )))
```

The complete program for FINDPATH, without comments, is

```
(FINDPATH (LAMBDA (ROOMST ROOMGO FEASIBLE) (PROG (NEWROOM DIR
NEWFUP NEWFDOWN UP DOWN DOORUP DOORDOWN CLEANUP CLEANDOWN)
(COND ((EQ ROOMST ROOMGO) (RETURN ROOMST)))
(MAPC (LIST T NIL) (FUNCTION (LAMBDA (BOOL)
 (PROG2 (PUTPROP (EVAL (ROOM BOOL)) (UP BOOL) T)
        (SET (FRONUP BOOL) (SET (CLEANUP BOOL) (LIST (EVAL (ROOM BOOL))))))
 ))))
SELECT
(SETQ DIR (COND ((GREATERP (LENGTH FRONDOWN) (LENGTH FRONUP)) T)
                (T NIL) ))
(COND ((GENC (EVAL (FRONUP DIR)) (FUNCTION (LAMBDA (NODE)
 (GENC (OPENINGS NODE) (FUNCTION (LAMBDA (PAIR)
  (COND ((GET (SETQ NEWROOM (CAR PAIR)) (UP DIR)) T)
        ((NOT (FEASIBLE (CDR PAIR))) T)
        ((GET NEWROOM (UP (NOT DIR))) (PROG2 (BOOKPG) NIL))
        (T (PROGN (BOOKPG)
                    (SET (NEWFUP DIR) (CONS NEWROOM (EVAL (NEWFUP DIR
))))))))))))))) (GO TRYAGAIN)))
(MAPC (LIST T NIL) (FUNCTION (LAMBDA (BOOL) (PROG (HOLD NEXT)
 (SET (FRONUP BOOL) (LIST (SETQ HOLD NEWROOM)))
CHECK
(COND ((EQ (SETQ NEXT (GET HOLD (UP BOOL))) T) (RETURN NIL))
      (NEXT (PROGN (SET (FRONUP BOOL) (CONS NEXT (CONS (GET HOLD
                        (DOORUP BOOL)) (EVAL (FRONUP BOOL)))))
                   (SETQ HOLD NEXT) (GO CHECK)) ) ))))))
(SETQ NEWROOM (NCONC FRONUP (CDR (REVERSE FRONDOWN))))
CLEANUP
(MAPC (LIST T NIL) (FUNCTION (LAMBDA (BOOL)
 (MAPC (EVAL (CLEANUP BOOL)) (FUNCTION (LAMBDA (NODE)
   (PROG2 (REMPROP NODE (UP BOOL))
          (REMPROP NODE (DOORUP BOOL)) )))))))
(RETURN NEWROOM)
TRYAGAIN
(COND ((NULL (EVAL (NEWFUP DIR))) (PROG2 (SETQ NEWROOM NIL)
                                         (GO CLEANUP))))
(SET (FRONUP DIR) (EVAL (NEWFUP DIR))) (SET (NEWFUP DIR) NIL)
(GO SELECT)  )))
```

1. In FINDPATH, as given, the new frontier could grow either from FRONUP or FRONDOWN. Another approach would be to allow growth only from FRONUP. If it happens that we want growth from FRONDOWN, we rename FRONUP as FRONDOWN and FRONDOWN as FRONUP. Rewrite FINDPATH along this alternative approach.

2. FEASIBLE checks only whether a passage (door, elevator, bridge, etc.) can be used. Show the changes in FINDPATH that are necessary if some of the passages are feasible in one direction but perhaps not in both. FEASIBLE then becomes a function of three arguments: (FEASIBLE (LAMBDA (FROMROOM PASSAGE TOROOM) ...)), which has value T if PASSAGE is feasible when going from FROMROOM to TOROOM and value NIL if the PASSAGE is not feasible when going from FROMROOM to TOROOM. You can no longer assume that

(FEASIBLE (LAMBDA (FROMROOM PASSAGE TOROOM) ...))

has the same value as

(FEASIBLE (LAMBDA (TOROOM PASSAGE FROMROOM) ...))

3. In FINDPATH, if FRONUP is larger than FRONDOWN, then the entire new frontier NEWFDOWN will be built. This strategy is acceptable if the new frontiers grow at about the same rate in both directions. If, for example, NEWFDOWN is enormous, it would be advantageous to switch to FRONUP and grow NEWFUP as soon as NEWFDOWN is larger than FRONUP and keep on building NEWFUP as long as it is not larger than NEWFDOWN. When NEWFUP becomes larger than NEWFDOWN, we switch back to growing NEWFDOWN. Rewrite FINDPATH along this more refined strategy.

12.5 Random Sentence Generators

Loneliness has become one of the illnesses of our times. For those sad moments when no gentle soul is there to soothe your heart with tender narrative, we shall describe a sentence generator. The sentence generator accepts as argument a grammar and can be set going to generate sentences in a random manner. We shall start with a very simple example that will be sufficient to construct the generator.

Let us assume that we want to generate simple sentences such as

AMINA SAW LAWALY
GEORGE REMARKED MARTHA
LAWALY GREETED LAURENT, etc.

The SENTENCEs are of the form NOUN VERB NOUN, where NOUN could be any of (AMINA LAWALY GEORGE MARTHA LAURENT) and VERB could be any of (SAW REMARKED GREETED). To make life harder, let us add another "verb," so that VERB could be (SAW REMARKED GREETED (WAS HAPPY TO MEET)).

The grammar could be read as the list

```
( (SENTENCE ((NOUN VERB NOUN)) )
  (NOUN (AMINA LAWALY GEORGE MARTHA LAURENT) )
  (VERB (SAW REMARKED GREETED (WAS HAPPY TO MEET) ) ) )
```

Notice that there is only one choice for expressing SENTENCE, while there are four choices for expressing VERB. To access the choices, we place the list of choices for an atom—referred to as a *nonterminal symbol*—as the property of the indicator CHOICES and immediately compute the number of CHOICES, which will be the property of the indicator NUMCHOICES. Assuming that the grammar is the value of GRAMMAR, it suffices to do

```
(MAPC GRAMMAR (FUNCTION (LAMBDA (GRAMMAR-RULE)
   (PROG2 (PUTPROP (CAR GRAMMAR-RULE) (QUOTE CHOICES) (CADR GRAMMAR-RULE) )
     (PUTPROP (CAR GRAMMAR-RULE) (QUOTE NUMCHOICES)
        (LENGTH (CADR GRAMMAR-RULE) ) ) ) ) ) )
```

It will be assumed that any atom which has CHOICES is nonterminal. If an atom has no CHOICES, it will be called a *terminal symbol*.

We can now outline the random sentence generator. We start with the list (SENTENCE). SENTENCE is replaced by one of its CHOICES. There is only one, so we obtain (NOUN VERB NOUN). The first NOUN is replaced by one of its CHOICES, using RANDOMINTFROMONE (see Section 12.1.2) with argument the NUMber of CHOICES of NOUN. Assume that we have picked GEORGE. The sentence becomes (GEORGE VERB NOUN). Since GEORGE has no CHOICES, we move down to VERB, which is replaced by one of its CHOICES, for example, GREETED. The sentence becomes (GEORGE GREETED NOUN). GREETED has no CHOICES, so we move down to NOUN. NOUN is replaced by one of its CHOICES, for instance, AMINA. The sentence becomes (GEORGE GREETED AMINA). AMINA has no CHOICES, and since there are no further atoms to process, the sentence generation terminates.

```
(GENSENTENCE (LAMBDA () (PROG (RESULT LOCAL CHOICES)
   (SETQ RESULT (SETQ LOCAL (COPY (QUOTE (SENTENCE) ) ) ) )
LOOP (COND ((NULL LOCAL) (RETURN RESULT) )
        ((SETQ CHOICES (GET (CAR LOCAL) (QUOTE CHOICES) ) )
         (REPLACE LOCAL (CAR (FINDNTHCDR (SUB1
            (RANDOMINTFROMONE (GET (CAR LOCAL) (QUOTE NUMCHOICES) ) ) )
               CHOICES) ) ) )
        (T (SETQ LOCAL (CDR LOCAL) ) ) )
   (GO LOOP)
   ) ) )
```

What would happen if COPY were missing in the definition of GENSEN-TENCE?

The sentence starts as (SENTENCE), and the original cell for (SEN-TENCE) is pointed to by RESULT. LOCAL points to the cell that is worked upon. If the CAR of the cell is terminal, i.e., has no CHOICES, LOCAL is advanced down the list. Otherwise, (CAR LOCAL) is RE-PLACEd by one of the CHOICES chosen at random, and LOCAL is not changed, but its CAR usually will be.

REPLACE changes the partial RESULT by doing appropriate RPLACA and RPLACDs. An auxiliary function LASTCELL finds the last cell of the nonempty list that is its argument.

```
(REPLACE (LAMBDA (CELL SEX)
    (COND ( (ATOM SEX) (RPLACA CELL SEX) )
             ( (RPLACA CELL (CAR (SETQ SEX (COPY SEX) ) ) )
               (PROG2 (RPLACD (LASTCELL SEX) (CDR CELL) )
                      (RPLACD CELL (CDR SEX) ) ) )
   ) ) )
```

Notice that, when SEX is a list, a copy was made so as not to destroy the storage structure of the second argument of REPLACE. If it is known that SEX is either an atom or a list of at least two elements—as would be the case for the forms of grammars that we adopted—then only the CDR of SEX needs to be copied:

```
(REPLACE (LAMBDA (CELL SEX)
    (COND ( (ATOM SEX) (RPLACA CELL SEX) )
             ( (RPLACA CELL (CAR SEX) )
               (PROG2 (RPLACD (LASTCELL (SETQ SEX (COPY (CDR SEX) ) ) )
                              (CDR CELL) )
                      (RPLACD CELL SEX) ) ) ) )
```

The auxiliary function LASTCELL would be written

```
(LASTCELL (LAMBDA (LIS)
    (COND ( (NULL (CDR LIS) ) LIS)
          (T (LASTCELL (CDR LIS) ) )
   ) ) )
```

It is also easily written using a LOOP, perhaps more efficiently depending on your LISP system:

```
(LASTCELL (LAMBDA (LIS) PROG ()
LOOP (COND ( (NULL (CDR LIS) ) (RETURN LIS) )
            ( (SETQ LIS (CDR LIS) ) (GO LOOP) ) ) ) ) )
```

To understand the effect of REPLACE, let us consider the programs

```
(SETQ RES (QUOTE (A CHIP THERE IS HEAVY)))
(SETQ LOC (CDDR RES))
(SETQ NEW (QUOTE (ON THE SHOULDER)))
```

At this point, the storage structures would be similar to

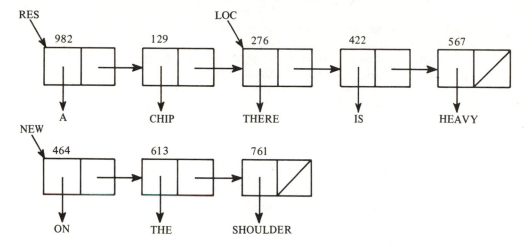

After the evaluation of (REPLACE LOC NEW), with the first version of REPLACE, the structures are

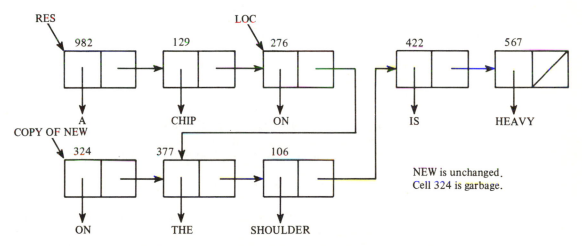

Notice that the cells at which RES and LOC are pointing are unchanged, but the value of RES would PRINT as (A CHIP ON THE SHOULDER IS HEAVY), and the value of LOC as (ON THE SHOULDER IS HEAVY). The CAR of LOC is the first of the new words that have REPLACEd the old (CAR LOC).

Let us now write a MONITOR which READs a grammar and writes a NUMBER of random sentences:

```
(MONITOR (LAMBDA (NUMBER) (PROG (GRAMMAR)
    (SETQ GRAMMAR (READ) )
```

initialize CHOICES and their number

```
(MAPC GRAMMAR (FUNCTION (LAMBDA (GRAMMAR-RULE)
  (PROG2 (PUTPROP (CAR GRAMMAR-RULE) (QUOTE CHOICES) (CADR GRAMMAR-RULE) )
         (PUTPROP (CAR GRAMMAR-RULE) (QUOTE NUMCHOICES)
               (LENGTH (CADR GRAMMAR-RULE) ) ) ) ) ) )
ONEMORE (COND ( (ZEROP NUMBER) (RETURN (QUOTE FINISHED) ) ) )
        (SETQ NUMBER (SUB1 NUMBER) ) (PRINT (GENSENTENCE) )
                                     (GO ONEMORE)
                                     ) ) )
```

EXERCISES

1. Run the MONITOR above to generate ten SENTENCEs with the GRAMMAR

```
( (SENTENCE (PRINC (PRINC COMPL) ) )
  (PRINC    ( (NVERB REL) ) )
  (NVERB    ( (N VERB) ) )
  (N        (HE SHE GEORGE MARTHA HENRY RICHARD) )
  (VERB     (THOUGHT KNEW GUESSED IMAGINED) )
  (REL      ( (N WOULD VOF) (N WOULD VWITH) (N WOULD VOF OF QUAL) (N WOULD
              VWITH WITH QUAL) ) )
  (VOF      (DIE FAINT) )
  (VWITH    (BURST BURN) )
  (QUAL     ( (ADJ QUALW) QUALW) )
  (QUALW    (EXCITEMENT JEALOUSY PASSION BOREDOM) )
  (ADJ      (BEAUTIFUL FAT SEXY VARICOSED BURNT SCARRED) )
  (COMPL    ( (WHEN N VSEE POSS ADJ PARTSW) ) )
  (VSEE     (SAW DISCOVERED REMARKED NOTICED KISSED CARESSED) )
  (POSS     (HIS HER) )
  (PARTSW   (LEGS THIGHS HANDS HAIR LIPS) )    )
```

2. Run the MONITOR to generate ten SENTENCEs with a GRAMMAR of your own choosing.

3. Given a grammar and a sentence, *parse* the sentence; i.e., determine the way in which the sentence was generated from the grammar. One representation of the parsing of the sentence is a tree rooted at SENTENCE and having the words of the input sentence as terminal nodes.

12.6   Robot Simulation

If your FINDPATH (Section 12.4) does not work, you may not be able to find your cat, which is certainly gloomy. A robot might replace the cat. Therefore, in this section, we shall outline some techniques that could be used to simulate a robot. The field of robot simulation is vast, and in this section we shall touch on only a very small fragment of the field.

12.6.1   Robot Worlds

We assume that the world of the robot is described by a set of true facts in the world. For example, the very simple world of Fig. 12.1 could be partially described as the set INITIAL–WORLD:

```
( (INROOM PAIL1 ROOMA) (INROOM BOX1 ROOMA) (INROOM DOORAB ROOMA)†
  (INROOM DOORAC ROOMA)
  (INROOM PLANT1 ROOMB) (INROOM ROBOT ROOMB) (INROOM BOX2 ROOMB)
  (INROOM DOORAB ROOMB)†
  (INROOM BOXO ROOMC) (INROOM PLANT2 ROOMC) (INROOM WATERTAP ROOMC)
  (INROOM DOORAC ROOMC)
  (MOVABLE PAIL1) (MOVABLE BOXO) (MOVABLE BOX1) (MOVABLE BOX2)
  (OPEN DOORAB) (OPEN DOORAC) (DRY PLANT1) (DRY PLANT2)
  (EMPTY PAIL1)
  (TYPE PLANT1 PLANT) (TYPE PLANT2 PLANT) (TYPE PAIL1 PAIL) ... )
```

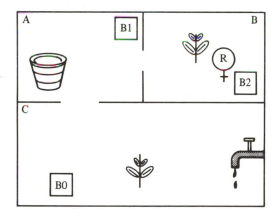

Figure 12.1

†It happens to be convenient to think of a door as being in the two rooms that it connects.

Of course, this is not a complete description. It does not say that the pail is rather close to DOORAC, while BOX1 is not.

12.6.2 Operators that Change the World

The robot can accomplish actions that change the world. For example, she can move around, open and close doors, push or carry movable objects from one place to another, fill the pail with water, water the plants, etc. Each of these actions is accomplished by an operator. Let us consider the example of the operator watering a plant. We shall use lowercase letters for variables in the description of operators.

The operator WATER(plant) can be applied to a world only when the world satisfies certain *conditions*. We want the robot to hold a pail filled up with water and to be next to the plant. Moreover, only dry plants may be watered. The conditions of WATER(plant) could be the *conditions–set*

```
( (HOLDING  ROBOT pail)  (TYPE pail PAIL)  (FULL pail)
  (NEXTTO  ROBOT plant)  (TYPE plant PLANT)  (DRY plant) )
```

Note that WATER(PLANT1) may not be applied to INITIAL–WORLD, since four out of the six conditions of WATER(PLANT1) are not satisfied.

Once the operator has been applied to an old–world, a new–world results. It is obtained by first deleting from the old world the facts which no longer hold. The *delete–set* of the operator WATER(plant) could be

```
( (FULL pail)  (DRY plant) )
```

The resultant set is augmented by the *add–set* of the operator. For WATER(plant), the add–set could be

```
( (EMPTY pail)  (WATERED plant) )
```

To resume: We have considered operators that are characterized by three sets: the conditions–set, the delete–set, and the add–set. For an operator to be applicable to old–world, its conditions–set must be a subset of the old world: conditions–set $\subseteq$ old–world. Once the operator has been applied, a new–world results, obtained from the old–world by first deleting the delete–set of the operator, and then adding its add–set:

new–world = ((old–world − delete–set) + add–set), where "−" and "+" are set difference and union, respectively.

As further examples, the operators GONEXTTO(object) and PUSH-NEXTTO(object to–object) could be axiomatized as

GONEXTTO(object):   the robot goes next to an object.
Conditions–set: ((INROOM object room) (INROOM ROBOT room)).
Delete–set: ((NEXTTO ROBOT $)).
Add–set: ((NEXTTO ROBOT object)).

In the above delete–set, the variable $ can be replaced by anything, i.e., from old–world we must delete every fact of the form (NEXTTO ROBOT something).

PUSHNEXTTO(object to–object):   The robot pushes object next to to–object.
Conditions–set: ((NEXTTO ROBOT object) (MOVABLE object) (INROOM object room) (INROOM ROBOT room) (INROOM to–object room)).
Delete–set: ((NEXTTO object $) (NEXTTO $ object)).
Add–set: ((NEXTTO object to–object) (NEXTTO to–object object)).

12.6.3 Difficulties with Operators

The least experience with programming should demonstrate how easy it is to write programs that are incorrect. Quite similarly, it is a matter of experience that mistakes are easily made in axiomatizations of robot worlds. For example, in the above descriptions of GONEXTTO and PUSHNEXTTO, nothing prevents the robot from going next to herself, by doing GONEXTTO(ROBOT), or from pushing BOX2 next to herself, by doing PUSHNEXTTO(BOX2 ROBOT). One's physical intuition may indicate that such actions are ridiculous and should not be permissible.

One way to prohibit GONEXTTO(ROBOT) would be to modify the description of the world to include a series of statements such as: (TYPE BOX2 OBJECT) (TYPE DOORAC OBJECT), etc., and to add (TYPE object OBJECT) to the conditions–set of GONEXTTO. Similarly, we could add (TYPE to–object OBJECT) to the conditions–set of PUSH-NEXTTO.

Another question relates to the redundancy with which one should describe operators. For example, in PUSHNEXTTO, one could argue that (INROOM ROBOT room) is redundant, since it is implicit in (NEXTTO ROBOT object) and (INROOM object room). However, some redundancy might help in achieving goals. Further, if ROBOT was NEXTTO other things besides object, these relations are not deleted by PUSHNEXTTO, leading to other errors.

EXERCISE

Describe the three sets characterizing your version of the following operators in the world of Fig. 12.1:

a. OPENDOOR(door)   f. GOTHRUDOOR(door)

b. CLOSEDOOR(door)   g. CARRYTHRUDOOR(object door)

c. OPENTAP(water–tap)   h. PUSHTHRUDOOR(object door)

d. CLOSETAP(water–tap)   i. PICKUP(object)

e. DRY(plant)   j. PUTDOWN(object)

                             k. FILL(pail)

12.6.4 Goal States

Starting from the world of Fig. 12.1, we may wish to attain a world in which the following facts are simultaneously true:

(NEXTTO ROBOT DOORAB) (INROOM PAIL1 ROOMB) (WATERED PLANT2)

There are many worlds which would satisfy the above conditions; for example, PLANT1 could be WATERED or DRY. It is sufficient to find *some* world to achieve our goal.

A solution to the problem will consist of a sequence of operators which transform the initial state of Fig. 12.1 into a state satisfying the three conditions above.

More generally, we shall consider problems of the following type: We are given an initial state and a partially specified final state. We wish to find a sequence of operators which transforms the initial state into a state in which all the partial specifications of the final state are satisfied.

One could consider many other types of robot tasks, for example,

a. All plants should be watered.

b. No two boxes should be next to each other, nor should any box be in room B.

12.6.5 A Strategy for Solving Robot Tasks

Restricting ourselves to the case of partially specified final states as in the example of the above section, we realize immediately that it is not possible to work on the three subtasks (NEXTTO ROBOT DOORAB), (INROOM PAIL1 ROOMB), and (WATERED PLANT2) in any order. If we first realize (NEXTTO ROBOT DOORAB), we notice that this property must be undone when we try to move the PAIL1 or water PLANT2. Similarly, if we put (INROOM PAIL1 ROOMB) before watering PLANT2, then the subgoal (INROOM PAIL1 ROOMB) must be undone. Hence, there is a desirable *hierarchy* in which the subtasks must be done: first, (WATERED PLANT2), next (INROOM PAIL1 ROOMB), and finally (NEXTTO ROBOT DOORAB).

The idea of hierarchy of subtasks extends to a hierarchy in which new goals must be solved as they are generated, for example, the new goals of the conditions–set of an operator which we wish to apply.

In the conditions–set of WATER(plant), we wish to first obtain (FULL pail), then (HOLDING ROBOT pail), and finally (NEXTTO ROBOT plant), without, of course, undoing what has already been achieved in satisfying the conditions–set of WATER(plant).

12.6.6. Desirable Operators

When we wish to obtain some specific goal in the world, we can usually find one or several operators which would achieve this specific goal. For example, if we wish (HOLDING ROBOT pail), PICKUP(pail) would do the trick. Presumably, if we carry the pail through a door, we would still be holding it, but it seems rather easier just to pick up the pail. Sometimes there are several possibilities: If we want (NEXTTO BOX1 BOX2), we could push BOX1 next to BOX2 or push BOX2 next to BOX1.

12.6.7 Outline of a Task Solver

We can now outline a monitor for solving simulated robot problems. Given a set of tasks T1, T2, T3, T4, T5, and T6, we first split them into various levels according to the hierarcy of subtasks. The various levels and the tasks they include could be

Level	Tasks
1	T2, T5
2	T6
3	T1
4	T3, T4

Hence, we want to do T2 and T5 first, but we don't know in which order. We might try the order T2, T5 first, and if that fails, then later try the order

T5, T2. Trying T2 first, we search for the desirable operators to accomplish T2. If there are several, we choose one (perhaps the most desirable)—OP4, for example—and try to apply it. If we cannot apply OP4, we generate as subtasks the conditions–set of OP4, etc.

Having accomplished T2 and T5, we accomplish T6. Let us assume that we succeeded. We then try to accomplish T1. Assume that we fail. Since T1 is alone in its hierarchical level, we need not backtrack to a previous level, for example, trying to accomplish T1 before T6 and after T2 and T5. In fact, the original task appears impossible, and the task solver stops.

12.6.8 Reference

The approach for robot problem solving outlined in Section 12.6 follows L. Siklóssy and J. Dreussi, "An Efficient Robot Planner which Generates its own Procedures," *Third International Joint Conference on Artificial Intelligence*, Palo Alto, Calif., 1973.

There are many difficulties associated with robot problem solving which we have not mentioned here.

12.7 Some More Difficult Exercises

In this section we shall offer a variety of exercises which are more demanding than the simple exercises previously encountered. We shall indicate cases when the exercises require substantial efforts for their solution, typically of the order of a class term project and sometimes much more.

We have purposefully left out references (when they existed) so that the reader will try to find solutions himself instead of just programming someone else's ideas.

12.7.1 Logic

EXERCISE

1. Write programs to transform expressions in predicate calculus to expressions in

a. Conjunctive normal form   b. Disjunctive normal form.

2. Write a theorem prover based on the resolution principle for proving theorems in

a. Propositional calculus.

b. Predicate calculus (substantial for a good theorem prover).

3. Write a system which can show that (some) expressions in predicate calculus are neither theorems nor unsatisfiable (substantial).

12.7.2 Trees

EXERCISE

Various types of information may be made available to describe a tree or a binary tree:

a. A description of the tree using subordinate (leftmost or youngest son) and predecessor (next right or next older brother) links and contents of each node.

b. The preorder traversal of the tree.

c. The postorder traversal of the tree.

d. The endorder traversal of the tree.

e. The level-by-level traversal of the tree.

f. The set of (father son) pairs of the tree.

Given any one description, write a program that will generate any other description, when possible. When the program is impossible, explain why, and try to make it feasible by enriching the description input to the program. The node of a tree could be represented as a GENSYM atom. The property list of the GENSYM atom contains information about the links, contents, and other information associated with the node.

12.7.3 Series Extrapolation

EXERCISE

Write a program that will continue a series. Examples of series are

A A A A A A A
A B A C A D A E
A B D G K P
A A B A B B A B B B

(Could become substantial.)

12.7.4 Calculus

All but the first exercise may be substantial.

EXERCISES

1. Differentiate a symbolic expression with respect to a variable.
2. Simplify a given expression according to some criteria of what is simpler
3. Integrate symbolically:

a. Simple integrals.

b. Multiple integrals.

c. Ordinary differential equations.

d. Partial differential equations.

e. Contour integrals.

4. Calculate the limits of symbolic expressions.

12.7.5 IQ Tests

EXERCISE

Write a system to solve

a. Verbal analogies.

b. Geometric analogies.

c. Arithmetic analogies, etc.

(All possibly substantial.)

12.7.6 Natural Language

All the exercises are substantial.

EXERCISES

1. Write a program to find

a. Synonyms

b. Antonyms

of words given a dictionary in the form of a network of relations among words.

2. Write an algebra (or other area) word problem solver.

3. Program a system to write

a. Puns.

b. Aphorisms.

c. Jokes (spicy, dirty, elephant, mother-in-law, LISP, corny, etc.).

d. Political speeches (right, left, up, down, middle, etc.).

e. Hard-core pornography.

f. Whodunits.

g. Shakespeare, etc.

4. Program a system to write synopses of chapters, books, plays, etc. (*very* substantial).

5. Write a program which pretends to be your

a. Boss.

b. Mother.

c. Lover.

d. LISP teacher.

e. Psychoanalyst, etc.

12.7.7 Programming

All the exercises are substantial.

EXERCISES

1. Write a program to prove properties of LISP programs. For example, for any lists A, B, and C,

(EQUAL (APPEND (APPEND A B) C) (APPEND A (APPEND B C)))

and

(EQUAL (REVERSE (REVERSE A)) A)

2. Prove that a program is correct.

3. Prove that a program is

a. Syntactically

b. Semantically

incorrect.

appendix

A

COUNTING PARENTHESES

It is so easy to miscount parentheses, thereby becoming unintelligible in LISP, that we shall describe three different algorithms to count parentheses. Personal taste will dictate the preferred one.

Let us consider a hard example of a list: Is ((A (B (C) (D))) ((E) (((E))) ((E)))) a list? A quick inspection is not conclusive. We must start counting parentheses. The following methods will work.

A.1 PARENCOUNT1

Scan the expression from left to right, and use a counter for the parentheses. The counter, initially zero, is increased by 1 for each left parenthesis encountered and is decreased by 1 for each right parenthesis encountered. Our example yields the following count:

```
( ( A  ( B ( C )  ( D ) ) )  ( ( E ) ( ( ( E ) ) )  ( ( E ) ) ) )
0 1 2    3   4 3 4   3 2 1  2 3 2   3 4 5 4 3 2   3 4 3 2 1 0
```

It is most important to be aware that we have a list if and only if both the following conditions hold:

a. The counter is 0 on the last parenthesis. Otherwise the number of right and left parentheses is not the same.

b. The counter is 0 only on the last parenthesis. Otherwise there may be

214

several lists, not just one, or there may be too many right parentheses before matching left parentheses.

Some additional examples will help clarify. The following are not lists:

<table>
<tr><td></td><td></td><td>Reason</td></tr>
<tr><td>a.</td><td>((A (B (C) (D)))</td><td>The counter has a final value of 1.</td></tr>
<tr><td>b.</td><td>((A (B (C)))) (D)</td><td>There are two lists, ((A (B (C)))) and (D). The counter has an intermediary value of 0.</td></tr>
<tr><td>c.</td><td>((A (B)))) (A (B)</td><td>The counter has an intermediary value of 0. Moreover, it becomes negative, indicating that some right parentheses occur before matching left parentheses.</td></tr>
</table>

Since parenthesis counting is one of the favorite pastimes of LISP speakers, this book offers two other ways to indulge in the sport. Our next algorithm is a variation of the algorithm that we have just described and also uses a counter. The rules on counting are somewhat more complicated than before.

A.2 PARENCOUNT2

1. Initialize counter to 0.

2. Scan left to right looking only at parentheses. If a right parenthesis is hit first, we do not have a well-formed list.

3. [Hitting ('s.] If hitting a left parenthesis, increase counter by 1 and go to 3.

4. [Hit) right after (.] If hitting a right parenthesis, do not change counter.

5. [Hit more)'s.] If hitting a right parenthesis, decrease counter by 1 and go to 5.

6. [Hit (right after).] If hitting a left parenthesis, do not change counter and go to 3.

Here are some results of the algorithm on several lists:

```
    (A (B (C) (D)))
    01   2   3  33   321
     ((E) (((E))) ((E)))
    01 2 2 234  432 23  321
      ((A (B (C) (D))) ((E) (((E))) ((E))))
    01 2   3    4  4 4  432 23  3 345  543 3 4  4321
```

A list is well formed if and only if the counter attains the value 1 exactly twice: once at the very beginning of the algorithm and once at the exit of the algorithm, when no further parentheses are left to be scanned.

EXERCISE

Apply the algorithm PARENCOUNT2 to the ill-formed expressions that illustrated PARENCOUNT1.

A.3 PARENCOUNT3

It is seen that PARENCOUNT2 pairs left and right parentheses that "match." The matching process can also be performed graphically, starting with the innermost parenthesis pairs that could be matched. We shall not describe this third algorithm, PARENCOUNT3 formally but shall illustrate it on the same examples that we have just used. The numbers across the lines indicate the order in which the parentheses are matched:

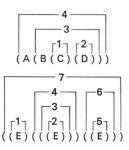

You should now take an enormous piece of paper and apply PAREN-COUNT3 on a list of the above two lists. Good Luck!

appendix

B

QUICKIE INTRODUCTION
TO LISP FOR
EXPERIENCED PROGRAMMERS

This appendix should allow the experienced programmer in languages such as ALGOL, PL/1, PASCAL, or SNOBOL to grasp the essence of most elementary LISP constructs and thereby avoid most of the slow pace of the first seven chapters. Description here is sketchy; it does not pretend to be a complete introduction. In particular, no discussion is made of fine points or of variations due to different implementations. We assume that all lists are well behaved.

The appendix can also be used by those who were once familiar with LISP but have become somewhat rusty and need to put their knowledge back into focus again.

The usual good programming habits should be adhered to: Do not redefine system functions; do not use system constants as variable names or local variables in function definitions; check your particular system for special features, available system functions, variations in spelling, number and order of arguments of functions, etc.

Only the EVAL supervisor EV-LISP—and not EVALQUOTE—is presented here.

B.1 Constructs

Atoms are alphanumeric identifiers or numbers, such as WERE, WE23R5E, 235, and 23.5. Alpha atoms start with a letter and are uniquely represented in memory.

217

```
‹S-expression› :: = atom | list
list :: = '(' inside ')'
inside :: = empty | S-expression | S-expression inside
empty :: =
```

So a list is a left parenthesis followed by any number of S-expressions separated by one or more blanks. The empty list ( ) is also written NIL and is both a list and an atom. The abbreviation of S-expression is SEX.

B.2   Elementary Predicates

NIL is used for false, and T for true.

B.2.1   EQ

EQ—EQual—has two arguments. Its value is T if the values of the two arguments represent the same pointer. Hence, EQ works for alpha atoms. On other constructs, it depends on how things are in memory.

B.2.2   ATOM

ATOM is T if the value of its unique argument is any sort of atom.

B.2.3   NULL

NULL is T if the value of its unique argument is NIL.

B.3   Elementary Functions

B.3.1   CAR

Its one argument should have as value a nonempty (i.e., non-NIL) list: (SEX1 SEX2 . . . SEXN), N > 0. The CAR of this is SEX1.

B.3.2   CDR

Its one argument should be a nonempty list, as for CAR. The value of CDR of (SEX1 SEX2 . . . SEXN), N > 0, is (SEX2 . . . SEXN).

B.3.3 CONS

CONS puts back together what CAR and CDR have undone. For any nonempty list X, (CONS (CAR X) (CDR X)) is EQUAL to X. EQUAL is a system function which checks whether two SEXes have the same value.

B.4   Function Form

LISP uses Polish parenthesized prefix notation for function evaluations. Arguments are evaluated left to right. Section B.3.3 gives an example.

The LISP system consists of a function EVAL that "listens" to input, i.e., reads a program to be evaluated, evaluates it, prints the value, then reads the next program to be evaluated, etc.

In a program, values of the arguments of a function are usually evaluated left to right, as with the ALGOL call-by-value. To stop EVALuation within a program, use the 1-argument function QUOTE. The value of (QUOTE (GODS WERE IMMORTAL)) is (GODS WERE IMMORTAL).

The use of EVALQUOTE is omitted here for simplicity.

B.5   Program Form

A program is a sequence of elementary programs given to EVAL. Each program is a single SEX that is read by EVAL and is evaluated, its value becoming output on the output device (printer, say) and the system cycles. The function DEFINE allows the definition of user functions.

B.6   DEFINE

This is the main function for defining new functions. DEFINE takes one argument, itself a list of possibly several function definitions. A program for EVAL using DEFINE would look like this:

```
(DEFINE (QUOTE (  definition-of-function1
                  definition-of-function2
                  . . .
                  definition-of-functionN  ) ) )
```

Functions can be defined recursively and in terms of each other.

B.7   Function Definition

Each definition of a function is of the form

```
(function-name LAMBDA-expression)
```

while a LAMBDA-expression is of the form

```
(LAMBDA list-of-LAMBDA-variables
        body-of-the-function)
```

The function-name is an alpha atom. The list-of-LAMBDA-variables is a list of different alpha atoms which are the dummy variables (arguments) of the function-name. The body-of-the-function is a program whose value is the value of the function. As mentioned above, upon entering the function, the values of the variables are calculated first as in the ALGOL call-by-value.

B.8   Conditional Expressions

The form of COND is

```
(COND  (left1 right1)
       (left2 right2)
       . . .
       (leftN rightN)  ), with N > 0
```

It is equivalent to the ALGOL-like construct

```
IF value of left1 ≠ NIL THEN value of right1 ELSE
IF value of left2 ≠ NIL THEN value of right2 ELSE . . . ELSE
IF value of leftN ≠ NIL THEN value of rightN ELSE error or NIL
```
(depending on implementation).

In a COND, arguments are EVALuated only as needed.

B.8.1   Example: APPEND

APPEND (usually a system function) concatenates two lists. A complete definition and subsequent two calls are

```
(DEFINE (QUOTE (
(APPEND (LAMBDA (LISTONE LISTTWO)
        (COND ( (NULL LISTONE) LISTTWO)
              (T (CONS (CAR LISTONE) (APPEND (CDR LISTONE) LISTTWO) ) )
        ) ) ))
```

```
)))
VALUE IS...
(APPEND)
(APPEND (QUOTE (BLACK PLUMS)) (QUOTE (ARE RED WHEN GREEN)))
VALUE IS...
(BLACK PLUMS ARE RED WHEN GREEN)
(APPEND (QUOTE ((GENERALLY SPEAKING))) (QUOTE (WOMEN (ARE))))
VALUE IS...
((GENERALLY SPEAKING) WOMEN (ARE))
```

The SEX following "VALUE IS . . ." is the output by EVAL.

B.9   PROG

PROG is a function of any number of arguments which allows ALGOL-like constructs: assignment statements, go-to's, local variables, etc. The format of PROG is

```
(PROG list-of-PROG-variables
        arg1  arg2  ...  argN)
```

The list-of-PROG-variables is a list of different alpha atoms. These serve as local variables inside the PROG. PROG variables are initialized to NIL upon entering the PROG. If some argM of the PROG is an alpha atom, it is considered as a label.

EVALuation of a PROG is ALGOL-like: It goes left to right, top to bottom. Labels are skipped. The normal sequencing can be changed by a transfer obtained by the function GO of one argument, which must be a label. Usually the argument of GO is not evaluated. Assignments are made by SET and SETQ (see Section B.10). The function RETURN of one argument forces exit from PROG with the value of its argument being the value of PROG. Otherwise, upon falling through, the value of PROG is NIL.

LAMBDA and PROG variables obey ALGOL-like rules of local and global variables.

B.10   SET and SETQ

The value of the first argument of SET should be an alpha atom.†
The value of this atom is changed to the value of the second argument of SET. The value of SET is the value of its second argument.

†Alpha atoms are nonnumeric atoms. The restriction guarantees that the values of numbers will not be changed.

(SETQ arg1 arg2) is equivalent to (SET (QUOTE arg1) arg2). Arg1 must be an alpha atom. In SETQ arg1 is *not* evaluated. Hence, SETQ is essentially the same as the ordinary FORTRAN or ALGOL assignment statement.

B.11   Constants

Constants are obtained by using SET or SETQ programs given directly to the system (or top-level) EVAL. In this way, a variable global to all functions is defined.

B.11.1   Example of a Constant

(SETQ VOWELS (QUOTE (A E I O U Y)))

B.11.2   Example of PROG Program

We repeat the example of APPEND (Section B.8.1) without using recursion, introducing an auxiliary function STICKINFRONT:

```
(DEFINE (QUOTE (
(APPEND (LAMBDA (LISTONE LISTTWO)
     (STICKINFRONT (STICKINFRONT LISTONE NIL) LISTTWO) ) )
(STICKINFRONT (LAMBDA (LISTONE LISTTWO) (PROG ()
  LOOP (COND ( (NULL LISTONE) (RETURN LISTTWO) ) )
       (SETQ LISTTWO (CONS (CAR LISTONE) LISTTWO) )
       (SETQ LISTONE (CDR LISTONE) )
       (GO LOOP)                      ) ) )
) ) )
 VALUE IS . . .
 (APPEND STICKINFRONT)
```

Notice that (STICKINFRONT LISTONE NIL) is just (REVERSE LISTONE), which has as value the reverse of a list.

B.12   Arithmetic Functions

See Section 5.3.6.

B.13   Functional Arguments

Function names and LAMBDA-expressions can be used as functional arguments. To avoid problems with variable context (the so-called

FUNARG problem) FUNCTION should be used instead of QUOTE to stop evaluation. See Sections 7.5, 7.6 and D.4.11.1.

B.14 MAP Functions

MAP functions go down one (or several) structure(s) in an orderly fashion and give each piece—substructure—of the structure to one (or several) functional argument(s). The values of the functional arguments may be collected. MAPCAR is the most used MAP function:

```
(MAPCAR (LAMBDA (LIS FUNCARG)
    (COND ((NULL LIS) NIL)
          (T (CONS (FUNCARG (CAR LIS)) (MAPCAR (CDR LIS) FUNCARG)))
)))
```

B.15 Generators

Generators are like MAP functions, except that all the substructures of a structure need not be generated, depending on values returned by the functional argument. GENC is the most used generator.

B.16 All the Rest

The experienced programmer should now be ready to study from Chapter 8 onward without too much difficulty. He may still find it profitable to skim through the first seven chapters and try his hand at a number of the exercises.

appendix
C

A LISP BIBLIOGRAPHY

1. J. McCarthy, "Recursive Functions of Symbolic Expressions and their Computation by Machine," Part I, *Comm. ACM*, *3*, 4 (1960), 184–195.

2. J. McCarthy, P. W. Abrahams, D. J. Edwards, T. P. Hart, and M. I. Levin, *LISP 1.5 Programmer's Manual*, The M.I.T. Press, Cambridge, Mass. 1962.
    (Description of the IBM 7090 LISP implementation.)

3. E. C. Berkeley and D. G. Bobrow (eds.), *The Programming Language LISP: Its Operation and Applications*, The M.I.T. Press, Cambridge, Mass., 1966.
    (Contains a variety of articles on uses and implementations of LISP.)

4. C. Weissman, *LISP 1.5 Primer*, Dickenson Publishing Company, Inc., Encino, Calif., 1966.
    (The first LISP primer.)

5. W. D. Maurer, *A Programmer's Introduction to LISP*, American Elsevier Publishing Company, Inc., New York, 1973.

6. D. P. Friedman, *The Little LISPer*, Science Research Associates, Inc., Palo Alto, Calif., 1974.
    (A programmed text approach to teaching elementary recursion.)

7. L. Siklóssy, *Let's Talk LISP*, Prentice-Hall, Inc., Englewood Cliffs, N.J., 1976.
    (A self-reference.)

8. D. Ribbens, "Programmation non numérique," *LISP 1.5*, Dunod, Paris, France, 1970.
    (With words like CONS, LISP is quite obscene in French!)

appendix
D

SOME ERRORS IN
LISP PROGRAMS

The number of errors that one can make in LISP is simply enormous, and we are not even thinking of logical errors. We shall list here some of the many common—and not so common—errors in programs. The reader's familiarity with these errors should help him play Sherlock Holmes as, magnifying glass and skewer in hand, he hunts down his program bugs, hoping to impale them.

Since LISP implementations vary greatly, the diagnostic of LISP systems when presented with faulty programs varies greatly too. A good idea might be to give your LISP system a series of faulty programs and observe its reactions.

A general remark is also in order: LISP tries to recover from errors. However, error recovery is often less than perfect, and diagnoses following an error may or may not be justified.

For every error that we list, an overly simple faulty "program" is given as illustration.

D.1 Parentheses and Dot Errors

Parentheses and dots have such an important function in LISP that they must be checked carefully. If extra right parentheses do not result in total errors, for example, at the end of a DEFINE, they should be used for security. Indeed, if some right parentheses are missing, READ would read a far different S-expression than was intended.

D.2   Awful Definitions

Some definitions are simply impossible. Here are some examples:

D.2.1   Awful EVQ-LISP Definitions

```
DEFINE A              No list of function definitions.
DEFINE   (A)
DEFINE ((
A                     Just an atom.
(A)                   No LAMBDA expression.
(A B)                 No LAMBDA expression.
(A (B))               No LAMBDA expression.
(A LAMBDA . . . )     Incorrectly formed LAMBDA expression.
))
```

D.2.2   Awful EV-LISP Definitions

Here are some samples that need few comments.

```
(DEFINE)
(DEFINE (A) )
(DEFINE ( (A (LAMBDA (Q K C) C) ) ) )      QUOTE is missing.
(DEFINE (QUOTE (
A
(A)
(A B)
(A (B) )
(A LAMBDA ... )
) ) )
```

Leaving these awful definitions, we look at some less extreme cases. We shall give examples of faulty lists that purport to be definitions. We must assume that the definitions are in a "clean" environment; i.e., there are no hidden constants, global variables, or function definitions that could make the definitions meaningful.

D.3 Redefinitions

A possible error occurs when a function is redefined.

```
(X44 (LAMBDA (S) S ) )
(X44 (LAMBDA (X) (LIST X) ) )
```

The first definition of X44 will be lost.

Redefining system functions is particularly ill-advised, although feasible:

```
(NOT (LAMBDA (TURN UNSTONED) ... ) )
```

D.4 Errors in the Definition Itself

D.4.1 Errors in the LAMBDA-Expression

The list of LAMBDA variables may be ill-formed:

a. (HH (LAMBDA X (CAR X)))   It is not even a list.

b. (AA (LAMBDA ((X)) (CAR X)))   The argument is not an atom.

c. (AB (LAMBDA (3) (QUOTE QUOTE)))   The variable name is a number.

d. (BB (LAMBDA (T NIL) (CAR T)))   Constants are used as variable names.

e. (CC (LAMBDA (X Y X Y) (CONS X Y)))   A variable name is repeated.

The binding of the first X, from left to right, will be lost when the second X is bound.

Something may follow the LAMBDA-expression:

```
(EE (LAMBDA (X) X DOGMATIC DOG MATING)
```

LAMBDA may have too many arguments,

```
(GG (LAMBDA (X) (CAR X) GEORGE (WAS NOT) A LETTUCE) )
```

or too few,

```
(DD (LAMBDA) ) ; (DDT (LAMBDA (OLD FOOLS HAVE EXPERIENCE) ) )
```

D.4.2 Errors in PROG

The PROG may lack a list of PROG variables:

```
(U (LAMBDA (QUICK ON THE DRAWL) (PROG)))
```

The list of PROG variables may be ill-formed:

```
(UR (LAMBDA () (PROG X ...)))
(URA (LAMBDA () (PROG ((PAN) C) ...)))
(URA2 (LAMBDA (FOOL) (PROG (2 Q KC) ...)))
(URANUS (LAMBDA () (PROG (T B Z) ...)))
(DESNOS (LAMBDA () (PROG (LO NMI LO NMI) ...)))
```

A PROG variable may overwrite a LAMBDA variable if it has the same name:

```
(V (LAMBDA (LET US SHAKE HEADS) (PROG (LET US SHAKE FINGERS) ...)))
```

Labels can cause problems. They should not be numbers:

```
(ZZAA (LAMBDA (EARLY BIRDS SLEEP LITTLE) (PROG () 7 (RETURN NIL))))
```

Repeated labels are not allowed in the same PROG:

```
(Y (LAMBDA (NO REDEEMING DEFECTS) (PROG () FAT (LIST) FAT (GO FAT))))
```

D.4.3 Errors in COND

The COND may lack arguments:

```
(AU (LAMBDA (PRACTICE MAKES MONOTONY) (COND)))
```

One of the arguments of COND is an atom:

```
(OH (LAMBDA (PUT DESCARTES BEFORE THE) (COND HORSE (T NIL))))
```

Additional errors may result if each argument of COND must be a list of exactly two SEXes.
Some part of the COND cannot be reached:

```
(Q (LAMBDA (POLICE FARCES EXERCISE) (COND (T NIL) (T T))))
```

D.4.4 Errors in GO

The use of GO is restricted to PROGs:

```
(GOOD (LAMBDA (LOVE IS) (GO EXERCISE)))
```

A label is missing:

(J (LAMBDA ( ) (PROG (VITAMIN) LUSH (RETURN NIL) (GO LUST))))

D.4.5 Errors in SETQ

The first argument of SETQ must be an alpha atom. It cannot be a number,

(ONLY (LAMBDA (DIRTY PEOPLE) (PROG (WASH THEMSELVES) (SETQ 7 PEOPLE))))

nor a system constant,

(DISAGREE (LAMBDA (WITH) (PROG (YOURSELF) (SETQ NIL WITH))))

nor a list,

(STUDY (LAMBDA (COEDS) (PROG (ROMANCE LANGUAGES) (SETQ (CAR COEDS) T))))

In some systems, SETQ cannot be used outside a PROG:

(HOLLAND (LAMBDA (IS) (SETQ IS (QUOTE DAMNED))))

D.4.6 Wrong Types of Arguments

In the previous section we showed some errors when SETQ is given the wrong types of first arguments. Similarly, errors occur when wrong types of arguments are given to some other functions:

Function	Bad Argument
SET	Value of first argument not an alpha atom
CAR, CDR	Atom
APPEND	Atomic first argument (and not NIL)
Numeric functions	
(PLUS, TIMES, etc.)	Nonnumeric argument
MAP, MAPCAR, GENC, etc.	Atomic first argument (and not NIL)
PRINT, LAST, etc.	Circular list

D.4.7 Wrong Number of Arguments

Many functions require a fixed number of arguments:

(HONOR (LAMBDA X (BUYS NO BEEF) (HONOR (CAR NO BEEF) BUYS)))

Both CAR and HONOR were given the wrong number of arguments.

D.4.8 Unbound Variables

The variable WAIST is unbound in

(NARROW (LAMBDA (MIND BROAD) (CAR WAIST)))

Sometimes the unbound variable is also a function name, perhaps a helpful hint to find the error:

(BROAD (LAMBDA (MIND NARROW) (PROG (WAIST) (CAR CAR) (CDR BROAD))))

Both CAR and BROAD are unbound variables.

D.4.9 Undefined Functions

The simplest case occurs when an undefined function is used. POOR is an undefined function in

(DYNAMITE (LAMBDA (HAS TEMPER) (POOR TEMPER)))

Numbers cannot be functions:

(MINUTES (LAMBDA (OF WASTED HOURS) (24 HOURS)))

If a variable is used as a function, an error occurs unless the variable is a functional argument or—in some systems—if the value of the variable is a function name.† Therefore, the definition

(PEDESTRIANS (LAMBDA (HAVE RUNDOWN) (RUNDOWN (QUOTE FEELINGS))))

may or may not be error-free.

Similarly, if a list is used as a function, an error occurs unless the value of the list is a functional argument or—in some systems—if the value of the list is a function name†:

(THE (LAMBDA (WONDERFUL DOGS US) ((WONDERFUL DOGS) US)))

D.4.10 Shared Function and Variable Names

There is danger in using an atom both as a function name and a variable. The following is a correct definition of the LAST of a nonempty list:

(LAST (LAMBDA (LAST) (COND ((NULL (CDR LAST)) (CAR LAST))
                          (T (LAST (CDR LAST))))))

†Or equivalent: LAMBDA-expression or LABEL-expression.

D.4.11 Problems with Functional Arguments

D.4.11.1 The FUNARG Problem

A LAMBDA-expression used as a functional argument might cause an error if it is not "quoted" by FUNCTION but by QUOTE, as in

```
(FNARG (LAMBDA (LIS FUN)
         (COND ( (NULL (CDR LIS) ) (FUN) )
               (T (FNARG (CDR LIS)
                         (QUOTE (LAMBDA ( ) LIS) ) ) )  ) ) )
```

The arguments of FNARG are a nonempty list and a function of no arguments. We trace

```
(FNARG (QUOTE (HULA HOOP) ) (QUOTE (LAMBDA ( ) NIL) ) )
VALUE IS . . .
(HOOP)
```

The actual functional argument on the top-level call is irrelevant. Since the CDR of (HULA HOOP) is not NIL, FNARG is called again with arguments (HOOP) and (LAMBDA () LIS). Since the CDR of (HOOP) is NIL, the value of the second call to FNARG is the value of (LAMBDA () LIS), which is the value of LIS. This value is retrieved from the binding that LIS has in the second call to FNARG, namely (HOOP).

But we feel dissatisfied. In the first call to FNARG, when we wanted to compute

```
(FNARG (CDR LIS) (QUOTE (LAMBDA ( ) LIS) ) )
```

the value of LIS was (HULA HOOP). That is the value we would have liked to see used both for (CDR LIS) and (LAMBDA () LIS). Replacing QUOTE by FUNCTION guarantees that the correct context will be saved for the functional argument. Indeed, defining

```
(FNARG2 (LAMBDA (LIS FUN)
 (COND ( (NULL (CDR LIS) ) (FUN) )
       (T (FNARG2 (CDR LIS)
                  (FUNCTION (LAMBDA ( ) LIS) ) ) )  ) ) )
```

we obtain

```
(FNARG2 (QUOTE (HULA HOOP) ) (QUOTE (LAMBDA ( ) NIL) ) )
VALUE IS . . .
(HULA HOOP)
```

EXERCISE

What are the values of the above programs for FNARG and FNARG2 when the first argument is (BLOW YOUR OWN STRUMPET)?

In short, FUNCTION must be used if the LAMBDA-expression contains a free variable whose binding may change by the time the LAMBDA-expression is executed. The problem that we encountered when QUOTE was used is called the FUNARG problem.

D.4.11.2 Functions of Arbitrarily Many Arguments

Often, a function of any number of arguments cannot be used as a functional argument of a fixed number of arguments. The function SUMSOFPAIRS makes a list of the sums of the corresponding elements in two lists of equal lengths. The definition

```
(SUMSOFPAIRS (LAMBDA (LISONE LISTWO)
 (DOUBLEMAPCAR LISONE LISTWO (FUNCTION PLUS)) ) )
```

might not work. Instead, one should build a LAMBDA-expression:

```
(SUMSOFPAIRS (LAMBDA (LISONE LISTWO)
 (DOUBLEMAPCAR LISONE LISTWO
  (FUNCTION (LAMBDA (LISONELEM LISTWOELEM)
                   (PLUS LISONELEM LISTWOELEM) ) ) ) ) )
SUMSOFPAIRS ( (0 20 100 0) (7 3 6 9) )
 VALUE IS ...
 (7 23 106 9)
```

D.4.12 Errors with QUOTE and EVAL

Many errors are caused by nonjudicious applications of QUOTE or EVAL.

D.5 Errors at the Top Level of EVQ-LISP

A variety of errors can occur at the top level of EVQ-LISP:

a. SETQ and QUOTE should not be used as top-level functions. To build constants, use SET.

b. The first argument of EVALQUOTE should usually be a function name, a LAMBDA-expression, or a LABEL-expression.

c. The second argument cannot be missing, or a non-NIL atom.

In addition, many errors already mentioned can occur at the top level of EVQ-LISP: wrong type or number of arguments, undefined variables and functions, etc. The errors at the top level of EV-LISP are the same as those encountered in function definitions.

D.6   Errors from READ

Numbers are a potential source of errors for READ. The range of the numbers is restricted. Some forms of floating-point numbers may not be acceptable, for example, .2 ,2., scientific notation, and perhaps others. Since "." is used both for dotted pairs and numbers, care must be exercised and blanks added liberally.

INDEX

Names of functions and constants are in capitals. References are to pages in the text. (sys) indicates a system function, (syscon) a system constant—at least in many LISP systems, check to make absolutely sure! A question mark indicates that the system function or constant may not exist in some LISP systems.